THE BEACH BOOK

ELEUTHERA, BAHAMAS EDITION

BRET SIGILLO ▪ GUNNAR EK

ACKNOWLEDGEMENTS

Without our designer, my sister Lissi, who seemed to always be preparing a meal, eating, or about to go out, during this project, and our map maker, Jiban, this book wouldn't have happened.

Without the love and support of our families — Solveig, Jessica, Josephine, Alex, Molly and Copi — who had the keen sense to know the difference between a boondoggle and a research project, this book would never have been made.

Without the spirit, great stories, and wonderful cooking of Rose Gibson we might never have had the energy to finish.

Without Saand.com and SeaDreams we would have had no place to stay.

Finally, if not for Strawberry, Coco and the makers of Alpo, canned chicken salad and Kalik we certainly would not have had the fortitude to finish.

Printed in the United States of America
First Printing, 2014

978-0-9915687-0-3 (Paperback edition)
978-0-9915687-1-0 (iBook edition)
978-0-9915687-2-7 (Kindle edition)
978-0-9915687-3-4 (ePub edition)
978-0-9915687-4-1 (.pdf edition)

Library of Congress Control Number: 2014903055

Book Design: Lissi Sigillo
Photography: Gunnar Ek, Bret Sigillo
Cartography: Jiban Dahal

The Beach Book, LLC
Self Published
www.bahamasbeachbook.com

We dedicate this book to the people of Eleuthera.

*Without your love, humility, wisdom, spirit
and ability to cut a road through the jungle
this book would not be possible.*

Contents

1 NORTHERN ELEUTHERA 1

2 CENTRAL ELEUTHERA

3 SOUTHERN ELEUTHERA...........................204

4 OFFSHORE ISLANDS 270

Preface

I became an Eleuthera homeowner in 1999 signing my ownership documents on the trip to assess damage after Hurricane Floyd. It was horrific, but steeled my resolve. Eleuthera is a special place, and indeed is not for everyone.

Back then I relied on advice and knowledge from longtime residents, locals, and my own sense of adventure to find new beaches. It became my personal mission to try every jungle road, and to learn and memorize what each one led to. I long held the notion that every road on Eleuthera led to either a beach or cemetery, and sometimes both! This, of course, is not true as we certainly learned during this project. As the years progressed it became harder and harder to keep track of each and every road I had traveled. More often than not, I found myself traveling down what I thought was a new jungle path only to end up on a beach that I might have discovered a decade or more ago. Still, I was driven to find them all, eagerly craning my neck as I drove by the roads trying to look down each path before making the decision to give the road a try, to see what lay at the end.

Vacationers to the island who I came in contact with often complained about the same things that frustrated me. Their vacations were short, their time precious, and they wanted to maximize their experience. That generally involved taking in all of the best beaches, or at least the nearest best beaches. They liked variety. They wanted to explore. They weren't necessarily planning on returning year after year. They usually had 7 days, two of which were spent traveling giving them only 4 or 5 days to explore. They didn't want to take wrong roads. They didn't want to take a poor road only to find out that there was a poor beach at the end, or worse, no beach at all. They wanted to know what beaches were the best, which ones were the closest, how to get there, and how long would it take. They craved maps showing them which jungle road led to which beach. They wanted to know what I knew.

The idea behind this project was simple. Make it easy for someone who was vacationing on the island to make a decision about which beaches to visit. Help them plan their trip. Give them that little bit of insider knowledge that can only come from someone who has traveled that road, been to that beach, knows what's good and bad about it, and can tell them how to get there in excruciating detail. We attempted 250 roads to find the 135 beaches cataloged in this book. We're going to save you from wasting time on the 115 that didn't lead to a beach. This book is worth every penny for that fact alone. Additionally, from our experience, you will able to wisely choose which beaches to visit because your vacation time is priceless.

This book is about giving Eleuthera vacation goers their vacation back. It's the definitive guide to ALL of Eleuthera's beaches. Use it to plan. Use it to prepare. Use it to find the best and have a great trip!

How to Use this Book

Start Here

First time visitors to Eleuthera and even those who visit regularly should familiarize themselves with our maps. Once you've oriented yourself on the island and have a basic understanding of the landmarks it's time to dive in and explore the various beaches. Each one is carefully described with essential information so you can fully enjoy each and every beach on the island.

You'll no doubt want to soak up the gorgeous pictures, and that is highly encouraged. However, the real practical use of the book is to help you decide which beaches to visit. Each beach page offers four main components:

1. How to find the beach and get there
2. What conditions you'll likely find
3. How the beach compares with others
4. A detailed description of the beach, its surroundings, pluses and minuses

It is important to note that beaches in this book can be reached by car or foot. Beaches only accessible by boat, or cutoff to safe travel for any number of reasons, have been purposely excluded.

There are a number of things which will help you make better use of this book and its various conventions:

Beach Ratings

Each beach was rated using a three star rating system with three stars being the highest and one star being the lowest score. What distinguishes a three star beach is something particularly special, usually in the form of unique geography. The three star beaches are also free from almost all blemishes including seaweed and debris, rocky water entry, and lack of privacy.

A one star beach had one or more noticeable blemishes with cleanliness and privacy playing significant roles. You'll still find sun, sand, and ocean but the conditions will probably make you question why you didn't heed our advice.

In between those extremes are all the rest. Most of the two star beaches are great beaches. They generally are not located in any type of major community so expect good privacy, but they also tend to have one or more blemishes. They can certainly be enjoyed, but the flaws will be noticeable. You'll find every kind of beach from small to large, sandy to rocky, private to semi-private, and shady to not shady in this category. What these beaches lacked was something that made them exceptional or truly unique.

Road Ratings

The same three star rating system is applied to each beach road, which is usually the road you take after leaving the highway. The ratings do not imply that once you leave the highway the road is going to maintain the same condition throughout. The ratings indicate the worst conditions you are likely to find on any particular beach road. I say 'likely' because road conditions do change. Paved roads can easily become significantly rutted and difficult to travel. If they don't receive regular maintenance, and that is quite common on the island, then expect even some paved roads to be poor.

A three star beach road is equivalent in comfort to that of the Queen's Highway, the main north to south thoroughfare on the island. A three star road is paved from end to end and doesn't require you to travel at a significantly decreased speed. You should consider it to be a normal paved road that can be driven at the speed limit. You can reach the beach easily with a car without any risk of damage due to road conditions.

A one star beach road has problems. It could be a rough jungle path, a poor dirt road, an uneven sandy road, or an extremely rutted paved road. You'll generally want a four wheel drive vehicle or at least a vehicle that has adequate underneath clearance. Roads with this rating will often lead to your vehicle getting scraped or scratched from tree branches, overhanging vegetation or long brush growing out of the middle of the road. The rating is indicative of the worst condition you will find and does not indicate that the entire road is of that condition. A one star road generally indicates that you will have to reduce speed significantly, sometimes to a crawl, to pass the worst road sections. The rating applies to driving conditions, predominantly, but there are also a few hike-to beaches that get this rating, for obvious reasons.

A two star road is a passable sand, dirt or paved road. It will require you to reduce speed, but you won't feel like you are taking your car for a walk. You can proceed with caution at a moderate continuous speed without having to come to a complete halt or otherwise have your foot on the brake the entire ride simply because of adverse road conditions. While a 4WD would be recommended you can reach the beach in a car if you are careful. The roads could have low lying brush or other vegetation that rubs against the vehicle.

Landmarks

Each landmark was carefully selected for use with driving directions, distances and driving times. The primary characteristic of the landmarks we used is permanence. A landmark is something that doesn't change and should always be there. There were a couple of noticeable exceptions where good visual geographic references could not be found. In those cases a reliable and somewhat permanent business / building in the community was used. Major intersections in towns are the most common landmarks along with airports, significant turning roads and major crossings. Below is a list of the landmarks used in this book including specific descriptions of where distance measurements were taken.

Harbour Island Government Dock / Three Island Dock

Regular water taxi service runs between the Three Island Dock on Eleuthera and the Government Dock in Harbour Island. The dock is a little more than a mile north of North Eleuthera Airport and is reached via the only north bound road that leads in that direction. There is a fee for the water taxi in each direction.

Spanish Wells Dock / Eleuthera Ferry Dock to Spanish Wells

If you proceed north on Eleuthera, following signs for Spanish Wells, you will inevitably end up at the ferry dock station, which is recognizable by its proximity to a brightly colored liquor store. The island of Spanish Wells is reached by water taxi and there is a toll in each direction.

North Eleuthera Airport (ELH)

Distances from North Eleuthera airport were measured from the main entry door on the terminal building. The airport is well marked by signage once you are north of the Glass Window Bridge.

Texaco Station (Between Bogue and Bluff)

In the northern part of the island there is a major fork in Queen's Highway. The fork has a Texaco gas station in its 'V'. When heading north, the fork to the right leads to North Eleuthera airport and the Three Island Dock. The fork to the left leads to the town of Bluff and the Spanish Wells Ferry Dock. Distance measurements were taken right at the fork.

Upper Bogue Turnoff

The town of Upper Bogue is a small northern community. Measurements were taken on the highway where a small sign marks the turn.

Glass Window Bridge

The bridge is a major tourist attraction due to its height and because it sits above where the Atlantic Ocean and Caribbean collide. You can see a brilliant contrast of water colors that transform from deep dark blue into a pale light turquoise. This man-made bridge takes the place of a naturally formed bridge of rock that was destroyed in a storm. Distance measurements were taken just past the northern tip of the bridge.

Gregorytown intersection

The town of Gregorytown is itself a major tourist attraction especially during its annual Pineapple Festival held each June. Right at the center of town there is an intersection with a 90-degree turn heading up a hill if you are going south, marked by a large pineapple shaped signpost pointing the way to various island towns. Measurements were taken at the heart of the intersection.

Hatchet Bay intersection (Alicetown)

The town of Alicetown sits just east of Hatchet Bay, a large protected body of water with a narrow mouth leading to the ocean. It is quite visible from the highway looking west. There is one major intersection in town which leads to the marina and back to the main residential section of the community. Distances were measured at the heart of the intersection.

Rainbow Bay Inn

The only discernible landmark in the residential community of Rainbow Bay is a small resort / restaurant called the Rainbow Bay Inn. Directions were measured from Queen's Highway directly perpendicular to the octagonal main building.

JC Fishing Pier

The Bahamian town of James Cistern, known affectionately to locals as JC, has at its center a large fishing pier that extends into the ocean. Measurements were taken on the highway in front of the pier.

Governor's Harbour Airport (GHB)

The Governor's Harbour Airport serves as the hub for most flights serving the island. Measurements were taken on Queen's Highway where you would turn in to enter the airport parking lot. To provide further reference, the entry is slightly past the international terminal (if heading north) and roughly perpendicular to the domestic terminal and Airport Liquor Store.

Governor's Harbour intersection

The Eleuthera capital, Governor's Harbour, has a main two-way intersection. The road that intersects with Queen's Highway leads around the harbor towards the peninsula of Cupid's Cay. There are a number of small businesses and shops at this junction. Measurements were taken from the center of the intersection.

Palmetto Point intersection

The town of Palmetto Point has one major, two-way intersection. Most of the businesses on the corners have been shut down as of this writing, but there is still a large sign on one of the corners listing the names of establishments in town. Distances were measured from the middle of the intersection.

Savannah Sound intersection

The major two-way intersection in the small town of Savannah Sound is best recognized by its single gas pump on the right hand side as you head south on Queen's Highway. Distances were measured from the middle of the intersection.

Tarpum Bay intersection

There is one 90-degree bend along the waterfront in the town of Tarpum Bay. It is near the fishing docks with a large signpost pointing towards the various Bahamian towns. Distances were measured at the turning point.

Rock Sound Market Place

Heading south, you will reach the Rock Sound Market Place. The Market Place has a hardware store, liquor store, supermarket, auto store, and gas station with a large parking area in front. Distance measurements were taken directly in front of the only Queen's Highway entry which is at the south end of the parking lot.

Chris Brown Boulevard / Cotton Bay

Probably the hardest landmark to identify is Chris "Fireman" Brown Boulevard. It is named after an Olympic track and field athlete who hails out of nearby Wemyss Bight. The road bearing his name is the back road, 7.5 miles south of the Rock Sound Marketplace, that leads from Queen's Highway to the original Cotton Bay community, with the remnants of its golf course, and then on to the town of Wemyss Bight. At the time of this writing the road had a small visible road sign. The large cement placard for Cotton Bay still exists, and the paved road is lined with a series of manicured palm trees designating its entrance.

Wemyss Bight T

If you continue south on Queen's Highway past the small towns of Green Castle and Waterford you will eventually end up at an east/west T intersection that leads to Cape Eleuthera to the west and Bannerman Town to the east.

Use of the Bank's Road (between Governor's Harbour and Palmetto Point) and Northshore Drive (between Rock Sound and Cotton Bay)

One well maintained back road runs along the east coast from Governor's Harbour to North Palmetto Point and is known as the Bank's Road. It serves as the main connecting point for beach roads leading to the ocean between those two towns. It extends further north past North Palmetto Point almost to Double Bay.

Northshore Drive is a newer road connecting the south part of Rock Sound along the eastern coast with the newer community of Cotton Bay Estates. It is still a bumpy dirt road, but serves as the gateway for several of the beaches between those two points.

Maps

The maps in this book were hand drawn with painstaking attention to detail. Drawn to scale, they include the beaches, jungle roads, landmarks, Queen's Highway, and other significant connecting roads. They are not meant as comprehensive maps of the island. Their sole purpose is to help you find the beaches and the roads that lead to them. Each beach is identified on the map. Its corresponding road uses the same number followed by a lower case 'r' designating the relationship between the two. In some cases, one road led to more than one beach. Rather than clutter the map with additional road labels, the beach road with the lowest number was used. When the road number differs from the beach number the GPS coordinates on each beach page indicate which road was used. Additionally, we purposely eliminated beach road markers from the maps when they shared the same coordinates as the beach and in places where they weren't helpful.

GPS Coordinates

Each beach and beach road is marked using GPS coordinates. Each coordinate was personally verified on the island for accuracy and then double checked again using various map software. The most accurate way to find a beach road is through the use of GPS, however, we recognize that not everyone will be traveling with such a device. If you don't have a GPS use the maps and directions.

Distances and travel times

Distances and travel times are actual driving or hiking times used by the authors when locating each road and its corresponding beach. However, they should still be considered as estimates that aid travel planning. While the measurements were done using digital, and highly accurate, GPS devices, the rental cars on Eleuthera rely on analog odometers, if they even have one that works. Odometer measurements may not accurately match the GPS measurements. Additionally, many of the driving times were measured while we were actively looking for tough-to-find roads, which required us to slow down noticeably while considering driving options. Oftentimes we had to reverse out the directions and driving times once we had positively located the beach after exploring several jungle paths. Thus, some of the driving times required us to proceed slowly while other times we knew exactly where we were going and could proceed at a normal speed. In other words, your mileage and trip time may vary.

What You Should Know

A handy table has been added to each beach page to provide critical tidbits of information so you know what to expect when you arrive at the beach. It should also be used to help you decide what to bring such as umbrella or water shoes, in case you don't feel like lugging those things around to every beach you go to. There is also some guidance on the quality of shelling and snorkeling. While we attempted to provide information in a yes/no manner some of the information required more detail. Here's a brief explanation of several important entries in the table.

Privacy

The beaches on Eleuthera are known for their privacy. Many beach goers are simply amazed that they can have an entire 3 miles of beach completely to themselves for the whole day. After a while you almost come to expect it.

A **secluded** beach is one that has no visible signs of civilization on or around it. There are no homes, resorts, or communities of any kind within eyesight.

A **public** beach is one where there should be no expectation of privacy. These are beaches that are in public areas, or situated within a community. You should expect to see people, houses, and other buildings. You should expect car noise and other forms of noise pollution.

A **semi-private** beach is one where you have a chance of seeing people, hearing sounds, or sharing the beach with others. There is a wide range of semi-private beaches. A single visible house is enough to receive this classification. Beaches that have small clusters of private homes, even if they are not directly on the beach, also fall into this category.

Litter, Seaweed

We recognize that there is both a high level of subjectivity in this category as well as a high probability of encountering different conditions due to changes in weather and currents. The volume of debris, litter, and seaweed on any given beach could be altered by any number of factors. Storms cause change. Human intervention causes change. Tides, currents, and any number of environmental conditions can alter the appearance of a beach. However, we felt it was such an important factor that we couldn't leave it out. How a beach looked from a cleanliness perspective significantly affected our entire opinion of the beach. It should also be noted that use of the word "litter" implies refuse left behind by humans not cleaning up after themselves. "Debris and wash-up", which were used more frequently in the beach descriptions, implies something discarded into the ocean that washed up on shore usually by cruise ships or passing vessels.

A beach with **no** litter/seaweed (**None** in the table) was just that. The beach was pristine and only traces of seaweed or debris, if any at all, are evident.

A beach with **light** litter/seaweed meant that it was noticeable, but not enough of an issue to be of any real concern. There will be ample places to sit and you won't feel like you have to move to avoid whatever was on the beach.

A beach with **moderate** litter/seaweed has a problem. The wash-up was severe enough that it might cause you to seek relief by moving to a cleaner and perhaps safer location, or even go to a different beach. A beach with this rating might cause concerns for families with children who would need to be supervised.

A beach with **extensive** litter/seaweed not only has a problem, it really has little in the way of offering relief. You might encounter a vast amount of debris or seaweed all over it to the point of it being unpleasant, unsafe, and unattractive.

Water Entry and Conditions

The water entry indicates whether water shoes might be needed to enter the water. The condition of the water can be used to determine if there is shallow water which might be a better choice for young children.

The Best Beaches of Eleuthera

We've included a handy list of beaches grouped by category and rated from 1 to 5, with 1 being the highest. A full description of the criteria used to evaluate them can be found with each list. But, please don't limit yourself to only the beaches on the list. Half the fun is exploring and finding beaches that you think are the best. Enjoy the adventure. We sure did!

Best 5 Beaches

In addition to having zero or only a single minor blemish, the beaches in this category offer something truly unique that set them apart. Privacy, cleanliness, and outstanding water access were all highly valued contributing factors. But, what set these beaches apart was some distinct memorable quality. These are the must-see beaches on the island.

1. Lover's Beach (27)
2. Lighthouse Beach Caribbean (129)
3. Harbour Island Pink Sands Beach (131)
4. Whiteland Beach 2 (106)
5. Deep Creek Beach (112)

Best 5 Beaches for Privacy

Having a huge beach all to yourself is what separates Eleuthera from many Caribbean islands. Beaches on this list were completely isolated with no visible resorts, houses, or communities. A number of other beaches on the island are also secluded. These are our choices for the best quality or most interesting beaches that are also extremely secluded.

1. French Leave Beach Central (69)
2. Lighthouse Beach North (128)
3. John Miller's Atlantic Beach North (120)
4. Red Pond Beach (101)
5. The Point at Half Sound Ocean Beach (96)

Best 5 Easy to Access Beaches

To earn a spot on this list a beach had to be both easy to find and easy to get to. Beaches on the list are accessible via smooth, well-maintained paved roads and are generally centrally located making them equally accessible from the north or south of the island.

1. Governor's Harbour Beach (67)
2. Oleander Gardens Beach (28)
3. Rainbow Bay Beach (38)
4. South Palmetto Point Beach (79)
5. Mid Rocks Beach (55)

Best 5 Beaches for Snorkeling

The volume, diversity, denseness and proximity of offshore reefs were the features that earned a beach a spot on this list.

1. Islandia Beach (88)
2. Catch Rock Beach (122)
3. Whiteland Beach 1 (105)
4. James Point Beach (42)
5. Between the Rocks Beach (80)

Best 5 Beaches for Children

The main characteristics of the good children's beaches are shallow calm water, wide sandy water entry, and short traveling time, mainly from the car to the beach. Other qualities such as ample shade were also considered.

1. Ten Bay Beach (83)
2. Rainbow Bay Beach (38)
3. Governor's Harbour Beach South (68)
4. Gaulding Cay Beach (25)
5. Spanish Wells Bayside Beach (134)

Best 5 Beaches for Food & Beverage

These are the beaches that had the closest proximity to the best food on the island.

1. Harbour Island Pink Sands Beach (131)
2. Nort'side Beach Resort (102)
3. French Leave Beach South (70)
4. French Leave Beach North (66)
5. Tie-Unique's Beach (77) & Bottom Harbour Beach (20)

The Commonwealth of the Bahamas

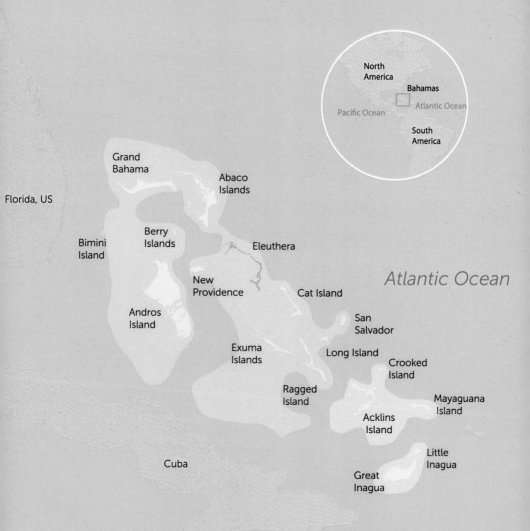

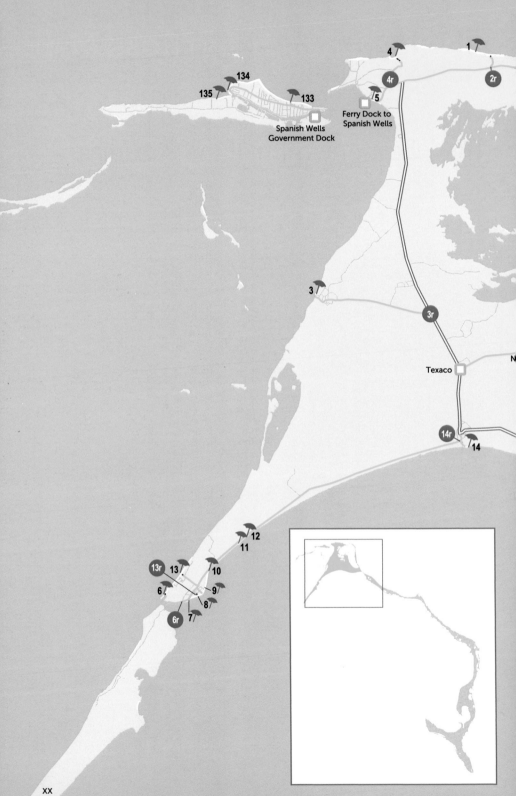

Eleuthera Beach Map Part 1

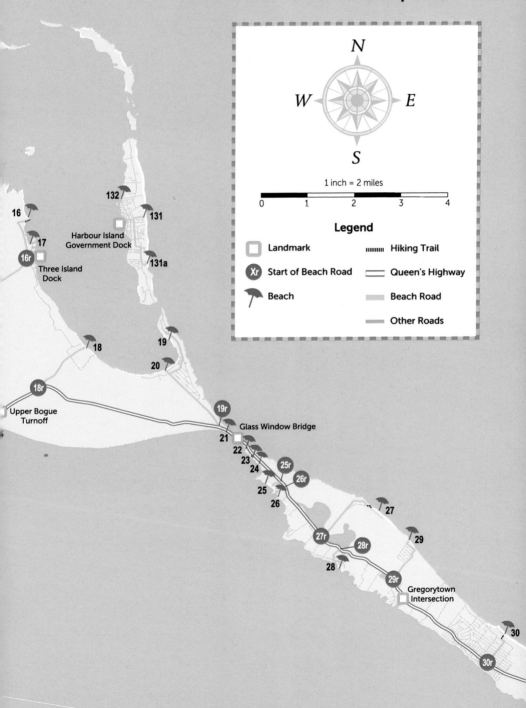

N
W · E
S

1 inch = 2 miles

0   1   2   3   4

Legend

☐ Landmark   ▥ Hiking Trail

Ⓧⁱ Start of Beach Road   Queen's Highway

⛱ Beach   Beach Road

Other Roads

16
17
16r
Three Island Dock

132
131
Harbour Island Government Dock
131a

18
18r
Upper Bogue Turnoff

19
20

19r
Glass Window Bridge
21
22
23
24
25r
25
26r
26
27
27r
27
28r
28
29r
29
Gregorytown Intersection
30
30r

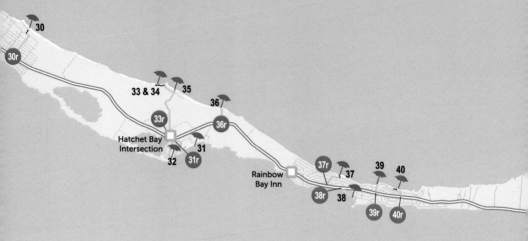

30
30r
33 & 34   35
36
33r
Hatchet Bay
Intersection
36r
32   31r   31
Rainbow
Bay Inn
37r   37
39   40
38r   38
39   40r

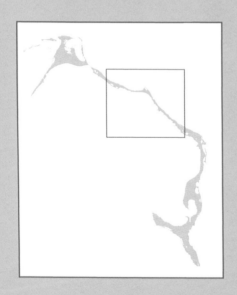

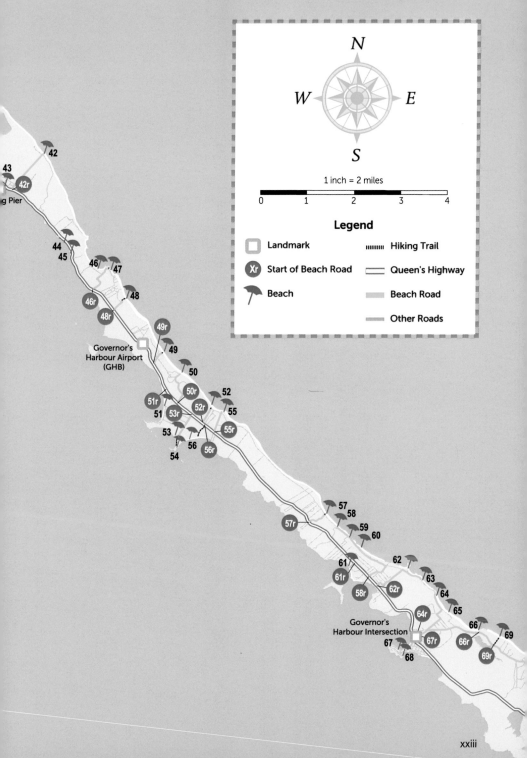

Eleuthera Beach Map Part 2

N
W   E
S

1 inch = 2 miles

0   1   2   3   4

Legend

☐ Landmark   ⫶⫶⫶ Hiking Trail

ⓧ Start of Beach Road   Queen's Highway

⛱ Beach   Beach Road

                         Other Roads

42
43
42r
g Pier
44
45
46
47
46r
48
48r
49r
Governor's
Harbour Airport
(GHB)
49
50
50r
52
51r
55
51
53r
52r
53
55r
54
56
56r
57
58
57r
59
60
61
62
61r
63
64
58r
62r
65
64r
66
66r
67r
69
Governor's
Harbour Intersection
67
69r
68

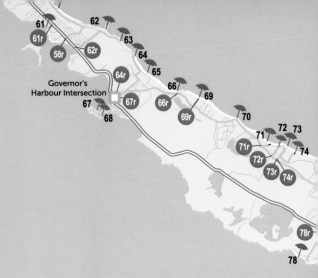

61
61r
58r
62
62r
63
64
65
64r
Governor's
Harbour Intersection
67
67r
66
66r
69
69r
70
71
71r
72 73
72r
73r 74r
74
78r
78
68

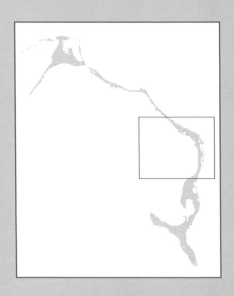

Eleuthera Beach Map Part 3

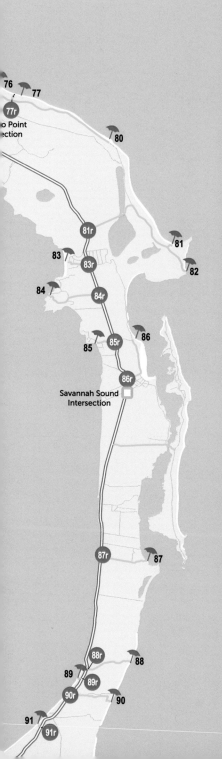

N
W E
S

1 inch = 2 miles

0 1 2 3 4

Legend

☐ Landmark
Xr Start of Beach Road
⛱ Beach

▥▥▥ Hiking Trail
── Queen's Highway
── Beach Road
── Other Roads

76
77
77r
o Point
ection
80
81r
81
83
83r
82
84
84r
85
85r
86
86r
Savannah Sound
Intersection
87r
87
88r
88
89
89r
90r
90
91
91r

Eleuthera Beach Map Part 4

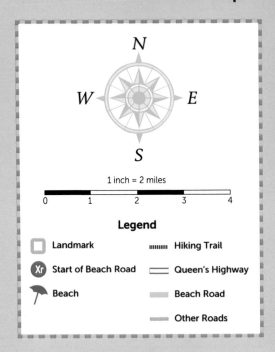

N
W   E
S

1 inch = 2 miles

0   1   2   3   4

Legend

☐ Landmark		⫶⫶⫶⫶ Hiking Trail	
Xr Start of Beach Road		▭ Queen's Highway	
⛱ Beach		▬ Beach Road	
		▬ Other Roads	

116

115
115r

114
114r

113

111
111r

Chris
Boule
Cotte

113r
112r

112

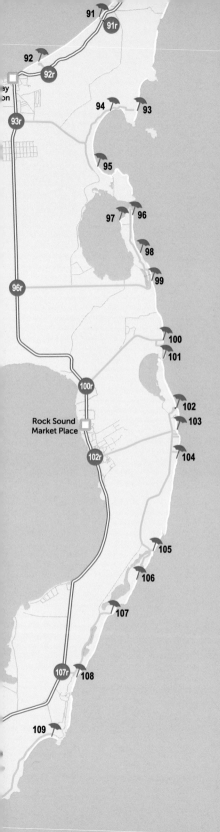

91

91r

92

92r

ay
on

93r

94

93

95

97

96

98

99

96r

100

101

100r

Rock Sound
Market Place

102

103

102r

104

105

106

107

107r

108

109

Eleuthera Beach Map Part 5

Legend

☐	Landmark	⊪⊪⊪	Hiking Trail
Xr	Start of Beach Road	═══	Queen's Highway
⛱	Beach	▬	Beach Road
		▬	Other Roads

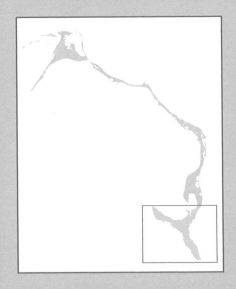

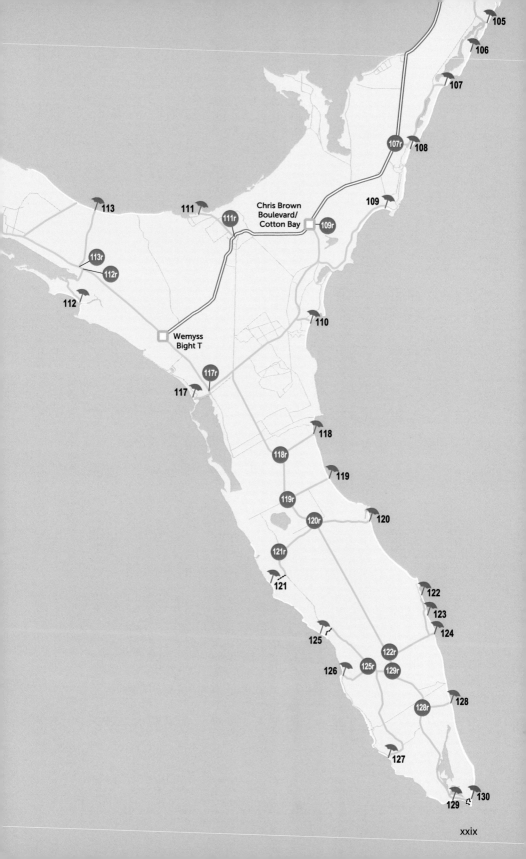

105

106

107

107r

108

109

Chris Brown
Boulevard/
Cotton Bay

109r

113

111

111r

113r

112r

112

110

Wemyss
Bight T

117r

117

118

118r

119

119r

120r

120

121r

121

122

123

124

125

122r

125r

129r

126

128r

128

127

129

130

1

Northern Eleuthera

The Northern Beaches

The sprawling northern section of the island is a diverse geography that forks in three directions from the pivotal northern landmark, the lone Texaco gas station. From there you can reach Current to the southwest, Preacher's Cave, Spanish Wells, and Russell Island to the north, and North Eleuthera Airport (ELH) and Harbour Island to the east.

Current, a sleepy little Bahamian town nestled at the stretch of a long, lonely strip of Queen's Highway, is best known for its famous drift dive, Current Cut. The area also serves as one of the drop off spots for the high-speed ferry service that shuttles passengers back and forth from Nassau. There is one cozy and colorful settlement there along with a handful of rather bland beaches.

There are no established Bahamian settlements north past the town of Bluff, which splits off to the west. You may come across several villages, inhabited mostly by resident Haitians. One in particular blocked us from reaching a beach due to a locked gate. You'll find water taxi service over to Spanish Wells, a simple fishing village and Russell Island, a private residential island boasting one sliver of pristine beach. The few beaches up this way are unique and worth the extra gas expense. Don't expect to find shops or restaurants, so plan accordingly.

Harbour Island, reached by water taxi from the Three Island station, is the main attraction when heading northeast. Pink Sands Beach being one of the finest and most well known in the Caribbean. The eclectic, upscale village offers an opportunity to experience everything Eleuthera is not; shops, restaurants, golf carts, a large number of crowing roosters and people.

The northern part of the island includes the settlements at Whale Point, Bottom Harbour, Gregorytown, Alicetown, and Rainbow Bay. You'll also find several natural attractions including the Glass Window Bridge, where two oceans collide, and the Queen's Baths, a series of cascading saltwater rocks pools with no discernible water source. A number of fascinating and high quality beaches can be found in and around these towns and tourist attractions. Unfortunately, Twin Bay Beach, one of the most unique cave beaches in this region, is no longer accessible due to the storm-induced collapse of both ceilings.

There are 40 beaches to the north. They offer a variety of choices ranging from big beaches with large surf to quaint half-moons that are smaller than your living room. You are sure to find at least one of each kind of beach in this fantastic region.

Tay Bay Beach

Tay Bay Beach is the easiest of the northern beaches to find, access and park by due to its proximity to Preacher's Cave. If you follow the signs to Preacher's Cave you will find Tay Bay on the opposite side of the large, grassy parking area. What isn't readily apparent is the variety of beaches you can find east and west of the main beach path. We recommend doing a little exploring because each beach section offers a slightly different experience. There is almost a half mile of sand alloted to Tay Bay, which sits between Current Bay to the east and Ben Bay to the west.

What each of the beaches has in common is very clear, shallow water with lovely turquoise hues turning into deep ocean blue just offshore. These are good beginner snorkeling areas due to their shallowness and small coral

heads, but this is an even better kayaking spot. That's because the road access back to the beach is perfectly paved, the beach path is wide and the water quality suitable for a smooth paddling session.

What you need to consider is whether or not you want to be in proximity to the cave since it will attract tourists who are likely to share the beach with you. If you want additional privacy then the pretty little cove just to the east is a perfect spot for a couple. The beaches further west offer more privacy, but come with the cost of additional debris, seaweed and fallen Casuarinas.

You can find some shade on most of the beach sections. The beaches to the west have a greater abundance of it The rock formations that must be crossed to reach these beaches

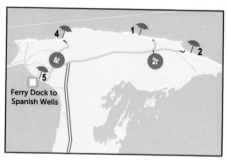

Ferry Dock to
Spanish Wells

Beach ★★☆   Road ★★★

Beach: 25° 33.502, -76° 41.757
Road: 25° 33.502, -76° 41.757

How to Get There

From points south
Total travel time: 7.8 mi. / 15 min
Drive north on Queen's Highway. Follow signs towards North Eleuthera airport to Texaco station. Bear left at fork and proceed 5.9 miles to T. Make right and proceed 1.7 miles. Make left at Preacher's Cave sign and proceed 0.2 miles on paved road to beach access to right of Preacher's Cave parking area.

Time / Distance
To beach road: 7.6 mi. / 14 min
Beach road to beach: 0.2 mi. / 1 min

are jagged and require some type of footwear. There is also a large rusted buoy on one of the western strips of sand that provides a defining and memorable visual.

There were really no blemishes on any of these beaches, but, once again, nothing overly special that would warrant the trip. What we like about Tay Bay is the ease of access. It is by far the easiest beach to find and get to in the north. There is plenty of space so you can find privacy. The water access is very easy. It is very inviting and makes you want to just jump in the water. Because of its proximity to the cave you may have to share the beach with other visitors so if privacy is your chief goal then hike east or west from the main beach or choose one of the other more difficult to reach beaches in the area.

What You Should Know	
Privacy	Semi-private
Shade	Some
Accessibility	Car
Beach Path	Sandy
Water Entry	Sandy
Water Condition	Deep ocean
Litter/Seaweed	Light
Nearest Town	Bluff
Snorkeling	Poor
Shelling	No
Length/Width	0.5 miles x 20 yards

Current Bay Beach

The northern beaches are generally worthy of a day trip and Current Bay Beach is no exception. A couple of exploratory wrong turns while driving didn't deter us from pursuing this series of beaches, each one separated by a low rocky pinnacle. Don't think you've found all beaches when you arrive at the first picnic area. There's plenty more to explore, but you have to go by land and sand, as there are no other access roads to drive to the more remote sections of beach.

The first beach is just a bit longer than a quarter of a mile. It sweeps in a swooshy kind of way from its western point to another rocky point that leads to…more beach! A picnic area with tables, benches, and BBQ pit at its center are its defining features. You have oodles of sand, shade and great shallow water

access to make this the perfect spot to hang out for the day if you aren't up to exploring. If you are a little more adventurous and don't mind some walking, proceed right (east) to find the additional beach sections that form the whole of Current Bay Beach.

During the course of your walk you'll notice that the beaches become more protected and have less seaweed. None of the beaches had any major amounts of debris, but each became more pristine as we ventured further east. The second bay stretches just shy of a quarter mile. The third is almost a half-mile long. The fourth requires a boat or a swim to reach. It extends another 0.15 miles and is not readily visible. All told you have about a mile and a quarter of some of the finest sand on Eleuthera.

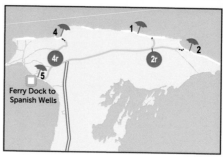

Beach ★★☆ Road ★★☆

Beach: 25° 33.312, -76° 41.211
Road: 25° 33.327, -76° 41.751

How to Get There

From points south

Total travel time: 8.2 mi. / 18 min

Drive north on Queen's Highway. Follow signs towards North Eleuthera airport to Texaco station. Bear left at fork and proceed 5.9 miles to T. Make right and proceed 1.7 miles. Continue straight onto dirt road by Preacher's Cave sign and proceed 0.4 miles. Make a left and proceed 0.1 mile. Bear to right and proceed another 0.1 miles to parking area by fence. Cross fence to access beach on left.

Time / Distance

To beach road: 7.6 mi. / 14 min
Beach road to beach: 0.6 mi. / 4 min

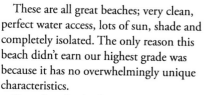

These are all great beaches; very clean, perfect water access, lots of sun, shade and completely isolated. The only reason this beach didn't earn our highest grade was because it has no overwhelmingly unique characteristics.

Even though it's a long ride to get here from most towns on Eleuthera, it's certainly worth it. Enjoy a leisurely 20-minute stroll down these gorgeous strips of sand. Accessing the picnic area required climbing over a broken metal fence. This is easy but you need to locate the fence to find the right place to set up camp. The road getting back to the beach is narrow and a little tricky, but if you follow the directions you will find this beautiful oasis with little trouble.

What You Should Know	
Privacy	Secluded
Shade	Some
Accessibility	Car, bumpy
Beach Path	Grassy
Water Entry	Sandy
Water Condition	Deep ocean
Litter/Seaweed	Moderate
Nearest Town	Bluff
Snorkeling	Poor
Shelling	No
Length/Width	1.0 miles x 30 yards

Bluff Public Beach

We didn't look for - or expect to find this beach. On a side trip to check out the town of Bluff we came across the government dock and this unassuming little community beach nestled under the protecting arm of the dock. This is also where water taxi service to Royal and Lobster Cays departs.

The beach sits under a large vacation home. The sand area is only 30 yards wide and 20 feet deep. It narrows even further in a triangular shape due to a rock wall that was built to offer additional protection from the waves. To the right a striated yet stunted rock wall forms a picturesque backdrop next to the colorful conch shack. It's a perfect little swimming spot for children with shallow, sandy water entry in a protected cove.

This is the smallest and quaintest of Bahamian public beaches. It is an interesting spot to discover in a community that is off the beaten path. If you are up this way and want a little side venture then check out the town of Bluff and its lone beach or take one of the water taxis to explore neighboring, less inhabited cays.

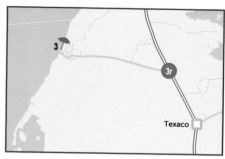

Beach ★☆☆   Road ★★★

Beach: 25° 29.449, -76° 44.860
Road: 25° 29.122, -76° 42.850

How to Get There

From points south

Total travel time: 3.8 mi. / 7 min

Drive north on Queen's Highway. Follow signs towards North Eleuthera airport to Texaco station. Bear left at fork and proceed 1.6 miles to sign for Bluff. Make a left and proceed 2.0 miles to T. Make right and proceed 0.2 miles around bend and Miss Annie's property. Make left into marina.

Time / Distance

To beach road: 1.6 mi. / 3 min
Beach road to beach: 2.2 mi. / 4 min

What You Should Know	
Privacy	Public
Shade	Plenty
Accessibility	Car
Beach Path	None
Water Entry	Sandy
Water Condition	Shallow cove
Litter/Seaweed	Light
Nearest Town	Bluff
Snorkeling	Poor
Shelling	Yes
Beach Size	15 yards x 10 feet

Ben Bay Beach

This idyllic 300 yards of sand is gorgeous. The water sits like a pool of quaint drinking water in a fine bowl, the light lapping of the waves creating a sensual rhythm that can easily put you in a melodic trance.

The day we evaluated this beach there had been flooding in the area that prevented us from driving all the way to the beach. Opting to walk the last few hundred feet through muddy puddles certainly saved our vehicle, but really should be an anomaly rather than the norm as the access road is generally quite passable. You may prefer a

4WD vehicle just so you have some clearance below as the road is not the best.

There are a number of beach shacks on the east end of the beach that offer shade, a place to grill, picnic tables and an elevated lookout. These dwellings cause us to believe that boaters from Harbour Island come here with some regularity to throw some good ol' fashioned beach parties. There are no houses around and the beach is otherwise completely isolated. It is also quite clean with only a little dried seaweed. Any wash-up that occurs is turned into some type of primitive

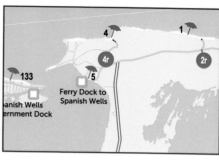

Beach ★★☆ Road ★☆☆

Beach: 25° 33.439, -76° 43.363
Road: 25° 32.997, -76° 43.571

How to Get There

From points south
Total travel time: 7.0 mi. / 19 min

Drive north on Queen's Highway. Follow signs towards North Eleuthera airport to Texaco station. Bear left at fork and proceed 5.9 miles to T. Make left and proceed 0.3 miles. Make right onto dirt road and proceed 0.3 miles. Bear right and proceed 0.3 miles. Make left and proceed 0.2 miles to beach. Stop short of big puddle at end if flooded.

Time / Distance
To beach road: 6.2 mi. / 14 min
Beach road to beach: 0.8 mi. / 5 min

What You Should Know	
Privacy	Secluded
Shade	Plenty
Accessibility	4WD recommended
Beach Path	Sandy
Water Entry	Sandy
Water Condition	Shallow cove
Litter/Seaweed	Light
Nearest Town	Bluff
Snorkeling	Poor
Shelling	No
Beach Size	300 yards x 30 yards

art project in the shacks. Casuarinas wrap around the entire beach and provide lots of shade regardless of the sun's direction. The water is quite swimmable with clumps of submerged rocks further out offering some decent snorkeling.

Choose this beach because of its interesting shape, good sandy water access and because of the beach huts. Beware of what could be a rough access road leading to a very small beach that offers little to do once you get there.

Spanish Wells Ferry Beach

The long and narrow Spanish Wells Ferry Beach starts at the dock where water taxis shuttle passengers to nearby Spanish Wells and Russell Island. The beach runs approximately 0.6 miles in a southeasterly direction. The beach access is a little up the road from the ferry docks, but is still right on Queen's Highway so expect to hear traffic noise. The bay offers an interesting view because of the nearby islands and sweeping view of Eleuthera, but that's about the only redeeming quality here. Water access is rocky and extremely shallow so it's a place to wade rather than swim. The sand is hard packed but there is ample shade under clusters of mangroves and Casuarinas.

Getting here is very easy because the access is right off of the highway and it's conveniently located near the ferry terminal. However, it's rocky, narrow, right by the highway and not very swimmable. This is not a destination beach but okay for killing time while waiting for the ferry.

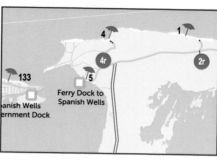

Beach ★☆☆   Road ★★☆

Beach: 25° 32.747, -76° 43.739
Road: 25° 32.747, -76° 43.739

How to Get There

From points south
Total travel time: 6.5 mi. / 11 min
Drive north on Queen's Highway. Follow signs towards North Eleuthera airport to Texaco station. Bear left at fork and proceed 5.9 miles to T. Make left and proceed 0.6 miles to access road on left well before ferry dock.

Time / Distance
To beach road: 6.5 mi. / 11 min
Beach road to beach: 0.0 mi. / 0 min

What You Should Know	
Privacy	Semi-private
Shade	Some
Accessibility	Car
Beach Path	Sandy
Water Entry	Rocky
Water Condition	Shallow bay
Litter/Seaweed	Light
Nearest Town	Bluff
Snorkeling	Poor
Shelling	No
Beach Size	0.6 miles x 20 yards

Riptide Beach

This is not a beach for kids or poor swimmers due to strong tides, mostly rocky water access, a high concentration of seaweed, and a long access walk. This is an excellent spot if you are up north looking to find some privacy and seclusion. Of all the beaches we found in the north this provides the best seclusion with good swimming and perhaps the best snorkeling.

From the beach you can see the awesome power of the tide surging through Current Cut, a swift moving channel that runs between Eleuthera and Current Island. Watch the oceans collide when the tides change direction with a mass of confused waves battling each other.

The beach sits to the southwest of the Current Northside beach and has many of the same characteristics in terms of sand and water sans private residences. Watch out for the occasional rock and the current, which can be intense at times.

Finding this beach is a challenge. The access road is poor and not well marked. You will pass what looks like a Roman pool that spills into the ocean, before finding a

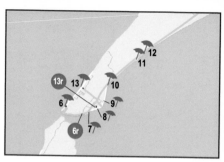

Beach ★★☆ Road ★☆☆

Beach: 25° 24.345, -76° 47.525
Road: 25° 24.326, -76° 47.068

How to Get There

From points south

Total travel time: 12.8 mi. / 28 min
From Glass Window Bridge drive north for 6.8 miles. Make left towards Upper Bogue and proceed 0.2 miles to Stop sign. Proceed 0.3 miles after Stop sign. Make left and proceed 4.7 miles. Leave paved road past town of Current and proceed 0.3 miles to Fast Ferry terminal / dock. Continue straight past dock on rough road another 0.4 miles passing ocean pool on left. Beach path is on right.

Time / Distance

To beach road: 12.1 mi. / 22 min
Beach road to beach: 0.7 mi. / 6 min

lone parking spot for the beach. From there you will need to cross some fallen trees and a wading pool to get onto the main beach. Proceed further to two half-moon beaches.

What makes this beach interesting is its view of the Cut and its privacy. However, it is difficult to get here and may not be worth the effort because the beach isn't all that great. If you were up here to scuba dive or to meet someone coming off of the Fast Ferry from Nassau then this is a perfectly fine beach to spend some time at, otherwise it's not worth the trip.

What You Should Know	
Privacy	Secluded
Shade	Some
Accessibility	4WD recommended
Beach Path	Rocky
Water Entry	Rocky
Water Condition	Deep with strong current
Litter/Seaweed	Moderate
Nearest Town	Current
Snorkeling	Average
Shelling	No
Beach Size	0.2 miles x 20 yards

Current Double Moon Beach

These quaint little cove beaches are not only quite pleasant, but easy to miss depending on the tide. Upon first inspection there didn't appear to be any sand at all, but later in the day, as the tide receded, the scenic beaches came into full view. From a location perspective they sit just west of the Current marina dock and are the last strips of sand you'll find before reaching the ferry dock. They are located close to the road so don't expect much privacy and you will definitely be subject to the noise from passing vehicles.

What they do offer is a perfect park-like setting ideal for a picnic. The first beach stretches a whopping 80 yards in half-moon shape. Casuarina needles provide a soft place to sit while the large trees offers ample shade. You can have a nice little lunch and a quick dip in the protected waters. Be cautious of leaving the protected swim area as the riptide from the Cut is lurking just outside the rocks.

The second 40 yards half-moon is less protected and perhaps a bit less interesting due to its shape and lack of shade. Still, it's a nice little exploration spot and provides some variety to the overall site with a good view of Current Island. Accessing these beaches is simple and when they're above water, they are quite nice. This is one of the better spots in or around Current.

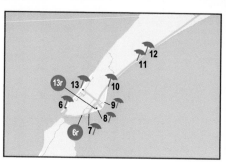

Beach ★★☆   Road ★★☆

Beach: 25° 24.250, -76° 47.119
Road (6r): 25° 24.326, -76° 47.068

How to Get There

From points south

Total travel time: 12.1 mi. / 22 min

From Glass Window Bridge drive north for 6.8 miles. Make left towards Upper Bogue and proceed 0.2 miles to Stop sign. Proceed 0.3 miles after Stop sign. Make left and proceed 4.7 miles. Leave paved road past town of Current and proceed 0.1 miles to parking area on left. Beaches are to right of dock.

Time / Distance

To beach road: 12.1 mi. / 22 min
Beach road to beach: 0.0 mi. / 0 min

What You Should Know	
Privacy	Semi-private
Shade	Some
Accessibility	Car, bumpy
Beach Path	Sandy
Water Entry	Sandy
Water Condition	Shallow cove
Litter/Seaweed	Light
Nearest Town	Current
Snorkeling	Poor
Shelling	No
Beach Size	150 yards x 15 feet

Marina Beach

The most distinguishable feature of this beach is the disheveled marina dock along with a smaller wooden dock, its pylons all that remains. Their stark contrast to the glowing turquoise of the water is a gentle reminder of how strong the major storms can be on this island and how long repairs can take.

The water access here is very good with a gently sloping sand ledge leading away from seaweed, sea lettuce and grass all along the flat shelf. The beach meanders about a quarter mile and while it seems secluded there are a few houses around. Beach access from the town of Current is quite easy and there is a sizeable parking lot just above the main beach access path. The riptides here can be dangerous as this beach is close to the Cut, but because the water is so shallow it shouldn't be a reason to not try this beach.

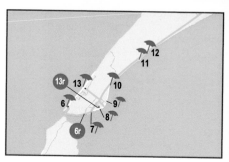

Beach ⭐⭐☆   Road ⭐⭐⭐

Beach: 25° 24.358, -76° 46.967
Road: 25° 24.358, -76° 46.976

How to Get There

From points south

Total travel time: 12.1 mi. / 22 min
From Glass Window Bridge drive north for
6.8 miles. Make left towards Upper Bogue
and proceed 0.2 miles to Stop sign. Proceed
0.3 miles after Stop sign. Make left and
proceed 4.7 miles. Make left and proceed 0.1
miles to parking area.

Time / Distance

To beach road: 12.1 mi. / 22 min
Beach road to beach: 0.0 mi. / 0 min

What You Should Know	
Privacy	Semi-private
Shade	Some
Accessibility	Car
Beach Path	Sandy
Water Entry	Sandy
Water Condition	Shallow with current
Litter/Seaweed	Moderate
Nearest Town	Current
Snorkeling	Poor
Shelling	No
Beach Size	0.25 miles x 15 feet

You can find shade away from the beach
under a long line of dense Casuarinas. The
beach has a rough grassy look to it, but no
other aesthetic appeal. If you are looking
for a long Caribbean side beach in Current,
then this is the one to go to as it has more
privacy than the public beach, however, it's
not a beach that you should go out of your
way to find.

Current Public Beach

One of the best public beaches on the island is alive and well in the charming old Bahamian town of Current. This well-kept beach area is similar to other public beaches in terms of its accessibility, but differs significantly in terms of how pristine and well maintained the beach area is.

A central dock marks the location. It seems active and vibrant with many boats moored there. A fish gutting station provides both color and charm with decorative signage announcing its use. This beach sits in front of the town of Current, which is quite visible from the sand. It is due east of

Marina Beach and is more or less an extension of that length of sand yet it maintains its own unique character.

A large beach pavilion with picnic tables, jungle gym, soccer field, volleyball courts, public bathrooms and showers offer a nice set of amenities for travelers with small children. Beware of the extremely strong currents that run along the shore out towards Current Cut. Fortunately, the water is shallow so escaping the current can be done by simply standing up.

There is no natural shade at this beach except inside the outdoor pavilion. The water entry is sandy and shallow. The beach, to the

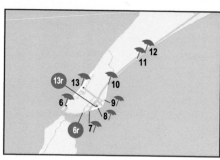

Beach ★★☆   Road ★★★

Beach: 25° 24.375, -76° 46.875
Road: 25° 24.405, -76° 46.910

How to Get There

From points south

Total travel time: 12.2 mi. / 24 min
From Glass Window Bridge drive north for 6.8 miles. Make left towards Upper Bogue and proceed 0.2 miles to Stop sign. Proceed 0.3 miles after Stop sign. Make left and proceed 4.6 miles. Make left and proceed to end. Proceed 0.1 miles onto dirt road to beach

Time / Distance
To beach road: 12.1 mi. / 23 min
Beach road to beach: 0.1 mi. / 1 min

What You Should Know	
Privacy	Public
Shade	None
Accessibility	Car
Beach Path	None
Water Entry	Sandy
Water Condition	Shallow with current
Litter/Seaweed	Light
Nearest Town	Current
Snorkeling	Poor
Shelling	No
Beach Size	0.25 miles x 15 feet

west of the deck, is free of seaweed and debris while the eastern beach had some minor seaweed. Lush grass and large sea lettuce form a bright green backdrop contrasting nicely with the pink sand, boats, and turquoise waters.

Overall, this is a very nice beach and probably the best community beach on the island. It lacks in privacy, but makes up for it by having a good set of child friendly amenities. This is not a beach you would go out of your way for, but is a nice stopping point if you happen to be in the northwest of the island.

Sand Banks Beach

If shade is what you crave then look no further than this hidden gem where it's almost impossible to find the sun unless you are in the water. The beach is completely hidden underneath a Casuarina tree forest with soft needles leading the way to the narrowest strip of sand you'll ever see. At times the beach was about 2' wide. When the waves receded it was about five to six feet at its maximum. Accessing the entire length of beach required walking into the water as the low lying branches would impede your ability to cleanly walk down the beach, which stretches 150 yards.

This beach is an excellent picnic spot with gentle lapping water. The crystal clear turquoise waters are perfect for swimming after you've waited the obligatory one-hour after eating to avoid cramps. Didn't your mother tell you that?

This excellent kayaking beach is set further back from the road than beaches 11

BEACH 10

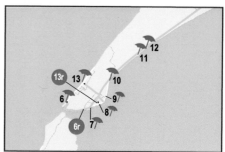

Beach ★☆☆   Road ★★★

Beach: 25° 24.699, -76° 46.806
Road: 25° 24.699, -76° 46.806

How to Get There

From points south
Total travel time: 11.7 mi. / 20 min
From Glass Window Bridge drive north for
6.8 miles. Make left towards Upper Bogue
and proceed 0.2 miles to Stop sign. Proceed
0.3 miles after Stop sign. Make left and proceed 4.4 miles to beach access on left.

Time / Distance
To beach road: 11.7 mi. / 20 min
Beach road to beach: 0.0 mi. / 0 min

What You Should Know	
Privacy	Semi-private
Shade	Plenty
Accessibility	Car
Beach Path	None
Water Entry	Sandy
Water Condition	Shallow cove
Litter/Seaweed	Light
Nearest Town	Current
Snorkeling	Poor
Shelling	No
Beach Size	150 yards x 4 feet

and 12, however, that won't totally protect
you from the road noise. There are also two
houses, one across the Queen's Highway
and one directly to the right, which limits
privacy. Still, of all the beaches in this area,
this was the best choice due its outstanding water entry, shade and size. It is easy to
find, offering a great opportunity to cool
off, relax, enjoy a good book and sip on a
cool beverage.

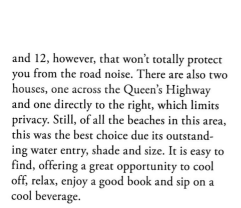

Upper Cove Beach

The best way to explain this beach is to compare and contrast it with beach #12, Ed's Bay. First of all, there are two beaches here rather than one, but they are both minute. The left or more easterly beach is about 30 yards long while the beach to the west is a mere 15 yards. These are come and sit beaches, for sure.

You will get more privacy here due to the beaches being set back from the road; however, these beaches are far from private or secluded. You are still very close to Queen's Highway so expect to hear road noise from passing vehicles. You will be partially visually obscured, but that's about it. The soft Casuarina needles under the trees offer a good place to sit with much more shade than up the road. This beach also offers excellent sandy water access and is much more swimmable than at other locations along this stretch of Queen's Highway.

It's an excellent spot to kayak because of

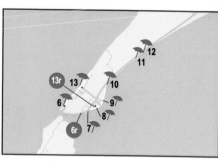

Beach ★☆☆ Road ★★★

Beach: 25° 25.242, -76° 46.227
Road: 25° 25.242, -76° 46.227

How to Get There

From points south

Total travel time: 11.5 mi. / 20 min
From Glass Window Bridge drive north for 6.8 miles. Make left towards Upper Bogue and proceed 0.2 miles to Stop sign. Proceed 0.3 miles after Stop sign. Make left and proceed 4.2 miles to beach access on left.

Time / Distance
To beach road: 11.5 mi. / 20 min
Beach road to beach: 0.0 mi. / 0 min

What You Should Know	
Privacy	Semi-private
Shade	Some
Accessibility	Car
Beach Path	None
Water Entry	Sandy
Water Condition	Shallow cove
Litter/Seaweed	Moderate
Nearest Town	Current
Snorkeling	Poor
Shelling	No
Beach Size	50 yards x 6 feet

good water access plus a short walk from the car. The chief negative, aside from the road noise, is the amount of seaweed and debris we encountered. I wouldn't characterize it as a huge problem, but it did hurt the overall appeal of the beach.

This is a nice little spot, easy to find and get to, with good water access, shade and some privacy. It is a good stopping point on the way to Current and a prime spot for kayaking.

Ed's Bay Beach

If you sneeze while passing by this beach you might miss it...so don't sneeze! This 30-yard plot of sand stretches out to almost kiss Queen's Highway. A sign on a nearby tree reveals the beach name at least until said tree or sign is no longer there.

This is a small half-moon carve out in the rocks on the Caribbean side of the highway with two rocky points offering a quaint and curious ocean access spot. The turquoise colors here are amazing and this is as fine of a kayak launch spot as you're likely to find. A nearby boat ramp can also be used if you are launching a larger vessel.

What you'll dearly miss here is privacy as the beach is right on the highway and there is

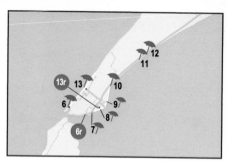

Beach ★☆☆   Road ★★★

Beach: 25° 25.348, -76° 46.090
Road: 25° 25.348, -76° 46.090

How to Get There

From points south

Total travel time: 11.3 mi. / 19 min
From Glass Window Bridge drive north for
6.8 miles. Make left towards Upper Bogue
and proceed 0.2 miles to Stop sign. Proceed
0.3 miles after Stop sign. Make left and proceed 4.0 miles to beach access on left.

Time / Distance

To beach road: 11.3 mi. / 19 min
Beach road to beach: 0.0 mi. / 0 min

What You Should Know	
Privacy	Semi-private
Shade	Some
Accessibility	Car
Beach Path	None
Water Entry	Rocky
Water Condition	Shallow cove
Litter/Seaweed	Moderate
Nearest Town	Current
Snorkeling	Poor
Shelling	No
Beach Size	30 yards x 6 feet

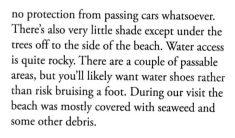

no protection from passing cars whatsoever.
There's also very little shade except under the
trees off to the side of the beach. Water access
is quite rocky. There are a couple of passable
areas, but you'll likely want water shoes rather
than risk bruising a foot. During our visit the
beach was mostly covered with seaweed and
some other debris.

Current Northside Beach

This well maintained beach resembles the northern version of some of the high-end residential beaches towards the center of the island such as Double Bay. The beach is only a half-mile long with a handful of well-maintained homes, which seem out of place for this area. The properties appear to be private residences rather than vacation rentals, but that is pure speculation.

You will find the nicest feature of the beach if you head to the northeast just past the first rocky point where you'll find two secluded mini beaches cut out amongst the rocks. If for some reason there is no privacy on the main beach, then take this trek to find these little private hideaways.

The houses along the main beach are set quite a ways back. Sea lettuce race towards the water where good sandy water access is met with large submerged boulders. You can find good places to enter the water, but watch out for those rock piles. There is a lot of seaweed but very little man-made debris.

Enjoy ample amounts of sun, but be aware

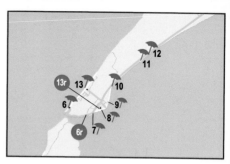

Beach ☆☆☆   Road ☆☆☆

Beach: 25° 24.689, -76° 47.221
Road: 25° 24.493, -76° 46.935

How to Get There

From points south

Total travel time: 12.2 mi. / 23 min
From Glass Window Bridge drive north for
6.8 miles. Make left towards Upper Bogue
and proceed 0.2 miles to Stop sign. Proceed
0.3 miles after Stop sign. Make left and proceed 4.5 miles to North Beach Road. Make a
right and proceed 0.4 miles through gate to
beach.

Time / Distance

To beach road: 11.8 mi. / 21 min
Beach road to beach: 0.4 mi. / 2 min

What You Should Know	
Privacy	Semi-private
Shade	Some
Accessibility	Car
Beach Path	Sandy
Water Entry	Sandy
Water Condition	Deep ocean
Litter/Seaweed	Moderate
Nearest Town	Current
Snorkeling	Poor
Shelling	No
Beach Size	0.4 miles x 40 yards

that shade is limited to the initial beach entry.
Current Northside is well marked, easy to
find, and easy to get to. Just pass through a
set of gates at the end of the paved road and
you're there. Due to high waves on the day
we visited this didn't appear to be a good
snorkel site. This is a true beach lover's beach
where you are going to work on your tan,
swim, and enjoy the view provided by the
numerous cays and islands off in the distance.

Lower Bogue Beach

What's nice about this settlement beach is the quality of the water access. You can really swim here and you'll want to if the conditions are good. The beach is nice and sandy with very little seaweed and hardly any debris. What is a bit unsettling is the state of the dock and the broken down tiki huts which give the area a very worn look.

The fairly short beach is set in front of a series of colorful Homecoming huts which glitter with an assortment of pastel pinks, blues and greens. The settlement, quite visible from the parking area and the beach, is located behind the huts.

Accessibility is excellent. The roads leading here are completely paved and there is a very large parking area. Because of the state of the dock, with broken cement and lots of exposed rebar, we wouldn't recommend it for families with small children. The tiki huts had no palm fronds left to offer shade, therefore, the only shade on the beach is back under a large tree at the entrance to the beach.

This is another beach that is better used as a photography spot as the colors of the pavilion are interesting set against the water and beach. The broken down dock is also a good photo subject. The water is quite swimmable.

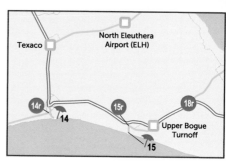

Beach ★☆☆   Road ★★★

Beach: 25° 26.861, -76° 42.250
Road: 25° 26.955, -76° 42.335

How to Get There

From points south
Total travel time: 7.2 mi. / 13 min
From Glass Window Bridge drive north for 6.8 miles. Make a left towards Upper Bogue and proceed 0.2 miles to Stop sign. Proceed straight and make your 2nd left. Proceed 0.2 miles to beach.

Time / Distance
To beach road: 7.0 mi. / 12 min
Beach road to beach: 0.2 mi. / 1 min

What You Should Know	
Privacy	Public
Shade	Some
Accessibility	Car
Beach Path	None
Water Entry	Sandy
Water Condition	Shallow Caribbean
Litter/Seaweed	Light
Nearest Town	Lower Bogue
Snorkeling	Poor
Shelling	No
Beach Size	100 yards x 30 yards

Upper Bogue Beach

Different than many of the Bahamian community beaches, tiny Upper Bogue Beach has several interesting qualities. It's still not the beach that you are going to choose to spend the day working on your tan, but if you happen to be passing by and want to see an interesting little spot then this might be your cup of tea.

What makes it interesting is a large grounded barge along with a broken down pier. They provide a very distinct backdrop, a vestige, perhaps, to the old Bahamas. They are both good photographic subjects. Set against the quaint town, large beach pavilion and small outcropping of sand, they are

good subjects to fill your frame; different than anything you'll find on other beaches.

The beach is very small stretching only about 50 feet long and 10 feet wide. The sand is not nice and was littered with an abundance of seaweed and other human litter. The nearby pavilion is a good place to rest and have a good drink out of the sun, but the lack of access to a working toilet and shower, both of which are just behind the beach, left us disappointed. I'm sure during Homecomings and other parties this location can be raucous, but simply as a beach spot there isn't much going on here.

The water is protected by a rocky

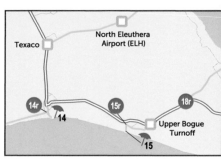

Beach ★☆☆   Road ★★★

Beach: 25° 26.611, -76° 40.879
Road: 25° 26.728, -76° 40.869

How to Get There

From points south
Total travel time: 5.4 mi. / 10 min
From Glass Window Bridge drive north for
4.8 miles. Make a left towards Upper Bogue
and proceed 0.4 miles. Make left and proceed
0.2 miles on paved road to parking area.

Time / Distance
To beach road: 5.2 mi. / 9 min
Beach road to beach: 0.2 mi. / 1 min

What You Should Know	
Privacy	Public
Shade	Some
Accessibility	Car
Beach Path	None
Water Entry	Rocky
Water Condition	Shallow Caribbean
Litter/Seaweed	Moderate
Nearest Town	Upper Bogue
Snorkeling	Good
Shelling	Yes
Beach Size	50 feet x 10 feet

shoreline, but was littered with seaweed.
Additionally, the beach area is unprotected
and not private at all. A couple of beachside
palms and Casuarinas at the water's edge are
quaint and picturesque.

To the left of the wreck there is a rocky
wall and sandy area that provides a good
place to experience the crashing waves when
the surf is high. Lots of fallen rocks in the
water offer a good safe snorkel spot for
beginners.

All in all this was an interesting spot for
photo opportunities and to have a cold
drink, but don't go out of your way to get
here unless you run out of beaches.

Three Rings Beach

Left of the boat loading docks is where you'll find the path to this series of beaches, the first stretching a quarter mile around a graceful half-moon following by a double half-moon that is only a tenth of a mile in length. The beaches are all narrow with extremely soft sand indicating that the sand is under water at high tide. To be able to walk comfortably stay close to the water's edge where the sand is firm and more compact.

The beach entrance showed evidence of being used for partying and it's likely that this is a stomping ground for some after-hours revelry. There is one occupied hut towards the end of the first beach followed by a series of signs hanging on trees showing evidence of undeveloped plots of land that have been claimed either legally or through squatting.

These beaches run south to north with views of Harbour Island and its northern neighbors becoming clearer as you move up the beach. If you are looking for a beach to kill a few hours while waiting for your flight this is the best choice as you have a much

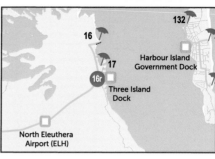

Beach ★★☆   Road ★★★

Beach: 25° 30.024, -76° 39.961
Road: 25° 29.355, -76° 39.916

How to Get There

From points south
Total travel time: 2.4 mi. / 4 min
From North Eleuthera airport drive north
1.4 miles. Make left and proceed 1.0 miles
on paved road to end. Beach path is on left
before loading dock.

Time / Distance
To beach road: 1.4 mi. / 2 min
Beach road to beaach: 1.0 mi. / 2 min

What You Should Know	
Privacy	Semi-private
Shade	Some
Accessibility	Car
Beach Path	Sandy
Water Entry	Sandy
Water Condition	Shallow bay
Litter/Seaweed	Extensive
Nearest Town	Harbour Island
Snorkeling	Poor
Shelling	No
Beach Size	0.4 miles x 10 yards

cleaner beach with better sand, shallow sandy
water access and decent privacy compared to
others in the vicinity. However, this is not a
beach that you would go out of your way for.

Continue north from the first half-moon
to find the other moons, which have much
less seaweed on the shore and some interesting mangrove vegetation. The area is peaceful
and appeared to be a good place to spot
wildlife. A small hawksbill turtle and a baby
lemon shark were feeding in the shallows during our visit.

Hiview Beach

If there was a category for the worst beaches on Eleuthera then this tiny plot of sand might be a contender. There are not many reasons to choose this location so let us save you the trouble of going there yourself by telling you what you'll find. You've got a clear view of the bayside of Harbour Island, and that's the best feature of the beach. It's also very close to the North Eleuthera Airport and Three Island Dock so you can quickly zip over here on a perfectly paved road, but why would you?

The beach stretches about 80 feet long, but there is so much construction debris and wash up that maybe half that area is useless. At one time this might have been a nice and well maintained little strip of beach since there is a formal parking lot and even a landscaped garden with a stonewall framing the beach, but it has fallen into complete disrepair. The seclusion and a rocky outcropping in the ocean

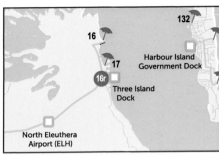

Beach ★☆☆   Road ★★★

Beach: 25° 29.746, -76° 40.036
Road (16r): 25° 29.355, -76° 39.916

How to Get There

From points south
Total travel time: 1.9 mi. / 3 min
From North Eleuthera airport head north 1.4 miles. Make left and proceed 0.5 miles on paved road. Parking area is on right.

Time / Distance
To beach road: 1.4 mi. / 2 min
Beach road to beach: 0.5 mi. / 1 min

What You Should Know	
Privacy	Semi-private
Shade	None
Accessibility	Car
Beach Path	Sandy
Water Entry	Sandy
Water Condition	Shallow bay
Litter/Seaweed	Extensive
Nearest Town	Harbour Island
Snorkeling	Poor
Shelling	No
Beach Size	80 feet x 8 feet

that serves as a garden for junior Casuarinas are good features, but are not enough reason to warrant coming here. The water is shallow and entry is mostly sandy.

To summarize, this beach is small and has so much debris that it feels like a dump rather than a beach. It is reasonably private, close to the water taxi and northern restaurants, and has an unobstructed view of Harbour Island. You can certainly find a better location even this far north.

Cistern Cay Beach

Maybe it was bad timing on our part, but at the time the beach was assessed it might have been in its worst condition. At high tide the only portion of the beach that remained above water was a solid mat of seaweed that ran the entire length of the beach. Coupled with the fact that it was a long, slow, bumpy ride back to the beach this is not a beach that you would seek out for any particular reason other than to experience a somewhat scenic view of Harbour Island, Whale Point and the cut that runs between the two.

The beach extends for almost four tenths of a mile to the south from the access point. There are several other sandy areas to the north that can be reached with a bit of climbing, but unfortunately there was not much reason to explore. The sandy areas to the north were even more littered with seaweed and debris. To the south there was one reasonably good sitting area set back underneath a small nest of palm trees and covered with a soft bed of Casuarina needles. Here you could at least set up camp and enjoy the shaded view.

There is one house being built at the

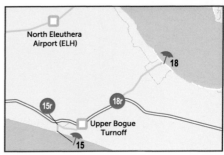

North Eleuthera
Airport (ELH)

18

15r   18r

Upper Bogue
Turnoff

15

Beach ★☆☆   Road ★★☆

Beach: 25° 27.842, -76° 38.958
Road: 25° 27.147, -76° 39.772

How to Get There

From points north
Total travel time: 2.1 mi. / 10 min
From Upper Bogue turnoff proceed south for 0.9 miles. Make a left and proceed 1.2 miles to turnabout parking area.

Time / Distance
To beach road: 0.9 mi. / 2 min
Beach road to beach: 1.2 mi. / 8 min

From points south
Total travel time: 4.9 mi. / 14 min
From Glass Window Bridge proceed north for 3.7 miles. Make a right and proceed 1.2 miles to turnabout parking area.

Time / Distance
To beach road: 3.7 mi. / 6 min
Beach road to beach: 1.2 mi. / 8 min

What You Should Know

Privacy	Semi-private
Shade	Some
Accessibility	4WD recommended
Beach Path	Sandy
Water Entry	Sandy
Water Condition	Shallow bay
Litter/Seaweed	Extensive
Nearest Town	Gregorytown
Snorkeling	Poor
Shelling	No
Beach Size	0.4 miles x 10 feet

circular parking area and another further down to the south. You'll need to move further south to have any privacy from the first house, but expect boat traffic in the bay from the Harbour Island marinas. The water was extremely shallow along the entire length of the beach.

The prime reasons to come to this beach are the unique views, ample shade and shallow bay waters. Unfortunately, the poor beach road, voluminous debris and lack of anything particularly endearing makes this a beach to avoid.

Whale Point Beach

This little gem is the best of the litter in this part of Northern Eleuthera owing to its flowing landscape, privacy and overall uniqueness. Whale Point Beach does come with a couple of caveats, however. First, it is not easy to find. You can drive past the small parking area on the opposite side of the street from the beach steps or even miss seeing the top of the steps, which are almost completely overgrown with ferns and brush. If you find the parking spot and the steps then make sure you leave a trail of breadcrumbs back because you can miss them in the opposite direction, too. Second, there are 33 steps down to the beach. Avoid this beach if going up and down a long set of relatively steep steps is going to be a problem.

Now, having the bad points out of the way, descend the steps to find a charming secluded spot with a large backdrop of Casuarinas, dense ferns, oyster plants and an abundance of other assorted greenery. The beach contour resembles a gently gliding ocean wave with a series of soft semi-horseshoe turns. At different points the beach is both wide and narrow depending on how far up the grass has crept giving the beach a unique rustic look. The locals have built a makeshift bench out of driftwood and there is also a homemade BBQ pit in front of a sign urging you to leave it as you found it.

The water is typical of the bayside — shallow, flat and sandy — with the notable distinction of being a turtle feeding area.

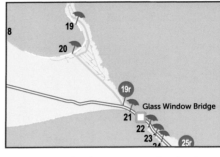

Beach ★★☆ Road ★★☆

Beach: 25° 28.087, -76° 37.538
Road: 25° 26.461, -76° 36.585

What You Should Know

Privacy	Semi-private
Shade	Plenty
Accessibility	4WD recommended
Beach Path	Stairs
Water Entry	Sandy
Water Condition	Shallow bay
Litter/Seaweed	Moderate
Nearest Town	Gregorytown
Snorkeling	Poor
Shelling	No
Beach Size	0.3 miles x 10 to 30 yds

The water is calm and shallow resembling a long wading pool. Homes to the south are at least a quarter of a mile away giving you a high degree of privacy. The beach also offers an excellent amount of both sun and shade.

In general, this rather clean beach seems natural and rugged owing to some dried seaweed to the back of the beach that, combined with the vegetation, gives an overall unkempt look. Whale Point Beach is picturesque, cute, quaint, and private. It is worth the extra half a mile drive from the Bottom Harbour Beach Club to find this very nice beach.

How to Get There

From points north
Total travel time: 5.8 mi. / 20 min
From Upper Bogue proceed south 3.6 miles. Make a left and proceed 1.4 miles. Make a right and proceed 0.6 miles making a left at T. Proceed several hundred feet to parking space on right with long set of steps on left in jungle down to beach.

Time / Distance
To beach road: 3.6 mi. / 6 min
Beach road to beach: 2.2 mi. / 14 min

From points south
Total travel time: 2.4 mi. / 15 min
From Glass Window Bridge proceed north 0.2 miles. Make right and proceed 1.4 miles. Make a right and proceed 0.6 miles making a left at T. Proceed several hundred feet to parking space on right with long set of steps on left in jungle down to beach.

Time / Distance
To beach road: 0.2 mi. / 1 min
Beach road to beach: 2.2 mi. / 14 min

Bottom Harbour Beach

The best characteristic of the Bottom Harbour beach is not the beach. The restaurant, bar and kayak rentals at the Bottom Harbour Beach Club are the chief reasons to come to this beach. Additionally, you will find your typical bay water access, shallow and sandy, very little actual exposed beach sand, lots of shade and not much privacy.

The fallen cement dock next to the colorful club provides a stark contrast to this lazy little setting. Even though there is a quarter mile of sand, tides play a huge factor in terms of usable beach area. You'll find that bringing chairs and setting up under the rows of tall Casuarinas will provide the best vantage for your view of North Eleuthera.

The bar/restaurant is cute and quaint with a full menu of typical Bahamian fare. The neighboring homes and restaurant eliminate your privacy, but that's not what you come to this beach for. You come here to use the restaurant and to have the convenience of its amenities next to a beach that is best suited as a wading area. You probably won't need too much sun protection here as the entire area is quite protected from harmful rays.

Bottom Harbour is easy to find and get to although the road can be extremely rutted in spots. Drop by for a spot of lunch, cold drink, or to kayak around the bay before heading out to some of the more beautiful beaches in the area.

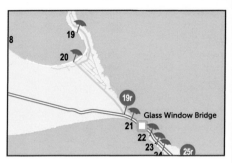

Beach ★☆☆   Road ★★☆

Beach: 25° 27.427, -76° 37.531
Road (19r): 25° 26.461, -76° 36.585

How to Get There

From points north
Total travel time: 5.1 mi. / 18 min
From Upper Bogue turnoff proceed south 3.6 miles. Make a left and proceed 1.5 miles to end. Park to right of Bottom Harbour Beach Club.

Time / Distance
To beach road: 3.6 mi. / 6 min
Beach road to beach: 1.5 mi. / 12 min

From points south
Total travel time: 1.7 mi. / 13 min
From Glass Window Bridge proceed north 0.2 miles. Make a right and proceed 1.5 miles to end. Park to right of Bottom Harbour Beach Club.

Time / Distance
To beach road: 0.2 mi. / 1 min
Beach road to beach: 1.5 mi. / 12 min

What You Should Know	
Privacy	Semi-private
Shade	Some
Accessibility	4WD recommended
Beach Path	None
Water Entry	Sandy
Water Condition	Shallow bay
Litter/Seaweed	Moderate
Nearest Town	Gregorytown
Snorkeling	Poor
Shelling	No
Beach Size	0.25 miles x 6 feet

Glass Window Bridge North / Cable Beach

This beach was nicknamed Cable Beach not because it bares any resemblance to its more famous Nassau counterpart, but because it serves the same function for telecommunications cables. The conspicuous conduit is quite visible both in the water and on land before being concealed underground. It's presence is almost reason enough to skip this location.

So, why come here? The view here is utterly delectable with beautiful turquoise water stretching as far as the eye can see. This is an excellent sunset spot and it has a very unique rock formation, a donut shaped cutout in an elevated rock pillar. This can be your private

cave for two, offering commanding views of the ocean from its narrow opening. It can be found by continuing south across the rocks towards the Glass Window Bridge. Be aware that you will have to climb up about 6 feet off the ground to get inside the donut.

Access to the sand, set amongst desert rock, is found by walking down a cement embankment just below Queen's Highway on the northern side of the bridge. The first two small beaches are each about 50 feet long and 10 feet wide. There is another small beach further south which is cleaner with better water access. You can access the water from

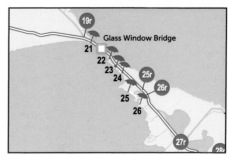

Glass Window Bridge

Beach ★☆☆   Road ★★☆

Beach: 25° 26.420, -76° 36.507
Road: 25° 26.420, -76° 36.507

How to Get There

From points north
Total travel time: 4.7 mi. / 8 min
From Upper Bogue turnoff proceed south for 4.7 miles to access road on right.

Time / Distance
To beach road: 4.7 mi. / 8 min
Beach road to beach: 0.0 mi. / 0 min

From points south
Total travel time: 0.1 mi. / 1 min
From Glass Window Bridge proceed north 0.1 mile to access road on left.

Time / Distance
To beach road: 0.1 mi. / 1 min
Beach road to beach: 0.0 mi. / 0 min

What You Should Know	
Privacy	Semi-private
Shade	None
Accessibility	Car
Beach Path	Cement walkway
Water Entry	Rocks and sand
Water Condition	Shallow Caribbean
Litter/Seaweed	Light
Nearest Town	Gregorytown
Snorkeling	Average
Shelling	No
Beach Size	160 yards x 10 feet

any of the beaches without water shoes.

The lack of trees coupled with the proximity to Queen's Highway means you will have neither protection from the sun nor privacy from passing cars. There is a nice secluded water cave across the highway, which can be reached from the same parking spot. It has crashing waves and lots of shade.

Cable Beach feels stark and desolate yet is easily accessed, has the cave and rock formation, and provides a nice panoramic view. It is also a good beginner snorkeling spot because of clear, shallow water littered with colorful tropical fish.

Glass Window Bridge South / Boiling Hole Beach

Just to the south of Glass Window Bridge is another of those beaches that barely qualifies as a beach. The most interesting attribute of this location is an active blowhole right by the road. The water will shoot either a stream of vapor or sometimes a two-story geyser out of a hole that is no more than a foot in diameter. This seems to occur constantly. Listen for the sound of rushing water at first and follow it to the Boiling Hole.

If you are intent on getting to the beach itself pull off of the Queen's Highway wherever there is space then hike down a fairly treacherous cement block and through the woods to two sandy patches of sand. There is no clear beach path either at the road or down through the trees so you just have to wing this one. It's about a 500-foot hike.

There are two small beaches that are each about 25 feet long and 10 feet wide. They are set in front of a forest of dead Casuarinas. These two beach pods were covered with a lot of seaweed and also had some other debris indicating that they don't get visited much.

Your view is of miles of beautiful turquoise Caribbean seas with one large rock outcropping that sits to the north of the more famous Twin Sisters rocks. The south beach pod has

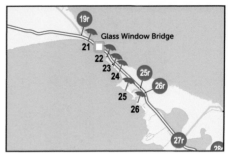

Glass Window Bridge

Beach ★★☆ Road ★★☆

Beach: 25° 26.123, -76° 36.092
Road: 25° 26.123, -76° 36.092

How to Get There

From points north
Total travel time: 0.1 mi. / 2 min
From Glass Window Bridge proceed south 0.1 mile to access point on right marked by large panels of cement. Park on side of road. Hike 500 feet to beach.

Time / Distance
To beach road: 0.1 mi. / 1 min
Beach road to beach: 500 foot walk / 2 min

From points south
Total travel time: 4.4 mi. / 23 min
From Gregorytown intersection proceed north 4.4 miles to access point on left marked by large panels of cement. Park on side of road. Hike 500 feet to beach.

Time / Distance
To beach road: 4.4 mi. / 21 min
Beach road to beach: 500 foot walk / 2 min

What You Should Know

Privacy	Semi-private
Shade	None
Accessibility	Car
Beach Path	Rocky
Water Entry	Rocky
Water Condition	Shallow Caribbean
Litter/Seaweed	Light
Nearest Town	Gregorytown
Snorkeling	Poor
Shelling	No
Beach Size	50 feet x 10 feet

an extremely rocky water entry while the northern beach is somewhat better. Still, this isn't a beach that you would seek out or plan to spend any significant time on.

The overall lack of privacy, poor beach access, and sub-standard beach conditions make this one to cross off the list unless you are looking for an adventure. The roadside Boiling Hole is the more interesting aspect of the site. You'll get a more picturesque view from nearby Cable Beach or a better overall experience by going just a little further south to nearby Twin Sisters.

Twin Sisters Beach

Tranquility is the first word that comes to mind when describing the view at lovely Twin Sisters Beach. The water has the luster of a fine sapphire. As it surrounds the contrasting darkness of the Twin Sisters rocks it seems to envelop and support them causing them to float on a sea of blue, the height and roundness of their adjoining shapes being their distinguishing features.

The beach can be tricky to find when heading south, but is much easier to find when going north. That's because the path leading down to the beach is nestled behind a tall set of roadside Casuarinas. The path extends all the way down to the beach, but due to its degrading condition we recommend parking close to the highway and walking the short way down the path to the beach. Plus, a visible car parked by the road will let others know that you are there, and perhaps cause them to choose another beach.

The beach is slightly rocky with smallish pebbles, rocks, and large rock ledges that provide an interesting landscape. It is littered with spindly dead Casuarinas that look like a bunch of beachside coat racks in front of the larger shaded Casuarina forest to the rear of the beach. You can find ample

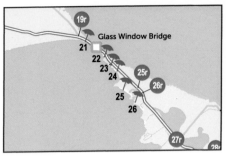

Glass Window Bridge

Beach ★★☆ Road ★★☆

Beach: 25° 25.988, -76° 36.005
Road: 25° 25.988, -76° 36.005

How to Get There

From points north
Total travel time: 0.2 mi. / 2 min
From Glass Window Bridge proceed south
0.2 miles to access road on right hidden
behind string of casaurina trees. It is much
easier to see the access road when heading
north as it looks like a long driveway just off
of the Queen's Highway.

Time / Distance
To beach road: 0.2 mi. / 1 min
Beach road to beach: 500 foot walk / 1 min

From points south
Total travel time: 4.3 mi. / 21 min
From Gregorytown intersection proceed
north 4.3 miles to access road on left hidden
behind string of casaurina trees. It is much
easier to see the access road when proceeding
north as it looks like a long driveway just off
of the Queen's Highway.

Time / Distance
To beach road: 4.3 mi. / 20 min
Beach road to beach: 500 foot walk / 1 min

What You Should Know

Privacy	Semi-private
Shade	Some
Accessibility	Car
Beach Path	Sandy
Water Entry	Rocks and sand
Water Condition	Shallow Caribbean
Litter/Seaweed	Light
Nearest Town	Gregorytown
Snorkeling	Poor
Shelling	No
Beach Size	120 yards x 20 feet

amounts of sun and shade with loads of soft
needles to nestle on.

The water quality is very good. Not only
is the beach very picturesque, the water is
quite alluring and swimmable. You'll have to
endure a little noise from passing cars, but
the trees provide ample protection to keep
you hidden from view.

Put Twin Sisters on your list of 'should-
visit beaches to see in the north' and hope
that you get there first before someone claims
this spot. The beach is only 120 yards long
and you'll want it all for yourself.

South Twins Beach

Referring to this location as a backup to Twin Sisters does not really do it justice as it has its own charm and ambience. This will still be your second choice and the beach you'd choose if you were headed to Twin Sisters, finding it occupied. It's just a bit south and still within view of the two cays, although from this vantage point they look like a single merged cay.

Getting to the beach is simple. Being just a few hundred feet from Queen's Highway, it makes more sense to park closer to the road and then walk back due to fallen trees

that you will have to climb over. Taking the short walk through the tall Casuarinas and over a bed of their needles will bring you to this little 100 yard patch of sand that merges with a number of small rocks and pebbles, especially towards the back of the beach.

At the time the beach was inspected it showed signs of having been used recently. There was a man-made BBQ pit along with a garbage bag that hadn't been carried out and that was probably the worst thing we found. Trees had been cut and harvested to make Casuarina briquettes, neither aiding nor

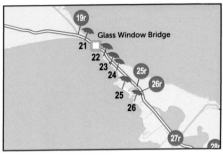

Glass Window Bridge

Beach ★★☆   Road ★★☆

Beach: 25° 25.870, -76° 35.877
Road: 25° 25.870, -76° 35.877

How to Get There

From points north
Total travel time: 0.4 mi. / 3 min
From Glass Window Bridge proceed south
0.4 miles miles to well hidden acces road on
right behind casuarinas. Walk down access
path that is overgrown and has fallen tree
limbs.

Time / Distance
To beach road: 0.4 mi. / 2 min
Beach road to beach: 500 foot walk / 1 min

From points south
Total travel time: 4.1 mi. / 20 min
From Gregorytown intersection proceed
north 4.1 miles to well hidden acces road on
left behind casuarinas. Walk down access
path that is overgrown and has fallen tree
limbs.

Time / Distance
To beach road: 4.1 mi. / 19 min
Beach road to beach: 500 foot walk / 1 min

What You Should Know

Privacy	Semi-private
Shade	Some
Accessibility	Car
Beach Path	Sandy
Water Entry	Sandy
Water Condition	Shallow Caribbean
Litter/Seaweed	Light
Nearest Town	Gregorytown
Snorkeling	Poor
Shelling	No
Beach Size	100 yards x 20 feet

detracting from the look of the beach. You'll
have a nice complement of sand, shade and
shallow, sandy water entry with no rocks. The
noise from Queen's Highway is a bit annoy-
ing, but you are visually protected. The only
houses within view are well to the south, and
barely within eyeshot.

All in all this is a great little beach, and
if not for the fact that there are other better
beaches nearby it would probably be an excellent choice for a tranquil day in paradise.

Gaulding Cay Beach

Lovely Gaulding Cay Beach came close to earning our highest grade, but a couple of notable blemishes kept if off the premier list. The main issue had to do with privacy and the number of houses that are built along the beach. In fact, this is one of only three beaches where we encountered live humans the entire time we were researching this book. There are also a fair amount of rocks on the beach and in the water. That's not to say that you can't get into the water without water shoes, you can, but if you don't want to step on or over rocks then you will either have to wade carefully or choose a more northern location on the beach.

The beach resembles Ten Bay in its straightness. It stretches a full quarter mile and is 20 to 30 yards wide. The sand is good and hard making it excellent for walking or even a short run. The view here is really special. Charming Gaulding Cay sits but a mere 30 yards offshore and is the only thing that breaks up what looks like your own Caribbean ocean infinity pool. It can be snorkeled or climbed with water shoes.

You'll find an abundance of sun along with plenty of shade. This is a decent shelling beach. The beach road is wide and the parking is ample. This is a very picturesque beach to see and contrast with Lover's, which is the epitome of Atlantic splendor. Its proximity to nearby establishments makes this beach even more desirable especially when traveling north on the island.

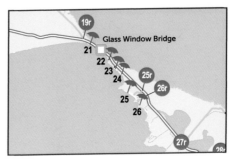

Glass Window Bridge

Beach ★★☆ Road ★★☆

Beach: 25° 25.487, -76° 35.690
Road: 25° 25.522, -76° 35.521

How to Get There

From points north
Total travel time: 1.3 mi. / 7 min
From Glass Window Bridge proceed south 1.0 miles. Make a right and proceed to fork. Make a right and follow road to end to beach.

Time / Distance
To beach road: 1.0 mi. / 5 min
Beach road to beach: 0.3 mi. / 2 min

From points south
Total travel time: 3.8 mi. / 13 min
From Gregorytown intersection proceed north 3.5 miles. Make a left and proceed to fork. Make a right and follow road to end to beach.

Time / Distance
To beach road: 3.5 mi. / 11 min
Beach road to beach: 0.3 mi. / 2 min

What You Should Know	
Privacy	Semi-private
Shade	Some
Accessibility	Car, bumpy
Beach Path	Sandy
Water Entry	Sandy
Water Condition	Shallow Caribbean
Litter/Seaweed	None
Nearest Town	Gregorytown
Snorkeling	Average
Shelling	Yes
Beach Size	0.25 miles x 25 yards

Small Bay Beach

How could the smallest of beaches turn out to be the one where we'd encounter the most people, a whopping five at one time? Small Bay physically sits between Twin Sisters and South Twins, but due to its rectangular shape with high rocky points you feel like you are completely boxed off from the outside. These walls make you feel completely isolated. The single houses on each side of the bay along with a boat storage hut at the center of the beach and what looks like continued construction in the community makes us think that this beach could be gated off in the near future, its use limited to

that of residents or renters of these dwellings.

The water here is its most attractive feature. It has a similar quaint look to that of Oleander Gardens, but is much smaller and much more protected. Lush palms, Casuarinas, and beds of Casuarina needles add to the ambience of a relaxing setting that is intensified by the swimming area and its view.

Privacy is obviously a factor here and construction noise in the community could be a problem until the houses are completed. Our recommendation is to give this beach a look before it becomes one of those lost beaches reserved only for the community.

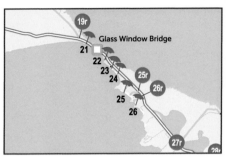

Glass Window Bridge

Beach ★★☆   Road ★★☆

Beach: 25° 25.350, -76° 35.588
Road: 25° 25.415, -76° 35.429

How to Get There

From points north
Total travel time: 1.4 mi / 8 min
From Glass Window Bridge proceed south 1.2 miles. Make a right and proceed 0.2 miles, making left at fork to beach.

Time / Distance
To beach road: 1.2 mi. / 6 min
Beach road to beach: 0.2 mi. / 2 min

From points south
Total travel time: 3.5 mi. / 11 min
From Gregorytown intersection proceed north 3.3 miles. Make a left and proceed 0.2 miles, making left at fork to beach.

Time / Distance
To beach road: 3.3 mi. / 9 min
Beach road to beach: 0.2 mi. / 2 min

What You Should Know	
Privacy	Semi-private
Shade	Plenty
Accessibility	Car, bumpy
Beach Path	Sandy
Water Entry	Sandy
Water Condition	Shallow Caribbean
Litter/Seaweed	Light
Nearest Town	Gregorytown
Snorkeling	Poor
Shelling	No
Beach Size	100 yards x 20 yards

Lover's Beach

Simply majestic and one of the best, if not THE best, beach on the island. I almost don't want to describe this beach for fear of depriving you of the experience of seeing it for yourself. Cleanliness is of extreme importance in terms of how we grade a beach and for an Atlantic-side beach this was the biggest and cleanest of the lot. The vast pristine sand stretches in a gentle curve around one of the tallest grassy dunes, which is probably only two stories high, but felt more like four.

The beach itself is not hard to find since you are way above it on the cliff as you drive in, and because it's so big it's easy to see. What is tricky to find is the beach path leading to the sand. Just past the very northern tip of this beach the beach road is sandy and very uneven giving you the impression

that you could tip your vehicle over if you aren't too careful. It is easy to pass the little turnoff where a slender sandy overgrown walking path takes you down onto the rocky shoreline. From there you have to walk a few hundred feet to the beach. Because of the walk through the grass, and the distance from where you park to where the beach is, this is not a great location for young children.

Once on the beach you will be impressed with just about everything. The sand color and texture is magnificent. The sandy water access is perfect the entire mile of beach. The wideness of the beach, reaching anywhere between 40' and 60' depending on how far the ocean recedes, makes the beach feel twice as big as it is. It's a good walking beach. It's a good running beach. It's an excellent sunning

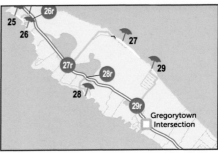

Beach ★★☆   Road ★☆☆

Beach: 25° 25.113, -76° 33.999
Road: 25° 24.596, -76° 34.807

What You Should Know

Privacy	Secluded
Shade	None
Accessibility	4WD recommended
Beach Path	Sandy
Water Entry	Sandy
Water Condition	Deep ocean
Litter/Seaweed	None
Nearest Town	Gregorytown
Snorkeling	Poor
Shelling	No
Beach Size	0.85 miles x 40 yards

and swimming beach. The elevated views before you get to the beach are outstanding. There are even a number of rocky vista vantage points to explore before you get onto the high beach dune which offer caves, cliffs and deep blue water views. On a clear day you'll be able to see all the way to Whale Point and past it to Harbour Island.

The area is completely private and isolated with no signs of life except for what nature has lovingly provided. Lover's Beach is one that you will want to spend the whole day on and hope to never leave. This beach is a must-see and we just hope that its pristine condition is consistent at all times. Bring a beach umbrella and your special loved one to experience the best of what Eleuthera has to offer.

How to Get There

From points north
Total travel time: 3.5 mi. / 19.5 min
From Glass Window Bridge proceed south 2.3 miles. Make a left and proceed straight for 0.6 miles. Bear left at fork and proceed 0.3 miles. Bear right, then continue another 0.3 miles, bearing right at forks, until you reach the beach path on the left through the dunes. Walk straight down path several hundred feet to sandy path at extreme north of beach and walk right several hundred feet across rocky point to beach.

Time / Distance
To beach road: 2.3 mi. / 11 min
Beach road to beach: 1.2 mi. / 8.5 min

From points south
Total travel time: 3.4 mi. / 15.5 min
From Gregorytown intersection proceed 2.2 miles. Make a right and proceed straight for 0.6 miles. Bear left at fork and proceed 0.3 miles. Bear right, then continue another 0.3 miles, bearing right at forks, until you reach the beach path on the left through the dunes. Walk straight down path several hundred feet to sandy path at extreme north of beach and walk right several hundred feet across rocky point to beach.

Time / Distance
To beach road: 2.2 mi. / 7 min
Beach road to beach: 1.2 mi. / 8.5 min

Oleander Gardens Beach

You should have no problem finding this quiet community beach, which might be the most idyllic looking Caribbean beach anywhere on the island. Oleander Gardens features a soft palm-lined backdrop and a high cliff wall perfectly framing a little quaint bay. If there is any beach that defines beach getaway more than Oleander Gardens I'd be surprised!

First, let's discuss what's problematic. The sand quality here is simply atrocious. It is rocky and pebbly throughout and the rocks extend for some ways into the water, making water shoes a requirement. Remarkably, there is one narrow path cut between the rocks in the water that might provide some safe passage out to deeper waters should someone neglect to take our advice on water shoes.

The beach is also very small. The whole waterfront area is only about 100 yards long with about 30 yards classifiable as beach. The bay is calm and shallow. A small picnic area to the left under some palm trees makes this an ideal setting for a picnic and a swim.

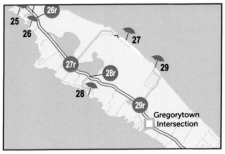

Gregorytown
Intersection

Beach ★☆☆   Road ★★★

Beach: 25° 24.147, -76° 34.492
Road: 25° 24.369, -76° 34.476

How to Get There

From points north
Total travel time: 3.2 mi. / 17 min
From Glass Window Bridge proceed south 2.8 miles. Make right into community of Oleander Gardens. Proceed to end of road and make left at T. Make next right into beach parking area.

Time / Distance
To beach road: 2.8 mi. / 15 min
Beach road to beach: 0.4 mi. / 2 min

From points south
Total travel time: 2.1 mi. / 6.5 min
From Gregorytown intersection proceed north for 1.7 miles. Make left into community of Oleander Gardens. Proceed to end of road and make left at T. Make next right into beach parking area.

Time / Distance
To beach road: 1.7 mi. / 4.5 min
Beach road to beach: 0.4 mi. / 2 min

What You Should Know

Privacy	Public
Shade	Some
Accessibility	Car
Beach Path	Cement walkway
Water Entry	Rocky
Water Condition	Shallow Caribbean
Litter/Seaweed	None
Nearest Town	Gregorytown
Snorkeling	Poor
Shelling	No
Beach Size	120 yards x 30 feet

Unfortunately, the fact that the beach is so rocky severely impacted the overall grade. Because this beach is set in front of a community with little privacy and ample worker noise, the number of negatives totally outweighs how scenic and picturesque it is here. If you don't mind these issues then Oleander is a perfectly quaint beach set amongst the scenic cliffs and swaying palms. It could be just the right tropical setting for you.

BEACH 28

Holiday Beach

If you like long, bumpy rides that end in not so spectacular beaches then Holiday Beach might be the one for you. The road leading back to the beach is very poor. It is rutted, bumpy and has loose gravel areas that are easy to lose traction on. After ascending the initial hill you have to almost walk your vehicle to the bottom before leveling out on a slightly better road. And, the experience doesn't get much better from there.

This beach is rugged with long rocky ledges dominating the landscape intermixed with an array of boulders just for laughs. There was a tremendous amount of debris in all directions making a very unattractive first impression. In fact, it was hard to find

a place that wasn't littered with wash up except on the rocks themselves. The beach does improve somewhat as you move south.

The most dramatic feature on the beach was a cut away with chiseled patterns to the left of the beach path as you face the water. On a calm day this little gateway would serve as the easiest and most unique way into the ocean, but on a rough day it's just too dangerous. Several hundred feet to the right is another sandy water access area that looked like the most logical spot to set up base camp. However, there is one solitary house on the dune just above that part of the beach which seems to always be within one's field of vision. Even though this beach is

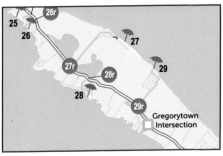

Beach ★★☆ Road ★☆☆

Beach: 25° 24.497, -76° 33.287
Road: 25° 23.856, -76° 33.539

What You Should Know

Privacy	Semi-private
Shade	None
Accessibility	4WD recommended
Beach Path	Sandy
Water Entry	Sandy
Water Condition	Deep ocean
Litter/Seaweed	Extensive
Nearest Town	Gregorytown
Snorkeling	Poor
Shelling	No
Beach Size	0.25 miles x 40 yards

How to Get There

From points north
Total travel time: 5.0 mi. / 29 min
From Glass Window Bridge proceed south
4.0 miles. Make left onto paved access road.
Proceed straight onto gravel road at 0.3 miles
and continue straight up hill. At fork bear
right and continue straight around bend
making a right at the T to the beach path.

Time / Distance
To beach road: 4.0 mi. / 20 min
Beach road to beach: 1.0 mi. / 9 min

From points south
Total travel time: 1.5 mi. / 10.5 min
From Gregorytown intersection proceed
north for 0.5 miles. Make right onto paved
access road. Proceed straight onto gravel road
at 0.3 miles and continue straight up hill. At
fork bear right and continue straight around
bend making a right at the T to the beach
path.

Time / Distance
To beach road: 0.5 mi. / 1.5 min
Beach road to beach: 1.0 mi. / 9 min

quite private that one house gave the impression that it wasn't.

If you do choose to go here then proceed
as far south by foot as possible where the
beach is more pleasant, scenic and less covered in debris. On the negative side, there is
no shade, excessive wash up, too many rocks
and boulders, and one house on a hill that
reminded me of a vulture waiting to take in
its meal. The one dramatic cutout and some
interesting shades of rock on the southern
end of the beach were its most interesting
features, but not enough to warrant a return
visit. Nearby Alicetown South or Surfer's
Beach are better choices.

Surfer's Beach

What you're first struck by is neither the waves nor the length of the beach. It's the height of the dune backing the beach, which looks to be almost 40' high, along with how wide the beach is, stretching to almost 50 yards at its widest. Then, when you see the mile and a quarter of some of the cleanest sand on the island and a continuous break of waves that must make a surfer drool like one of Pavlov's dogs, you probably have to pinch yourself a little as a reminder that this is real.

Getting to this beach is the worst part. There are a number of ways to get here, and we chose the shortest, most direct route, which also might be the bumpiest. Arriving at the final sandy beach path we thought better of taking the chance of driving up the hill, as it was soft sand with deep impressions.

We parked at the bottom of the hill, and took a leisurely five-minute walk to the first beach path, which spilled us out right next to the Surfer's Beach shack. This is an assortment of wood, palm fronds and fishnets that provide support for various colorful beach wash up. Don't leave this spot if you require shade, as this is all that's to be found.

The sand stretches out in a loving embrace of the ocean, meandering in a concave fashion both north and south from this point. There is a large, rocky outcropping to the north, which is definitely worth exploring. In addition to it providing almost perfect protection from the constant battering of waves, it acts as a waterfall of sorts with gently flowing water cascading into tidal pools that were almost big enough to bathe in. Either

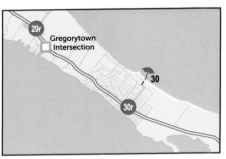

Beach ★★★ Road ★☆☆

Beach: 25° 22.826, -76° 31.616
Road: 25° 22.425, -76° 31.854

What You Should Know	
Privacy	Secluded
Shade	None
Accessibility	4WD recommended
Beach Path	Dune
Water Entry	Sandy
Water Condition	Deep ocean; waves
Litter/Seaweed	Light
Nearest Town	Alicetown
Snorkeling	Poor
Shelling	Yes
Beach Size	1.25 miles x 50 yards

How to Get There

From points north

Total travel time: 2.5 mi. / 19 min

From Gregorytown intersection proceed south for 2.0 miles. Make a left onto access road. Proceed 0.4 miles on rough road to next right leading up sandy hill. Either proceed cautiously up this hill for 0.1 miles or park at base and walk up hill to beach path on right. There are several beach paths on this road.

Time / Distance

To beach road: 2.0 mi. / 10 min
Beach road to beach: 0.5 mi. / 9 min

From points south

Total travel time: 3.9 mi. / 15 min

From main intersection in Hatchet Bay just before marina proceed north for 3.4 miles. Make a right onto access road. Proceed 0.4 miles on rough road to next right leading up sandy hill. Either proceed cautiously up this hill for 0.1 miles or park at base and walk up hill to beach path on right. There are several beach paths on this road.

Time / Distance

To beach road: 3.4 mi. / 6 min
Beach road to beach: 0.5 mi. / 9 min

side of the point was quite swimmable even with rough surf, but on days when the ocean is calm you can enter pretty much anywhere you want as the only difficult area is at the northernmost part of the beach where a ring of rocks stretches all the way to the cliffs.

The beach is extremely private and secluded with only one lone house way up on the furthest, north cliff. While surfing is certainly in order, this is an ideal beach for any number of reasons or activities. It's great for walking, running, swimming, shelling, body surfing and tanning. This vast beach brings with it a great sound experience with the constant drone of crashing waves restoring clarity of thought and mind. The only negatives are the rough beach roads coupled with the lack of shade. Surfer's Beach is one of the best the island has to offer.

Alicetown Beach Public North

It is often said that every road in Eleuthera leads to either a beach or a cemetery. Sometimes it leads to both. The northern, public beach in Alicetown is one of the latter. Coming off of the road the first thing to greet you is the cemetery, which stretches almost 100 yards down the back of the beach before ending in a Casuarina forest. The next thing you notice is how rocky the beach is, but for some, the rocks are an advantage. They serve as a barrier retaining numerous shells on shore. In fact, you'll have about a ten-foot swath of shells that runs the entire length of the beach. These shells are very small! While several beaches in the Tarpum Bay area are better overall for shelling, this is one of, if not the best for that activity to the north.

You'll need water shoes if you intend to swim in its shallow bay waters. The rock ledge extends about ten feet deep on land and another ten feet into the ocean before leveling out to sand. While the ledge itself is also flat with no sharp edges, it is slippery, so always wear water shoes as a precaution. The front of the beach lacks privacy with a few private homes in the area. The further down the beach you go, especially after you reach the Casuarinas, the more privacy and shade you'll have. However, we did find some squatter shacks set up at the far end of the woods. They weren't occupied at the time we were there, but they did look active.

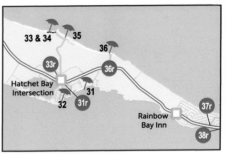

Beach ⭐☆☆ Road ⭐⭐⭐

Beach: 25° 20.879, -76° 28.825
Road: 25° 21.054, -76° 29.094

How to Get There

From points north
Total travel time: 6.0 mi. / 11 min
From Gregorytown intersection proceed south 5.4 miles to main intersection in Hatchet Bay just after marina. Make a right onto paved road. Make 1st left and proceed 0.6 miles on paved road to cemetery and beach path.

Time / Distance
To beach road: 5.4 mi. / 9 min
Beach road to beach: 0.6 mi. / 2 min

From points south
Total travel time: 3.3 mi. / 6 min
From Rainbow Bay Inn proceed north 2.7 miles to main intersection in Hatchet Bay just before marina. Make a left onto paved road. Make 1st left and proceed 0.6 miles on paved road to cemetery and beach path.

Time / Distance
To beach road: 2.7 mi. / 4 min
Beach road to beach: 0.6 mi. / 2 min

What You Should Know

Privacy	Semi-private
Shade	Some
Accessibility	Car
Beach Path	None
Water Entry	Rocky
Water Condition	Shallow Caribbean
Litter/Seaweed	Light
Nearest Town	Alicetown
Snorkeling	Average
Shelling	Yes
Beach Size	0.25 miles x 20 yards

The beach is very easy to find and get to. All you have to do is make your first left after entering the community and then follow a well-paved road to the end where you'll find an ample parking area by a small shaded beach pavilion. Of the two beaches in Alicetown, this is the better choice unless the rocks or cemetery bother you. The beach is almost a quarter of a mile long, so it's good for walking. The wide beachcombing field gives you an extra activity to do. There was little seaweed and some leftover litter along with an abandoned dinghy right in the middle of the beach, but they were minor inconveniences in exchange for a very eclectic beach with a wide Caribbean view.

Alicetown Beach Public

This small public beach seems ill-fitted at the end of its concrete jungle. It is located at the back end of a populated Bahamian town and offers no privacy. There are houses all around and the three palm trees at the back of the beach provide little protection either from sight or sound. Since it is on the Caribbean side of the island the water is both shallow and clear with no significant drop off for several hundred feet from shore. Small sand bars poke through the ocean surface in several places except when the tide is high.

The left side of the beach is quite rocky, but to the right side there is a good snorkel spot. You'll want to stay right in the center of its 40 yards to have the best water access.

There are several picnic tables under the palm trees with a few dilapidated palapas. The beach gives off an aura of being a popular night party spot.

This is a good beach for young children because it's easy to get to on perfectly paved roads. Since the beach is right on the road you have a very short walk to a sandy, shallow area that would be a perfect kids' wading pool. There was some minor seaweed and debris, but nothing significant. The biggest problem with this beach is where it's located relative to the town. We might have caught it on the wrong day, but the constant noise from the neighborhood made us long for the peace and quiet of a more secluded area.

Beach ★☆☆   Road ★★★

Beach: 25° 20.688, -76° 29.057
Road (31r): 25° 21.054, -76° 29.094

How to Get There

From points north

Total travel time: 5.8 mi. / 11 min
From Gregorytown intersection proceed south 5.4 miles to main intersection in Hatchet Bay just after marina. Make a right onto paved road and proceed 0.4 miles to Stop sign. Make a left and proceed 400 feet to beach on left.

Time / Distance
To beach road: 5.4 mi. / 9 min
Beach road to beach: 0.4 mi. / 2 min

From points south

Total travel time: 3.1 mi. / 6 min
From Rainbow Bay Inn proceed north 2.7 miles to main intersection in Hatchet Bay just before marina. Make a left onto paved road and proceed 0.4 miles to Stop sign. Make a left and proceed 400 feet to beach on left.

Time / Distance
To beach road: 2.7 mi. / 4 min
Beach road to beach: 0.4 mi. / 2 min

What You Should Know	
Privacy	Public
Shade	None
Accessibility	Car
Beach Path	None
Water Entry	Sandy
Water Condition	Shallow Caribbean
Litter/Seaweed	Light
Nearest Town	Alicetown
Snorkeling	Average
Shelling	No
Beach Size	40 yards x 20 yards

Slide Beach and Round Hole Beach

This single location features two of the most unique beaches on the island. From a cool and wow perspective these two little gems stand out. Upon arriving at the site there seems to be no real beach. It looks like one of those dead end rock ledges that we often found on our quests. Off in the distance we spied what looked like something of interest.

About a tenth of mile to the north we found the first oasis, Slide Beach. Carved between the striated rocks was a triangular shaped patch of sand leading to a white rock ledge that led to another plot of sand that angled into the water. The water dramatically rushes through the twenty-foot cutout. The view from the back of the beach provides just enough elevation to soak up the cliffs to the north. On a calm day this is probably a lovely little swimming hole, but we weren't able to fully evaluate it due to the dangerously high waves.

Trekking another 200 feet north led to the discovery of hidden Round Hole. It looks like a sandy cave pit that had its lid removed leaving it exposed to the air and sun. You can climb down into the bowl, which is about ten feet deep. It's not a perfectly symmetrical 360 degree circle, but reminded us of a circular gladiator pit where instead of predators being led into the stadium you get a rush of ocean water from a hole at the front of the cave. From inside Round Hole you have no view of the ocean, as the walls are too high. Plenty of sun comes in and you also have a couple of ledges that you can sneak under to escape the sun. While you wouldn't go swimming here, there is enough water let in that you can dip your feet or even wade a bit towards the deeper part. Consider this beach your own private sanctuary.

We can guarantee one thing—you'll never find anything like this anywhere else on the island. These beaches are truly unique and the area is extremely secluded. The negatives are no real ocean view from inside of Round Hole and because the beaches are so small with little to do you might get bored quickly. Also, be aware that you will have to hunt for shade. Swimming access will depend on ocean conditions. If you don't mind doing a little exploring then this is a venture you should place on your must-see list.

How to Get There

From points north

Total travel time: 6.3 mi. / 12 min
From Gregorytown intersection proceed south 5.4 miles to main intersection in Hatchet Bay just after marina. Make left and proceed straight for 0.5 miles onto dirt road. Continue straight for 0.2 miles. Make left onto rough jungle path. Proceed 0.2 miles to small parking area on left. Walk 0.1 miles left to beaches.

Time / Distance

To beach road: 5.4 mi. / 9 min
Beach road to beach: 0.9 mi. / 3 min

From points south

Total travel time: 3.6 mi. / 4 min
From Rainbow Bay Inn proceed north 2.7 miles to main intersection in Hatchet Bay just before marina. Make right and proceed straight for 0.5 miles onto dirt road. Continue straight for 0.2 miles. Make left onto rough jungle path. Proceed 0.2 miles to small parking area on left. Walk 0.1 miles left to beaches.

Time / Distance

To beach road: 2.7 mi. / 4 min
Beach road to beach: 0.9 mi. / 3 min

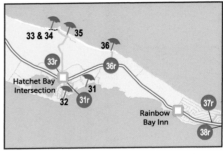

Beach ★★☆ Road ★☆☆

Beach: 25° 21.949, -76° 29.186
Road (33r): 25° 21.062, -76° 29.100

What You Should Know	
Privacy	Secluded
Shade	None
Accessibility	Car, bumpy
Beach Path	Rocky
Water Entry	Rocky
Water Condition	Deep ocean; cave
Litter/Seaweed	Light
Nearest Town	Alicetown
Snorkeling	Poor
Shelling	No
Beach Size	2-20 yards x 20 yards

Alicetown Beach Northside

The most prominent features of Alicetown Northside are its massive boulders. Sometimes they are solitary, but mostly they are piled on top of each other like a violent game of dominos played by the ancient Gods. What you will enjoy about this beach is its isolation. It's a bit of work to make it back to the beach, but there is absolutely no sign of life within eyeshot. The flipside of that, however, is that the beach is loaded with debris and litter. The boulders act as collection points for anything the sea tosses onshore, and its isolation ensures that none of what washes up gets removed ever.

There's not much to do at this beach other than take in the sun. Its about a quarter mile long and 20 yards wide, but because of where

the rocks are placed you really can't do much other than climb over them. Water access is good amongst the rocks with the beach seeming to be fit in like a complex jigsaw puzzle between all the boulders.

Overall, this is not an attractive location. If you like the look of boulders and are willing to trade a lot of debris for privacy then you might pick this beach. With so many other great choices around you can safely move this one towards the bottom of your list. It should be noted that by walking around the southern rocky point you can gain access to the northern portion of Alicetown South. We found no way to drive over a private sand pit blocking any reasonable access to the other beach from here.

Beach ★★☆ Road ★★★

Beach: 25° 21.848, -76° 29.003
Road (33r): 25° 21.062, -76° 29.100

How to Get There

From points north
Total travel time: 6.2 mi. / 12 min
From Gregorytown intersection proceed south 5.4 miles to main intersection in Hatchet Bay just after marina. Make left and proceed straight for 0.5 miles onto dirt road. Continue straight for 0.3 miles. Make left before gate. Proceed a few hundred feet to beach path.

Time / Distance
To beach road: 5.4 mi. / 9 min
Beach road to beach: 0.8 mi. / 3 min

From points south
Total travel time: 3.5 mi. / 7 min
From Rainbow Bay Inn proceed north 2.7 miles to main intersection in Hatchet Bay just before marina. Make right and proceed straight for 0.5 miles onto dirt road. Continue straight for 0.3 miles. Make left before gate. Proceed a few hundred feet to beach path.

Time / Distance
To beach road: 2.7 mi. / 4 min
Beach road to beach: 0.8 mi. / 3 min

What You Should Know	
Privacy	Secluded
Shade	None
Accessibility	Car, bumpy
Beach Path	Rocky
Water Entry	Sandy
Water Condition	Deep ocean
Litter/Seaweed	Moderate
Nearest Town	Alicetown
Snorkeling	Poor
Shelling	No
Beach Size	0.25 miles x 20 yards

Alicetown Beach South

This beach requires a keen eye and a little fortitude in order to get through the initial overgrown entry off of the highway. The entry point resembles nothing more than tall grass. If you are worried about underbrush or other types of vegetation coming in contact with your vehicle then avoid this particular beach. However, once you find the beach road then it's almost a straight shot and very easy to get back to the beach on a road that is generally good quality by Eleuthera standards. Making a left at the fork takes you almost immediately to the parking area where you cross a small dune to reach the beach. It only took us 2 minutes

from the point where we left the road before we had our toes in the sand.

The beach stretches for approximately three quarters of a mile. This is one of those big, rugged beaches that is completely isolated. While the beach is long, the water access here is somewhat limited to an initial entry area that is only 20 yards wide and 30 yards deep. From there you have 300 yards of rock ledge at the water's edge before having a place where you can enter the water and we found no way by driving to gain access anywhere else.

At this southern point there is a cutaway between rocks where you can access the

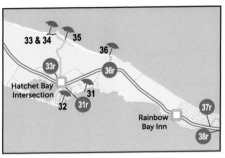

Beach ★★☆   Road ★★☆

Beach: 25° 21.530, -76° 28.201
Road: 25° 21.304, -76° 28.206

What You Should Know

Privacy	Secluded
Shade	None
Accessibility	4WD recommended
Beach Path	Sandy
Water Entry	Sandy
Water Condition	Deep ocean
Litter/Seaweed	Light
Nearest Town	Alicetown
Snorkeling	Poor
Shelling	No
Beach Size	0.75 miles x 40 yards

ocean. There is lots of sun, but no shade. Extremely tall swaying palms and Casuarinas dot the landscape in the background fronted by a short sandy dune. There was some minor wash up and almost no seaweed. A rocky point to the right provides an interesting place to explore.

This is a good beach for privacy with a limited patch of sandy water access leading to deep ocean. The beach is good for walking or jogging, and it's an excellent place to take in lots of rays. As with most Atlantic side beaches, be wary of the direction of the wind as a strong easterly breeze makes water access extremely dangerous due to rough seas.

How to Get There

From points north
Total travel time: 1.3 mi. / 3 min
From Hatchet Bay intersection proceed south for 1.0 miles and make left onto access road. Proceed 0.3 miles through very overgrown path to end. Make left at T. Proceed a few hundred feet to access on right.

Time / Distance
To beach road: 1.0 mi. / 1 min
Beach road to beach: 0.3 mi. / 2 min

From points south
Total travel time: 2.0 mi. / 5 min
From Rainbow Bay Inn proceed north for 1.7 miles and make right onto access road. Proceed 0.3 miles through very overgrown path to end. Make left at T. Proceed a few hundred feet to access on right.

Time / Distance
To beach road: 1.7 mi. / 3 min
Beach road to beach: 0.3 mi. / 2 min

Smuggler's Beach

This beach has the nicest parking area on the island. It's so well groomed that you almost don't want to leave it to go to the beach. With prominent signage, a surrounding rock wall, tall palm, and large grassy area you are tempted to just soak in the gorgeous elevated views from here. It looks more like a putting green than a parking lot.

Once you get over how nice the parking area is you have to walk down a flight of stairs to reach the beach. In approximately 70 paces you will descend about 20 to 30 feet where are you are greeted by a purposeful collection of debris. The sign designates 'Lost Soles' and that's where all the various sandals, shoes, sneakers and water shoes have ended up. Near that is a second debris field that seems to claim any litter that cannot be worn on one's feet.

What make this beach interesting are its angles. Behind the beach is a high lush dune set at a 45-degree angle. Then there is a small, sandy flat ridge. From that point the beach drops off again at 45 degrees into the water. The lower sand and dune seem to form parallel lines. With no visible houses or road noise you have good privacy. At the time this beach was assessed the wind was whipping from

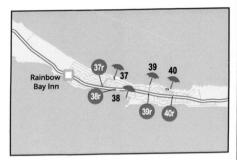

Rainbow
Bay Inn

Beach ★★☆   Road ★★★

Beach: 25° 20.385, -76° 26.122
Road: 25° 20.233, -76° 26.356

What You Should Know

Privacy	Secluded
Shade	None
Accessibility	Car
Beach Path	Stairs and rocky
Water Entry	Sandy
Water Condition	Deep ocean
Litter/Seaweed	Moderate
Nearest Town	James Cistern
Snorkeling	Poor
Shelling	No
Beach Size	300 yards x 20 yards

the east generating huge dangerous waves crashing on the beach and making swimming impossible. You will want to come here when the wind is coming from the west at which time the deep sandy water access will be excellent.

The length of the beach is about 300 yards, its widest swath about 20. There is lots of sun here, but no shade whatsoever. Other than the debris, the steep walk down, and a bit of a rock scramble to get onto the beach there is little else wrong. If you like seclusion and the sound of the surf then this is a good beach for you.

How to Get There

From points north
Total travel time: 1.0 mi. / 2 min
From Rainbow Bay Inn proceed south 0.6 miles to Cross Island Drive. Make a left and proceed 0.3 miles to end. Make a right and proceed 0.1 miles to large grassy parking area on left. Beach access is in middle of back wall of parking area.

Time / Distance
To beach road: 0.6 mi. / 1 min
Beach road to beach: 0.4 mi. / 1 min

From points south
Total travel time: 5.3 mi. / 11.5 min
From JC Fishing Pier proceed north 4.9 miles to Cross Island Drive. Make a right and proceed 0.3 miles to end. Make a right and proceed 0.1 miles to large grassy parking area on left. Beach access is in middle of back wall of parking area.

Time / Distance
To beach road: 4.9 mi. / 10.5 min
Beach road to beach: 0.4 mi. / 1 min

Rainbow Bay Beach

This is one of the most beautiful beaches on the island, and certainly one of the best on the Caribbean side. What makes it special is its cleanliness, which is valued above almost all other attributes that we considered. When you combine that with its unique park-like setting you have something very different and special.

So few beaches on the island are really well maintained. While this beach is not large or overly dramatic, it is completely free of seaweed and debris. The bay has a picturesque double set of beaches protected by a peninsula to the south and a rock wall to the north.

Getting to Rainbow Bay Beach is very easy. The roads are in perfect condition, the beach is well marked, there is ample parking, and there is even a cement walkway to the beach with a handrail making it accessible to most. Picnic tables and tiki huts are available on the beach for those who get there first. The water is inviting and perfectly swimmable, however, the beach does have pebbles throughout and there is a ring of rocks just offshore in the water. Water shoes are not mandatory, but not a bad idea especially if you choose to use the more southerly of the two beaches.

This is a good shelling beach. Piles of

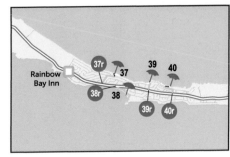

Beach ★ ★ ★   Road ★ ★ ★

Beach: 25° 20.054, -76° 25.894
Road: 25° 20.191, -76° 26.098

How to Get There

From points north
Total travel time: 1.2 mi. / 3 min
From Rainbow Bay Inn proceed south 0.9 miles to Wandering Shore Drive. Make a right and proceed 0.3 miles to large parking area on right.

Time / Distance
To beach road: 0.9 mi / 2 min
Beach road to beach: 0.3 mi. / 1 min

From points south
Total travel time: 4.9 mi. / 10.5 min
From JC Fishing Pier proceed north 4.6 miles to Wandering Shore Drive. Make a left and proceed 0.3 miles to large parking area on right.

Time / Distance
To beach road: 4.6 mi / 9.5 min
Beach road to beach: 0.3 mi. / 1 min

What You Should Know

Privacy	Public
Shade	Some
Accessibility	Car
Beach Path	Cement walkway
Water Entry	Pebbly
Water Condition	Shallow Caribbean
Litter/Seaweed	None
Nearest Town	James Cistern
Snorkeling	Average
Shelling	Yes
Beach Size	200 yards x 20 yards

miniature shells can be found in pods near the rocks especially by the southern pinnacle. A peninsula to the south makes this beach look like an unreal painting; you will have to pinch yourself to realize that you really are in paradise.

Enjoy the great water, wonderful views, perfect conditions and cleanliness of the beach. Be aware that there are houses all around, pebbles on the beach, a ring of rocks in the water, and a sparse amount of shade. Regardless of its minuses this beach received our highest rating.

Hidden Beach

We should really rename this location Unhidden Beach since its complete exposure to the road, community and nearby houses makes you immediately wonder how it got its name in the first place. Perhaps the hidden sandy spot beneath the boulders to the right is the real hidden beach even though the main beach is exposed to all.

The beach itself is divided in two by a large set of boulders that runs from back to front through its mid-section. Each beach section measures 50 by 30 yards, giving it the

appearance of two side-by-side rectangles. They almost look like a pair of twin blocks that face north towards the awesome cliffs that form the wall against the Atlantic side of Rainbow Bay.

A nice picnic table set up under a lone palm tree greets you as you enter this very easy-to-find beach. Bring suntan lotion and an umbrella, as this tree is the only shade you'll find. The water entry is classic deep Atlantic Ocean. You'll have no trouble avoiding the large rocks that sometimes jut out of

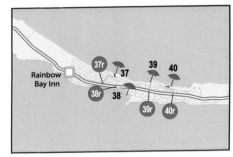

Rainbow
Bay Inn

37r 37 39 40

38r 38

39r 40r

Beach ★★☆ Road ★★★

Beach: 25° 20.241, -76° 25.471
Road: 25° 20.115, -76° 25.503

How to Get There

From points north
Total travel time: 1.7 mi. / 5 min
From Rainbow Bay Inn proceed south 1.5 miles to Hidden Beach Drive. Make a left and proceed 0.2 miles to beach access on left.

Time / Distance
To beach road: 1.5 mi. / 4 min
Beach road to beach: 0.2 mi. / 1 min

From points south
Total travel time: 4.2 mi. / 9 min
From JC Fishing Pier proceed north 4.0 miles to Hidden Beach Drive. Make a right and proceed 0.2 miles to beach access on left.

Time / Distance
To beach road: 4.0 mi. / 8 min
Beach road to beach: 0.2 mi. / 1 min

What You Should Know

Privacy	Semi-private
Shade	None
Accessibility	Car
Beach Path	Sandy
Water Entry	Sandy
Water Condition	Deep ocean
Litter/Seaweed	Light
Nearest Town	James Cistern
Snorkeling	Average
Shelling	No
Beach Size	100 yards x 30 yards

the sand as you access the water. Tides here can be problematic as can crashing waves. However, on days when the wind comes from the west this can be a lovely swimming beach with a nice sandy hidden beach between the boulders just north of the main beach access.

Because of its location and lack of privacy it didn't receive a high grade. It does, however, have a very interesting look and should be considered if you want an Atlantic side beach with picnic table and dramatic rocks.

Driftwood Beach

The Rainbow Bay community has many beach options making this an ideal spot to explore from. Driftwood Beach is a study in contrasts. Its dark rock surroundings seem to reach out and swallow its smallish beach, which resembles a pink tongue extending out into the ocean. The beach is super sandy in places, but also has rocks intermixed, a balance of two masses competing for space. Debris has concentrated into ugly pits that are both amazing works of natural art as well as modicums of society's ills.

The main beach, with perfect sandy water access, is a perfect complement to two high sandy back beaches further south that offer good sunning spots with no water access. The beach has no houses on or around it, although it is centered in the community and several homes come into view further north. Since it's so easy to find and get to, you shouldn't necessarily expect to have it all to yourself. All the roads are well paved and there is ample parking.

The debris on the main beach is scattered, but there is a fair amount of seaweed. Because this beach is small, only 120 yards x 30 yards, you may find the wash up a little imposing. The other negative aspect is the lack of shade

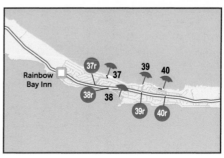

Beach ★★☆   Road ★★★

Beach: 25° 20.184, -76° 25.188
Road: 25° 20.050, -76° 25.069

What You Should Know	
Privacy	Semi-private
Shade	None
Accessibility	Car
Beach Path	Sandy
Water Entry	Sandy
Water Condition	Deep ocean
Litter/Seaweed	Light
Nearest Town	James Cistern
Snorkeling	Poor
Shelling	No
Beach Size	120 yards x 30 yards

How to Get There

From points north
Total travel time: 2.2 mi. / 6 min
From Rainbow Bay Inn proceed south 2.0 miles to Sea to Sea Drive. Make a left and proceed 500 feet to T. Make a left and proceed 0.2 miles to parking area on right. There is an alternate parking area that can be reached by making a right at the T. Proceed 100 feet to path for south part of beach and rocky point.

Time / Distance
To beach road: 2.0 mi. / 5 min
Beach road to beach: 0.2 mi. / 1 min

From points south
Total travel time: 3.7 mi. / 8 min
From JC Fishing Pier proceed north 3.5 miles to Sea to Sea Drive. Make a right and proceed 500 feet to T. Make a left and proceed 0.2 miles to parking area on right. There is an alternate parking area that can be reached by making a right at the T. Proceed 100 feet to path for south part of beach and rocky point.

Time / Distance
To beach road: 3.5 mi. / 7 min
Beach road to beach: 0.2 mi. / 1 min

as this beach sits well in front of any vegetation or trees. Also, when the wind is whipping from the east this beach can turn into a violent meshing of water with land. Seas can be high if the conditions are right.

All in all, this is a good beach to choose for sunning and swimming when the wind is coming from the west. There were some interesting places to explore that could be good sandy hangouts amongst the rocks. The back beaches provide nice sitting areas for sunrises or to view the last of the day's light.

The Central Beaches

Some of the best beaches and also the most accessible can be found in the central region. Here, the roads are easier to find (sometimes even labeled with signs), better developed, used more frequently and maintained to a much higher degree than either north or south. This is due to both the larger population in this section of the island along with the popularity of the region among tourists and second homeowners. Travelers coming to the island generally favor the central region due to the quantity of beaches with shorter driving distances along with the best shopping, restaurants, lodging choices and other island amenities. Did someone say Friday night Fish Fry in Governor's Harbour?

The central region includes the towns of James Cistern, Governor's Harbour, (the island's capital), North and South Palmetto Point, Savannah Sound, and Tarpum Bay. Windermere Island, reachable by a small bridge from the main island, was not included due to the fact that private residents or those renting there can use those beaches. One of our criteria for inclusion in this book is that the beach had to be reachable by foot or by car with unrestricted access thus making Windermere off limits.

There are a large number of smaller residential communities that also make this region unique. They include Winding Bay, Little Bay, Ten Bay, Double Bay, Balara Bay, Twin Coves, Tranquility Bay, and Hut Pointe. Each of these communities typically centers on a beach. While the beaches are generally less private, they are usually of high quality thanks to their cleanliness and the quality of their access roads.

What you'll ultimately find here is the densest number of beaches within 38 miles of north to south driving. In addition to having the most choices, you'll have the least amount of travel time and the fewest number of car abrasions by avoiding those dense jungle paths found in the other regions. Central Eleuthera is about convenience.

The Beaches at Moray Pond

These lovely beaches are worth the extra work to get to. It's not that these beaches are particularly hard to find. But, the road leading back to them is a little more than a mile and is one of the classic bumpy island beach roads that will make you feel like a well-shaken James Bond martini by the time you finish the ride. It's manageable with a car, but a 4WD vehicle is recommended. What you get is a secluded pristine large beach. The setting is complemented to the north by a small, rocky beach that is more picturesque than swimmable. There are also miles of exploratory rock ledges for the more adventurous. The large horseshoe, to the right of the parking area, is a quarter mile long and spreads a full 270 degrees around the bay. It looks and

feels like a Caribbean beach due to its water depth, quality, color, and placidness owing to how well protected it is. Yet, it still maintains that big beach Atlantic feel due to the deep blue ocean just beyond the edges of the bay. The bay resembles a big bowl, its waterline sitting six feet below the sandy upper rim of the beach. You'll want to walk a few hundred feet from where you first access the beach to avoid a large rock outcropping that spills into the water. Because the bay is so protected from wind we recommend packing bug spray. Walking north from the parking area leads you to the little horseshoe, a mere 100 yards long. It's very rocky on the beach and also rocky into the water making it more interesting visually, but not a place that you'll be

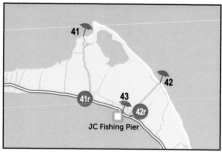

Beach ★★★ Road ★☆☆

Beach: 25° 20.857, -76° 22.625
Road: 25° 19.732, -76° 22.582

What You Should Know	
Privacy	Secluded
Shade	None
Accessibility	4WD recommended
Beach Path	Sandy
Water Entry	Rocks and sand
Water Condition	Shallow and deep
Litter/Seaweed	Light
Nearest Town	James Cistern
Snorkeling	Poor
Shelling	No
Beach Size	0.3 miles x 30 yards

How to Get There

From points north
Total travel time: 6.2 mi. / 18.5 min
From Rainbow Bay Inn proceed south 4.7 miles. Make a left and proceed 0.2 miles. Make a left and proceed 0.1 miles to dirt road. Proceed 1.2 miles to beach access area. Horseshoe Beach is on the right. Little Horseshoe Beach is on the left.

Time / Distance
To beach road: 4.7 mi. / 9.5 min
Beach road to beach: 1.5 mi. / 9 min

From points south
Total travel time: 2.3 mi. / 11 min
From JC Fishing Pier proceed north 0.8 miles. Make a right and proceed 0.2 miles. Make a left and proceed 0.1 miles to dirt road. Proceed 1.2 miles to beach access area. Horseshoe Beach is on the right. Little Horseshoe Beach is on the left.

Time / Distance
To beach road: 0.8 mi. / 2 min
Beach road to beach: 1.5 mi. / 9 min

galloping into the water. If you choose to swim over here you'll want water shoes or be selective about where you step. Sand is intermixed amongst boulders and formations, and you can spot numerous fossils in the rocks. If you continue hiking along the rocks to the north you can see one cave off in the distance. There is more to explore in that direction including what could be a hike-to beach and several other little swimmable coves. These beaches offer several combined experiences wrapped into one. Plan on spending some time here and don't forget that beach umbrella. The entire setting is very dramatic adding to its appeal and overall grade.

James Point Beach

Rivaling the large Airport Beach to the south, James Point overcomes the usual Atlantic beach problems of debris and seaweed just because of its massive size making those issues seem small in comparison. This beach sits in front of a tall sloping dune, and while there are several beach paths down to the beach they are really spread out and almost not worth trying to find. It's easier to just get on the beach to walk around and explore all it has to offer.

Below the dune is a flat plateau where all of the seaweed and debris seems to concentrate, but below that, on a sloping shelf leading to the water, is nothing but soft pink sand that absorbs your feet like a loving, soft sponge. Most of the beach has good sandy water access, but there are a couple of rocky points that can easily be avoided.

As you head south you'll find the most distinctive feature of this beach, a shipwreck that protrudes from the water like a rusty dragon approaching its beachside lair. Enjoy a good snorkel around its various submerged and exposed pieces, but be careful as old steel vessels like this are extremely jagged and can cause nasty cuts. Rows of coral heads provide lots of snorkeling opportunities, their distances from shore varying greatly depending on what part of the beach you are on.

The beach turns ever so gently in an inverted half-moon shape obscuring parts of it from view the further down the beach you go. Bring an umbrella and plenty of suntan lotion, as there is no shade whatsoever.

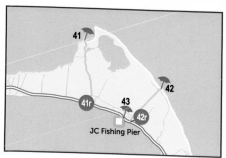

Beach ★★☆　　Road ★★☆

Beach: 25° 20.012, -76° 21.229
Road: 25° 19.421, -76° 21.769

What You Should Know

Privacy	Secluded
Shade	None
Accessibility	Car, bumpy
Beach Path	Dune
Water Entry	Rocks and sand
Water Condition	Deep ocean
Litter/Seaweed	Moderate
Nearest Town	James Cistern
Snorkeling	Average
Shelling	No
Beach Size	3.5 miles x 50 yards

From a privacy standpoint, James Point gets an odd, mixed review. It is completely isolated and private, however, its proximity to a major town needs to be considered. While it will take an effort for someone to make the trek back to this beach the likelihood of someone showing up is much greater as it abuts the back of the JC settlement.

All in all, this is a very nice beach that is distinct because of its size and the shipwreck. If you are looking for a long, wide sunny beach that is not far from the amenities of a community then this is the beach for you. If you are concerned about rough waters, no shade, and the likelihood of other people on the beach then continue to seek. Eleuthera has plenty of other options.

How to Get There

From points north
Total travel time: 1.0 mi. / 8 min
From JC Fishing Pier proceed south for 0.2 mile. Make left on paved road. Proceed 0.1 miles bearing right at fork and onto dirt road. Proceed 0.7 miles to beach path.

Time / Distance
To beach road: 0.2 mi. / 2 min
Beach road to beach: 0.8 mi. / 6 min

From points south
Total travel time: 4.8 mi. / 14 min
From GHB proceed north for 4.0 miles. Make right on paved road. Proceed 0.1 miles bearing right at fork and onto dirt road. Proceed 0.7 miles to beach path.

Time / Distance
To beach road: 4.0 mi. / 8 min
Beach road to beach: 0.8 mi. / 6 min

JC Settlement Beach

This 30-yard long beach sits right in the center of town in the bustling (by Eleuthera standards) Bahamian town of James Cistern, known affectionately as JC. As you would expect of the settlement beaches, there is no privacy and with this one, even less so. The beach sits adjacent to the long JC fishing dock, which is a constant source of comings and goings. It is right on Queen's Highway, right across from Kel-D's bar, and offers no protection from either noise or the sights as there are no trees except for a lone small palm behind a picnic table. Despite all the obvious shortcomings, this is a quaint, picturesque beach that offers interesting photo opportunities because of its location. At some point during your trip you are probably going to pass through the area. We wouldn't recommend bringing a beach blanket and setting up an umbrella, but we would recommend grabbing a Kalik from Kel-D's and snapping a couple of pictures for the scrapbook.

In addition to being uniquely picturesque in a truly Bahamian way, the beach offers convenience. It's right on the road,

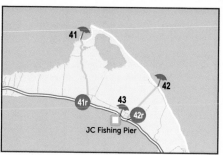

JC Fishing Pier

Beach ★★☆ Road ★★★

Beach: 25° 19.470, -76° 21.882
Road: 25° 19.470, -76° 21.882

How to Get There

From points north
Total travel time: 5.5 mi. / 9 min
From Rainbow Bay Inn proceed south for 5.5 miles. Beach is on right next to fishing dock.

Time / Distance
To beach road: 5.5 mi. / 9 min
Beach road to beach: 0.0 mi. / 0 min

From points south
Total travel time: 4.2 mi. / 9 min
From GHB proceed north for 4.2 miles. Beach is on left next to fishing dock.

Time / Distance
To beach road: 4.2 mi. / 9 min
Beach road to beach: 0.0 mi. / 0 min

close to the restaurants and next to the fishing dock where locals come in to sell their catch of the day.

Water access here is rocky at the shoreline, but the water gets deeper quicker than usual for a Caribbean side beach so good for a quick dip. It's also a neat place to talk to the locals and get a feel for what Eleuthera really is like.

Give this beach a try if you are passing through and then head over to the other side of the island for the majestic beach at James Point to spend the day.

What You Should Know	
Privacy	Public
Shade	None
Accessibility	Car
Beach Path	None
Water Entry	Rocky
Water Condition	Shallow Caribbean
Litter/Seaweed	Light
Nearest Town	James Cistern
Snorkeling	Poor
Shelling	No
Beach Size	100 feet x 20 feet

JC Caribbean Beach Central

JC Caribbean Central is set back a couple of hundred feet from Queen's Highway. This offers a bit more protection from the road as compared to JC Caribbean South. Due to a grove of Casuarina trees between the road and the sand, you'll get a little more shade and a little more privacy. However, you will see and hear cars passing on the road.

The beach has no distinguishing traits or outstanding features. If you want to go swimming here you'll probably want water shoes, as it is narrow and quite rocky. If not for the enticing color of the clear aquamarine water there would be almost no reason to stop.

There are better beaches just a short drive away, but if you are desperate to cool off or don't want to go through the trouble of either finding a beach road or managing one of the bumpier ones, this beach could work. Most people probably want to find something a bit more private after taking a quick dip here.

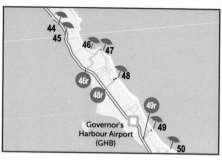

Beach ★☆☆   Road ★★★

Beach: 25° 18.605, -76° 20.927
Road: 25° 18.643, -76° 20.938

How to Get There

From points north

Total travel time: 1.3 mi. / 4 min
From JC Fishing Pier proceed south 1.3 miles to access road on right. Continue down path to shaded area to park.

Time / Distance

To beach road: 1.3 mi. / 4 min
Beach road to beach: 200 feet / 0 min

From points south

Total travel time: 2.9 mi. / 7 min
From GHB proceed north for 2.9 miles to access road on left. Continue down path to shaded area to park.

Time / Distance

To beach road: 2.9 mi. / 7 min
Beach road to beach: 200 feet / 0 min

What You Should Know	
Privacy	Semi-private
Shade	Plenty
Accessibility	Car
Beach Path	Sandy
Water Entry	Rocky
Water Condition	Shallow Caribbean
Litter/Seaweed	Light
Nearest Town	James Cistern
Snorkeling	Poor
Shelling	No
Beach Size	0.25 miles x 10 yards

JC Caribbean Beach South

JC Caribbean South is one of those places you stop by when it is extremely hot and you need to take a dip in the ocean for fear of melting. Fortunately, there are plenty of other beaches around, but if you're in a pinch, why not pull off on the side of Queen's Highway and cool off.

This beach classifies as a beach in our book, but just barely. It's right on the highway, which is convenient. In other words, you can't miss it, but neither will any other car driving up and down the road. Don't expect any privacy from cars passing by. Expect road noise as well.

There is sand, shade and gorgeous water here. You can go swimming in very shallow turquoise water or have a little picnic in the shaded area looking out to the Caribbean Sea. But why do that when you can simply drive a few minutes either north or south and find one of the better beaches that are just a stone's throw away?

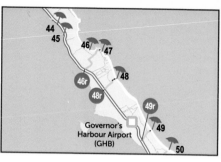

Beach ★☆☆   Road ★★☆

Beach: 25° 18.399, -76° 20.717
Road: 25° 18.399, -76° 20.717

How to Get There

From points north
Total travel time: 1.7 mi. / 5 min
From JC Fishing Pier proceed south 1.7 miles to access road on right.

Time / Distance
To beach road: 1.7 mi. / 5 min
Beach road to beach: 0.0 mi. / 0 min

From points south
Total travel time: 2.5 mi. / 6 min
From GHB proceed north for 2.5 miles to access road on left.

Time / Distance
To beach road: 2.5 mi. / 6 min
Beach road to beach: 0.0 mi. / 0 min

What You Should Know	
Privacy	Semi-private
Shade	Some
Accessibility	Car
Beach Path	Sandy
Water Entry	Rocky
Water Condition	Shallow Caribbean
Litter/Seaweed	Light
Nearest Town	James Cistern
Snorkeling	Poor
Shelling	No
Beach Size	0.25 miles x 10 yards

Round Cove Beach

This beach epitomizes a blend of good and bad; the result, a mediocre review. After driving on a very poor road for almost six minutes to travel a mere half a mile you encounter an exquisite private setting. If not for the church pew sized seaweed piles and almost continuous field of debris around its 270-degree circumference this beach would probably be one of the highest rated. However, you might need a 4WD vehicle to get here and you might wish you had brought along a backhoe to clean up the debris.

The location of Round Cove is really exquisite. There is a shady area that leads to ample sun and sand for a half-mile as you move north around the semi-circle. As would be expected of a beach that's a little tricky to get to, you have all the privacy you could want with good sandy water entry and an interesting view provided by the rocky outcroppings at either end of the beach.

Coral heads and grassy areas litter the water, but don't interfere with swimming or wading. Good snorkeling can be found around the corals and sunken rocks. An anchored boat mooring line indicates use of this

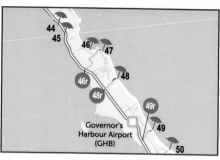

Beach ★★☆ Road ★★☆

Beach: 25° 18.062, -76° 20.119
Road: 25° 17.719, -76° 20.337

How to Get There

From points north
Total travel time: 3.4 mi. / 14 min
From JC Fishing Pier proceed south for 2.9 miles. Make a left and go straight bearing right at 0.2 miles. Proceed 0.3 miles on rough road to beach. Round Cove Beach is on left. Long Point Beach is on right.

Time / Distance
To beach road: 2.9 mi. / 8 min
Beach road to beach: 0.5 mi. / 6 min

From points south
Total travel time: 1.8 mi. / 12 min
From GHB proceed north for 1.3 miles. Make a right and go straight bearing right at 0.2 miles. Proceed 0.3 miles on rough road to beach. Round Cove Beach is on left. Long Point Beach is on right.

Time / Distance
To beach road: 1.3 mi. / 6 min
Beach road to beach: 0.5 mi. / 6 min

What You Should Know

Privacy	Secluded
Shade	Plenty
Accessibility	4WD recommended
Beach Path	Sandy
Water Entry	Sandy
Water Condition	Shallow entry
Litter/Seaweed	Moderate
Nearest Town	James Cistern
Snorkeling	Good
Shelling	No
Beach Size	0.5 miles x 30 yards

area as a launch pad for fishing. In general, this is a good walking and exploring beach, but be careful where you walk if you leave the sand as there are enough hidden burs to wreck your vacation.

You'll enjoy the isolation, the protected feel of the cove and the sandy water access. The debris and seaweed reduced the appeal of the location considerably. Combined with a rough road and a lot of burs the overall rating had to be just average.

Long Point Beach

To the right of the beach path to Round Cove is another short sandy path that at first wasn't visible, but was found to lead to another beach with a completely different set of characteristics. Two beaches for the price of one long lousy drive!

Long Point is about a quarter mile long and is uncharacteristically straight with large rocky outcroppings throughout. This makes finding easy water entry a little more challenging, but not impossible. Similar to its more rounded sister beach to the north, Long Point is extremely private. There is a house set about a quarter mile away from the beach, which is barely visible and the only dwelling in sight.

Since this beach is not well protected you can expect much rougher surf, deeper water and larger waves. The benefit of those factors is that big ocean sound that you don't get at the more rounded and protected beaches.

The beach here, as you might expect, is unkempt. There is ocean debris and seaweed on most of the back of the beach. You'll find no shade here. Behind you is a low dune that provides some wind coverage, but nothing more.

Choose Long Point for its privacy, big ocean sound and copious amounts of sun. If you want calmer water, shade and a shallower entry then stick with Round Cove to its immediate north.

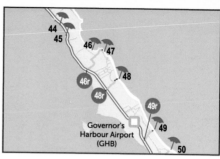

44
45
46 47
48
46r
48r
49r
Governor's
Harbour Airport
(GHB)
49
50

Beach ★★☆   Road ★☆☆

Beach: 25° 18.062, -76° 20.119
Road (46r): 25° 17.719, -76° 20.337

How to Get There

From points north
Total travel time: 3.4 mi. / 14 min
From JC Fishing Pier proceed south for 2.9 miles. Make a left and go straight bearing right at 0.2 miles. Proceed 0.3 miles on rough road to beach. Round Cove Beach is on left. Long Point Beach is on right.

Time / Distance
To beach road: 2.9 mi. / 8 min
Beach road to beach: 0.5 mi. / 6 min

From points south
Total travel time: 1.8 mi. / 12 min
From GHB proceed north for 1.3 miles. Make a right and go straight bearing right at 0.2 miles. Proceed 0.3 miles on rough road to beach. Round Cove Beach is on left. Long Point Beach is on right.

Time / Distance
To beach road: 1.3 mi. / 6 min
Beach road to beach: 0.5 mi. / 6 min

What You Should Know	
Privacy	Semi-private
Shade	None
Accessibility	4WD recommended
Beach Path	Sandy
Water Entry	Rocky
Water Condition	Deep ocean
Litter/Seaweed	Moderate
Nearest Town	James Cistern
Snorkeling	Poor
Shelling	No
Beach Size	0.25 miles x 20 yards

Airport Beach North

Of all of the access points on Airport Beach the northern access is the least desirable. This is the same 3.5 mile long beach as locations 49, 50, and 52, but the difference is that there are several houses here. While they may be seldom occupied it still feels like you've given up the privacy and seclusion that you have at the southern access points.

From a beach road standpoint, the last quarter mile of the road is steep and sandy. While it can be traversed with a four-wheel drive vehicle you should be cautious if driving all the way down the hill to the beach path. A better option might be to park towards the top of the hill and walk down. The path from the top of the hill is littered with burs so watch where you step.

This access point has debris and a high concentration of seaweed. Ocean access is quite good although the reef system is less developed. A narrow rocky ocean outcropping provides something different from a snorkeling perspective as compared to just reef.

This should be your last option for going to the Airport Beach. There is no shade, less privacy, lots of burs, and an access road that could be a problem depending on what type of vehicle you are driving. The beach does have lots of sun, great water access and a massive body of sand to its south. On a positive note, the view from the top of the hill offers a very nice photo opportunity.

Beach ★★☆   Road ★★☆

Beach: 25° 17.526, -76° 19.821
Road: 25° 17.367, -76° 19.960

How to Get There

From points north
Total travel time: 3.8 mi. / 13 min
From JC Fishing Pier proceed south 3.6 miles. Make a left and proceed 0.1 miles bearing left where road goes into jungle. Make immediate first right. Park at top of hill or proceed cautiously to lower hill. Follow sandy path to beach.

Time / Distance
To beach road: 3.6 mi. / 10 min
Beach road to beach: 0.2 mi. / 3 min

From points south
Total travel time: 0.8 mi. / 5 min
From GHB proceed north 0.6 miles. Make a right and proceed 0.1 miles bearing left where road goes into jungle. Make immediate first right. Park at top of hill or proceed cautiously to lower hill. Follow sandy path to beach.

Time / Distance
To beach road: 0.6 mi. / 2 min
Beach road to beach: 0.2 mi. / 3 min

What You Should Know	
Privacy	Semi-private
Shade	None
Accessibility	4WD recommended
Beach Path	Sandy
Water Entry	Sandy
Water Condition	Deep ocean
Litter/Seaweed	Moderate
Nearest Town	James Cistern
Snorkeling	Average
Shelling	No
Beach Size	3.2 miles x 50 yards

Airport Beach Central

The central access point on Airport Beach offers the same high level of privacy that is experienced up and down this impressive 3.5-mile stretch of sand with a few subtle differences. First, parking is limited and you will need to traverse a narrow overgrown sandy beach path that was loaded with burs at the time of our visit. Beware of these rough, prickly seed casings that can penetrate your skin and break off underneath. They seem to stick to everything that touches them including sandals, socks, or any other article of clothing. The dry burs cause the most

problems. Bringing a pair of tweezers along is not a bad idea to aid in extraction, as they will often get imbedded into your fingers while you try to pull them from other parts of your body and clothing.

There is a rope at the final leg of the beach path, which seems like a bit of overkill, as this little dune is not very steep, and the path can easily be walked down without additional assistance. The beach itself has most of the same beach attributes as #50 with the main difference being the lack of shade. The high dune provides an excellent vantage point for

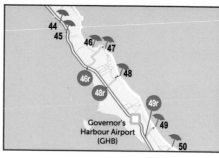

Beach ★★☆ Road ★★☆

Beach: 25° 16.620, -76° 19.138
Road: 25° 16.457, -76° 19.265

How to Get There

From points north
Total travel time: 0.6 mi. / 5 min
From GHB proceed south 0.4 miles. Make a left and proceed cautiously 0.4 miles to parking area. Walk trail to beach. Walk down final steep beach path. A rope is tied off there to assist.

Time / Distance
To beach road: 0.4 mi. / 1 min
Beach road to beach: 0.2 mi. / 4 min

From points south
Total travel time: 8.0 mi. / 16 min
From Governor's Harbour intersection proceed north 7.8 miles. Make a right and proceed cautiously 0.4 miles to parking area. Walk trail to beach. Walk down final steep beach path. A rope is tied off there to assist.

Time / Distance
To beach road: 7.8 mi. / 12 min
Beach road to beach: 0.2 mi. / 4 min

What You Should Know	
Privacy	Secluded
Shade	None
Accessibility	4WD recommended
Beach Path	Dune
Water Entry	Sandy
Water Condition	Deep ocean
Litter/Seaweed	Moderate
Nearest Town	James Cistern
Snorkeling	Average
Shelling	No
Beach Size	3.2 miles x 50 yards

some nice photos, but is covered with low lying vegetation rather than the tall shade Casuarinas that beach 50 has.

The reef system here is mature and closer to shore so a good snorkeling spot. There is debris and seaweed, but it is manageable. Overall, this is a great location for tanning, sweeping elevated views, and lots of privacy. The main trade-off is accessibility. The beach road has a high degree of tilt and the beach path is a little trickier to navigate than at other places on this big beach.

Airport Beach South / Navy Beach

A Naval facility was built on Eleuthera in the late 1950's as part of a project to track Soviet submarines in the Atlantic. Many of its old dilapidated buildings, roads, and operating structures still exist and look like a skeleton of a time long forgotten. While the facility has been closed for decades, the huge driveway with parking for hundreds of vehicles make this is a very easy find and a good score for beachcombers. The massive parking lot is starting to collapse at the front, as the sand supporting it erodes, so choose your parking spot wisely and then walk over the 15' dune down to the 3.5 mile by 50 yard wide beach. As you can imagine, a parking lot of this size is very distinguishable if you make the correct turns. If you make incorrect turns you can quickly get lost in the labyrinth of roads that become overgrown and impassable.

Airport Beach is a big sunny beach, but it is also surrounded by dunes that serve as plateaus for tall Casuarina trees. This means you can get a lot of shade on the back of the beach. The beach is extremely isolated with no houses or establishments nearby. The main negative is the pollution both inside the old facility and on the beach. What is left from the Navy is still there... in abundance. A decayed old dock and other litter can be found in the sand. The parking area is strewn with cables, clothing, electronics etc. Seaweed is mostly located towards the back of the beach. If you are willing to sit by the water in the sun neither the debris nor the seaweed will cause any concern, however

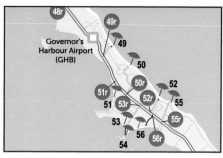

Beach ★★☆ Road ★★★

Beach: 25° 16.278, -76° 18.813
Road: 25° 15.785, -76° 18.831

What You Should Know

Privacy	Secluded
Shade	Some
Accessibility	Car
Beach Path	Dune
Water Entry	Sandy
Water Condition	Deep ocean
Litter/Seaweed	Extensive
Nearest Town	Governor's Harbour
Snorkeling	Average
Shelling	No
Beach Size	3.2 miles x 50 yards

if neatness is of prime importance then you can find other beaches that are better.

There is nice sandy water access along the entire length of the beach. A moderate reef system exists offshore that is reachable by swimming, plus a few large coral heads closer to shore for snorkeling.

There is nothing overly exciting or unique at this beach. The old facility provides some history and a unique backdrop, but it is simply a vestige of the past. In 1980 the base was officially decommissioned after the United States could not secure a favorable lease renewal for the land. The facilities and equipment that were left behind have gone to waste, rusting in the salt spray. Come to this beach for a bit of nostalgia, seclusion, and a great combination of sun and shade.

How to Get There

From points north
Total travel time: 1.8 mi. / 6 min
From GHB proceed south 1.2 miles. Make a left on paved access road and proceed 0.3 miles bearing left past abandonded guard gate. Proceed 0.1 miles and make right. Make immediate left into massive cement parking lot. Proceed 0.2 miles to beach access. Park and walk over dune to beach.

Time / Distance
To beach road: 1.2 mi. / 4 min
Beach road to beach: 0.6 mi. / 2 min

From points south
Total travel time: 7.4 mi. / 11 min
From Governor's Harbour intersection proceed north 6.8 miles. Make a right onto paved access road and proceed 0.3 miles bearing left past abandonded guard gate. Proceed 0.1 miles and make right. Make immediate left into massive cement parking lot. Proceed 0.2 miles to beach access. Park and walk over dune to beach.

Time / Distance
To beach road: 6.8 mi. / 9 min
Beach road to beach: 0.6 mi. / 2 min

Alabaster Beach

The Caribbean side beaches are known for their bright turquoise water, flat sandy water entry and remaining shallow away from shore. But what makes Alabaster, also known as Receiver's Beach, different is its 1-mile length, very long by Caribbean beach standards, coupled with the seemingly endless variety of access points. Park wherever you want up or down the beach and simply cross a small patch of trees to access the beach. Additionally, the central beach path is right next door to Cocodimama, an excellent eatery and bar, one of the few establishments of its kind on the western shore of the island.

Alabaster is a good walking beach. Normally we classify good walking and running beaches as the same, but because much of the sand on Alabaster sits below water level during high tide, the sand, especially closer to the water, is sponge-like causing you to sink a good 3 to 4 inches with each footstep making it extremely tough to run in.

The pink sand is of nice quality, although there is some seaweed and fallen trees to the southern end of the beach. Much of the seaweed from recent storms has been collected and piled up so it should not be a problem. The water is crystal clear, shining like a turquoise sapphire, very vibrant and very alive, serving as a natural shallow wading pool. You won't find debris, rocks or shells to inhibit your water entry.

There is lots of sun, but limited shade except back under the trees. This is not the most scenic of beaches. Parts of it are close to Queen's Highway and the Governor's

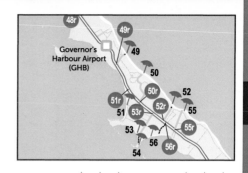

Beach 51 ★★☆ Road ★★★
Beach: 25° 15.811, -76° 19.046
Road: 25° 15.914, -76° 18.982

Beach 51a ★☆☆ Road ★★★
Beach: 25° 16.207, -76° 19.134
Road: 25° 16.207, -76° 19.134

Beach 51b ★★☆ Road ★★★
Beach: 25° 16.067, -76° 19.075
Road: 25° 16.067, -76° 19.075

Beach 51c ★★☆ Road ★★★
Beach: 25° 15.990, -76° 19.037
Road: 25° 15.990, -76° 19.037

What You Should Know

Privacy	Semi-private
Shade	Some
Accessibility	Car
Beach Path	Sandy
Water Entry	Sandy
Water Condition	Shallow Caribbean
Litter/Seaweed	Moderate
Nearest Town	Governor's Harbour
Snorkeling	Average
Shelling	No
Beach Size	1.0 miles x 20 yards

Harbour airport, which will be experienced audibly and visually. The only decent snorkeling is far down on the southern rocky shoreline. Don't expect privacy because of the resort, but do take advantage of a good meal and cold drink while you visit.

There are several alternate access points that have also been cataloged. The northernmost, 51a, is right on the road. You will see highway traffic and hear road noise. The water access is rocky and there is a nearby house. The access points at 51b and 51c are much better. There is plenty of shade under the Casuarinas, a hair more privacy, and better sandy water entry. You also get some protection from road noise while still being within a short walk or drive to Cocodimama.

How to Get There

From points north
Total travel time: 1.2 mi. / 4 min
From GHB proceed south 1.0 miles. Make a right and proceed 0.2 miles to start of beach access just past Cocodimama Resort.

Time / Distance
To beach road: 1.0 mi. / 3 min
Beach road to beach: 0.2 mi. / 1 min

From points south
Total travel time: 7.2 mi. / 11 min
From Governor's Harbour intersection proceed north 7.0 miles. Make a left and proceed 0.2 miles to start of beach access just past Cocodimama Resort.

Time / Distance
To beach road: 7.0 mi. / 10 min
Beach road to beach: 0.2 mi. / 1 min

Jono's Beach

This elongated swath of beach stretches for 3.5 miles, from Mid Rocks to the south, all the way to the northern tip of Airport Beach, making it ideal for walking, running, or even ATVing. The beach is 50 yards wide providing a seemingly endless supply of sand. What's also nice about this beach is its level of seclusion. From this access point you can still see the one building on Mid Rocks northern beach off in the distance, but that is the only one you'll see. There are no other houses visible from the beach in any direction.

The trade-off is debris. The beach was littered with cruise ship debris, and a fair amount of seaweed. A moderate formation of coral heads provides some opportunity for snorkeling, but this is not one of the best spots. The landscape here is different than other locations, too. Low-lying dunes behind the beach lead up to a plateau that then leads up to a cliff. That helps to augment the privacy, but also presents one of the lone problems with this beach. If you have trouble walking up and down hills then this is a beach you probably want to avoid. The parking area at the end of a very bumpy paved beach road

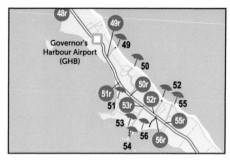

Beach ★★☆   Road ★★☆

Beach: 25° 15.680, -76° 18.281
Road: 25° 15.437, -76° 18.400

How to Get There

From points north
Total travel time: 2.2 mi. / 7 min
From GHB proceed south 1.8 miles. Make a left and proceed 0.2 miles bearing left at the end. Park in shaded area and follow path to beach.

Time / Distance
To beach road: 1.8 mi. / 5 min
Beach road to beach: 0.4 mi. / 2 min

From points south
Total travel time: 6.6 mi. / 10 min
From Governor's Harbour intersection proceed north 6.2 miles. Make a right and proceed 0.2 miles bearing left at the end. Park in shaded area and follow path to beach.

Time / Distance
To beach road: 6.2 mi. / 8 min
Beach road to beach: 0.4 mi. / 2 min

What You Should Know

Privacy	Semi-private
Shade	Some
Accessibility	Car, bumpy
Beach Path	Dune
Water Entry	Sandy
Water Condition	Deep ocean
Litter/Seaweed	Moderate
Nearest Town	Governor's Harbour
Snorkeling	Good
Shelling	No
Beach Size	3.2 miles x 50 yards

is set back away from the beach. You have to walk about 100' to a short, but fairly steep embankment that takes you to the beach.

Water access is good everywhere and if not for the amount of debris this would be an ideal setting although there is nothing particularly unique here. Choose this beach for its privacy and its great length. Avoid it if walking up and down the beach path will give you trouble or if you are looking for a perfectly clean beach.

Esso Beach

This tiny pimple of a beach wins the award for most pluses combined with the most negatives. Its overall rating ended up being low, but there are some reasons you might want to give this beach a visit, not the least of which that this is the best, and perhaps only way to access nearby HideAway Beach (54).

The sandy part of the beach is only about 100 yards long if even that. You will zip down a very well maintained paved beach road, but the reason it's so well maintained is because there is an oil refinery at its end, just before the beach. You may find the access blocked off by a gate up at Queen's Highway so only head back this way if the gate is open, and make sure you don't get locked in, which is a possibility. I was fortunate enough to have

one of the plant workers come out and let me know that I would have to leave at a certain time because he was locking up shortly.

The beach forms an almost complete 360-degree circle with mangrove roots growing out of the water. This little cove is littered with cement stanchions poking out of the water, old oil drums and other sorts of refinery debris. The combination of lack of privacy, lots of debris, and a lot of seaweed make this a very unattractive location. There are also lots of rocks making water entry difficult, but there were also a fair amount of miniature shells to collect, too.

There were several above average features. First, if you walk out to the left past the beach and onto its rocky point you will be

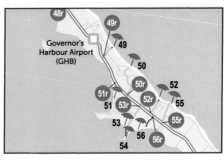

Beach ★★☆ Road ★★★

Beach: 25° 15.207, -76° 18.833
Road: 25° 15.573, -76° 18.589

What You Should Know

Privacy	Public
Shade	Plenty
Accessibility	Car
Beach Path	Sandy
Water Entry	Rocky
Water Condition	Shallow Caribbean
Litter/Seaweed	Moderate
Nearest Town	Governor's Harbour
Snorkeling	Poor
Shelling	Yes
Beach Size	100 yards x 10 feet

How to Get There

From points north
Total travel time: 2.0 mi. / 7 min
From GHB proceed south 1.6 miles. Make a right and proceed 0.4 miles to end of road. Parking area is straight off of paved road past Esso refinery.

Time / Distance
To beach road: 1.6 mi. / 5 min
Beach road to beach: 0.4 mi. / 2 min

From points south
Total travel time: 6.8 mi. / 10 min
From Governor's Harbour intersection proceed north 6.4 miles. Make a left and proceed 0.4 miles to end of road. Parking area is straight off of paved road past Esso refinery.

Time / Distance
To beach road: 6.4 mi. / 8 min
Beach road to beach: 0.4 mi. / 2 min

amazed by the water hues with blues ranging from light turquoise to glowing aqua to deep blue. Those colors, offset by several cays and a peninsula in the distance, make this a very attractive spot. If you have water shoes, the shallow bay extending past the beach is quite inviting and highly swimmable. The beach also offers a high amount of shade with lots of soft Casuarina needles.

If you don't mind the debris in the cove or that Eleuthera Petroleum Limited is right behind the beach, then this is an interesting spot with some beautiful water, a rock ledge at the point worthy of exploring, and hike-to access over to the much nicer HideAway Beach.

Hide Away Beach

This small and seemingly inaccessible beach is tucked away on the tip of Tranquility Bay on the northern shore facing Alabaster Bay. We found it almost by accident while taking a peek at the water access by the rocky point of Esso Beach (53). Off in the distance to the south of Esso is a tiny patch of barely visible sand with a junction of land that connects to a small peninsula.

A 5-minute hike across the shoreline brings you to this cute little spot that is no more than 50 yards long and 20 feet wide.

The sand is pink and clean. An abundance of shade is available beneath the Casuarinas that connect this beach with Tranquility Bay. Be aware that large piles of seaweed had collected back under the trees.

The peninsula was readily accessible by land or water for some exploring. Additionally, there is a ledge over somewhat deeper water to dive from.

The beach features nice water access, interesting views and copious amounts of shade. Depending on where the sun

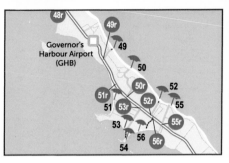

Beach ★★☆ Road ★☆☆

Beach: 25° 15.040, -76° 18.851
Road (53r): 25° 15.573, -76° 18.589

How to Get There

From points north
Total travel time: 2.0 mi. / 12 min
From GHB proceed south 1.6 miles. Make a right and proceed 0.4 miles to end of road. Parking area is straight off of paved road past Esso refinery. Walk past and to left of first beach to rocky point, then walk left about 5 minutes across rocky shelf to beach.

Time / Distance
To beach road: 1.6 mi. / 5 min
Beach road to beach: 0.4m plus hike / 7 min

From points south
Total travel time: 6.8 mi. / 15 min
From Governor's Harbour intersection proceed north 6.4 miles. Make a left and proceed 0.4 miles to end of road. Parking area is straight off of paved road past Esso refinery. Walk past and to left of first beach to rocky point, then walk left about 5 minutes across rocky shelf to beach.

Time / Distance
To beach road: 6.4 mi. / 8 min
Beach road to beach: 0.4m plus hike / 7 min

What You Should Know

Privacy	Secluded
Shade	Plenty
Accessibility	Car; Hike
Beach Path	Rocky
Water Entry	Sandy
Water Condition	Shallow Caribbean
Litter/Seaweed	Moderate
Nearest Town	Governor's Harbour
Snorkeling	Good
Shelling	No
Beach Size	50 yards x 20 feet

is positioned you might choose to walk through the trees to the Tranquility Bay side and work on your tan from over there. Just be aware that to access this beach you need to go through the refinery access road which may be closed off. The hike is not difficult, but you do have to be careful crossing some of the sharp rocks. Also, depending on what activities are going on at the refinery there may be ships coming and going. This adventurous beach is fun to find - a tucked away little gem.

Mid Rocks Beach

Rip on down Knowles Drive, one of the most clearly marked and easily passable beach roads around. The road leads to two beaches separated by a large rocky point at the end of the beach road. While you'll have no problem getting here you won't find a clearly marked parking area so just park at the end, walk past the pylons and proceed either left or right depending on your taste of beaches.

To the left is a quarter mile of mostly deserted beach that extends for miles past the visible 'end' of the beach. Besides what looks like a new bar/restaurant being built immediately to the left there are no other homes or establishments. The dunes are low lying and the landscape is mostly shade-bearing Casuarinas.

To the right, or south, you have a completely different experience. The walk is a little bit longer in this direction, about 300', and a little more treacherous over the rocks. What you get is a dune cliff with tall palms and several private homes as your backdrop. You will sacrifice a little bit of privacy in exchange for a more scenic landscape.

Both beaches are flat with good sandy water access. An abundance of reef and fallen rocks off the point make this a highly

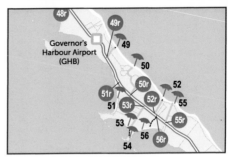

Beach ★★☆   Road ★★★

Beach: 25° 15.624, -76° 18.061
Road: 25° 15.287, -76° 18.194

What You Should Know

Privacy	Semi-private
Shade	None
Accessibility	Car
Beach Path	Rocky
Water Entry	Sandy
Water Condition	Deep ocean
Litter/Seaweed	Moderate
Nearest Town	Governor's Harbour
Snorkeling	Good
Shelling	No
Beach Size	1.0 miles x 50 yards

How to Get There

From points north
Total travel time: 2.5 mi. / 8 min
From GHB proceed south 2.1 miles to Knowles Road. Make a left and proceed 0.4 miles to pilons. Park and walk straight to rocky point between beaches.

Time / Distance
To beach road: 2.1 mi. / 6 min
Beach road to beach: 0.4 mi. / 2 min

From points south
Total travel time: 6.3 mi. / 9 min
From Governor's Harbour intersection proceed north 5.9 miles to Knowles Road. Make a right and proceed 0.4 miles to pilons. Park and walk straight to rocky point between beaches.

Time / Distance
To beach road: 5.9 mi. / 7 min
Beach road to beach: 0.4 mi. / 2 min

promising snorkel spot especially on a calm day. While the beach is not as well protected as Hut Pointe, as evidenced by some wash-up and seaweed, you get two different beaches for the price of one. These beaches are fun to explore, easy to get to, and quite interesting visually. The northern beach has an additional beach path at the middle of the beach. Just be careful, as there was a fair amount of construction debris and fallen trees making access a little more difficult. The only real negative at this location is that you will have to walk away from the rocky point to find a sandy base camp.

Tranquility Bay Beach

The beach at Tranquility Bay was a real challenge to get to, as all the beach roads seemed to be so poorly maintained that they were barely passable. Others were marked with foreboding signs and delineated by unwelcoming chains aimed at keeping us out. We have a hard time being denied access to a public beach and Tranquility Bay wasn't going to be an exception. There's nothing quite so inviting as your friendly Keep Out, Private Road, and No Trespassing signs confronting you at each and every turn. Nevertheless, we did find a couple of ways down to the beach. After trying both, this beach was not worth the trouble unless you want to collect shells.

The first access road starts at an old abandoned food store called Burrow's Seafood and Chicken. We hiked to the beach on the road behind it. Although it was probably passable with a vehicle, the road was very overgrown, so foot passage was a better option. However, upon leaving the beach, we discovered a very well paved and super wide road that turned out to be chained off at Queen's Highway. There were no signs prohibiting someone from entering so if you have to make it back to this beach you are better off parking at its entrance on Queen's Highway proceeding by foot on this paved road.

The beach itself is a typical Caribbean half-moon that stretches about a half mile and is about 30' at its widest. The bay is well protected and shallow. Two distant cays provide a nice scenic view. However, the biggest problem with the beach is the poor

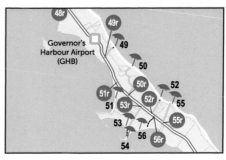

Beach ★☆☆   Road ★☆☆

Beach: 25° 15.193, -76° 18.484
Road: 25° 15.398, -76° 18.359

What You Should Know

Privacy	Semi-private
Shade	Plenty
Accessibility	Car; Hike
Beach Path	Dirt
Water Entry	Rocky
Water Condition	Shallow Caribbean
Litter/Seaweed	Moderate
Nearest Town	Governor's Harbour
Snorkeling	Good
Shelling	Yes
Beach Size	0.4 miles x 30 feet

How to Get There

From points north
Total travel time: 2.1 mi. / 10 min
From GHB proceed south 1.9 miles to access road. Look for road on right that has chain across it. Park in front of chain and walk 0.2 miles down wide road to beach.

Time / Distance
To beach road: 1.9 mi. / 5 min
Beach road to beach: 0.2m hike / 5 min

From points south
Total travel time: 6.3 mi. / 13 min
From Governor's Harbour intersection proceed north 6.1 miles. Look for road on left that has chain across it. Park in front of chain and walk 0.2 miles down wide road to beach.

Time / Distance
To beach road: 6.1 mi. / 8 min
Beach road to beach: 0.2m hike / 5 min

appearance due to a lot of seaweed, along with a rocky ledge in the water that starts about 5' offshore. While the ledge is mostly flat and low-lying you would probably want water shoes to go for a dip and there didn't seem to be a way to bypass those rocks. The bay is quite private except for one house and its beach hut. The best thing about the beach was its abundance of shade offered by the wall of towering Casuarinas.

Given the difficulty of accessing this beach coupled with rocky water access, and lots of seaweed, we think you can find better places to spend your day. If you want a bit of an adventure and some good shells then this might be worth a half hour of your time.

Hut Pointe Beach

This long and super-wide beach is perhaps the most inviting, most swimmable beach on the island. Of all the beaches that we visited, Hut Pointe has a unique combination of beach qualities — color, sandy water access, cleanliness, zero rocky entry points — that almost draws you into its irresistible lightly lapping waves. It failed to get the highest beach grade only because it fronts a substantial community with visible houses running almost its entire length, making it hard to find any privacy.

The Wykee Estates community, marking the turn off to Hut Pointe, makes it easy to find. The beach is easy to access although it has changed somewhat. What used to be a short road at the end of a steep paved drive that led to various beach paths behind the community has now turned into a service road to Skye Beach Club, one of the more upscale and intimate boutique resorts on the island which also offers the decidedly splendid bar and restaurant known as The Bistro. Now, to access the beach you must park outside a locked gate that guards the service road and walk an extra 50' to the main beach path.

The cool, clean sand runs at least a mile to the northern point with a multi-tiered pitch. The back of the beach is flat leading to a rim that drops off and slopes gradually into the water. On a good day the beach is rhythmic, its smallish waves providing a constant lyrical harmony, almost like background music. The quaint little beach cabana, decorated colorfully in the nouveau wash-up motif, provides one pocket of shade on an otherwise sunny beach.

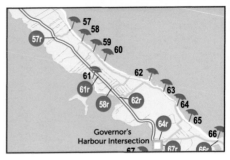

Beach ★★☆　Road ★★★

Beach: 25° 13.867, -76° 16.263
Road: 25° 13.747, -76° 16.523

What You Should Know	
Privacy	Semi-private
Shade	None
Accessibility	Car
Beach Path	Sandy
Water Entry	Sandy
Water Condition	Deep ocean
Litter/Seaweed	None
Nearest Town	Governor's Harbour
Snorkeling	Poor
Shelling	No
Beach Size	2.0 miles x 50 yards

The view is quite nice and on a clear day you can see far south, almost to Twin Coves. To the north the shore rounds out, but there is a lot of beach in that direction mostly fronting high cliffs. This beach is extremely clean and ranks as one of the cleanest on the island.

To summarize, the water is what makes Hut Pointe special. You'll want to take a dip as soon as you get there. Its convenient location, cleanliness, and overall beach quality make it a super special spot and if it wasn't for the lack of privacy it would receive our highest grade. As a side note, there is also some historic significance to the community itself. Many of the old stone buildings were built in the 40's by the first Premiere of the Bahamas, Sir Roland Symonette.

How to Get There

From points north
Total travel time: 5.4 mi. / 11 min
From GHB proceed south 5.1 miles. Make left at Wykee Estates sign and proceed 0.3 miles on steep paved drive to gate. Park outside gate and walk 50' to beach entrance.

Time / Distance
To beach road: 5.1 mi. / 8 min
Beach road to beach: 0.3 mi. / 3 min

From points south
Total travel time: 3.2 mi. / 8 min
From Governor's Harbour intersection proceed north 2.9 miles. Make right at Wykee Estates sign and proceed 0.3 miles on steep paved drive to gate. Park outside gate and walk 50' to beach entrance.

Time / Distance
To beach road: 2.9 mi. / 5 min
Beach road to beach: 0.3 mi. / 3 min

Hut Pointe Beach South

This large beach dovetails into Hut Pointe over at Wykee Estates and is located just north of the Bistro restaurant at the Skye Beach Club. It's one of those big, wide, long Atlantic-side beaches that stretches south contiguously for almost 2 miles. The best feature is its commanding unobstructed, northeastern view.

The water is very nice and almost seems like the Caribbean on a calm day. Don't be fooled, though. This is a good beach for body and traditional surfing when the wind is blowing in the right direction. The better snorkeling is to the very southern end of this beach as the reef tapers off significantly to

the north. Scattered palms provide shade and are the dominant feature of the landscape.

The biggest problem here is seaweed and debris. There were signs that this was being managed with debris being collected into piles, but with this much beach it's difficult to keep up. It looked like whoever was trying was losing a never-ending battle.

A separate hidden beach that sits between Coconut Cove and this access spot can be found by walking around the point to the south. There you'll find a backdrop of big boulders in the back with a small plot of sand in front, and this might be your best

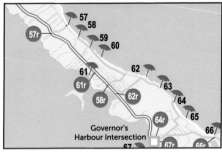

Governor's
Harbour Intersection

Beach ☆☆☆   Road ☆☆☆

Beach: 25° 13.654, -76° 16.037
Road: 25° 12.818, -76° 15.484

How to Get There

From points north
Total travel time: 8.0 mi. / 21 min
From GHB proceed south for 6.3 miles.
Make left just past Worker's Complex buildings and proceed 0.4 miles straight through
intersection to end. Make left at T and
proceed 1.3 miles to parking area next to tall
palms.

Time / Distance
To beach road: 6.3 mi. / 10 min
Beach road to beach: 1.7 mi. / 11 min

From points south
Total travel time: 3.4 mi. / 14 min
From Governor's Harbour intersection
proceed north for 1.7 miles. Make right just
before Worker's Complex buildings and proceed 0.4 miles straight through intersection
to end. Make left at T and proceed 1.3 miles
to parking area next to tall palms.

Time / Distance
To beach road: 1.7 mi. / 3 min
Beach road to beach: 1.7 mi. / 11 min

What You Should Know

Privacy	Semi-private
Shade	Some
Accessibility	4WD recommended
Beach Path	Sandy
Water Entry	Sandy
Water Condition	Deep ocean
Litter/Seaweed	Moderate
Nearest Town	Governor's Harbour
Snorkeling	Good
Shelling	No
Beach Size	2.0 miles x 50 yards

bet if you want a smaller secluded beach.
Once you reach this beach you can find any
number of access points onto it through the
trees.

The best thing about this beach is its location relative to the Skye Beach Club bar and
restaurant, which is only a quarter mile walk
away. This big, flat, sandy beach is excellent
for walking and running. Due to its proximity to Skye Beach and Wykee you should
have no expectations that this beach will be
completely unoccupied, but it's so big that it
should not be a problem.

Coconut Cove Beach

This is another one of those special private hideaways where words won't do it justice. You will know you've arrived at the right spot because all of a sudden there's a dense coconut grove just behind a plot of sand made even more interesting by its rocky foundation. It's only 1/10th of a mile north from Sandpiper Beach (60).

This beach feels more private and protected due to all of those beautiful palm trees, which tower above a massive bed of palm fronds covering the ground beneath them. While not overly comfortable to sit or lie on, they draw you in by the sheer thickness of the surrounding shade.

The beach is small, probably only 30 yards wide and even less deep. Large boulders stacked on top of each other at the back of the beach lead to the sand where isolated rocks and small rock ledges are exposed. You can still find easy sandy water access out to the extensive nearby reef system. This beach is extremely clean with no seaweed and very little debris.

Several houses up the hill from this beach have easy access here so you'll want to get here first and claim it for yourself. It's truly picturesque and very unique. The coconut trees are just icing on the cake for this lovely beach.

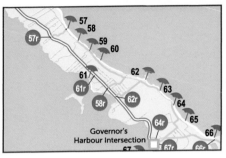

Beach ★★☆   Road ★☆☆

Beach: 25° 13.479, -76° 15.813
Road (58r): 25° 12.818, -76° 15.484

How to Get There

From points north
Total travel time: 7.6 mi. / 17.5 min
From GHB proceed south for 6.3 miles. Make left just past Worker's Complex buildings and proceed 0.4 miles straight through intersection to end. Make left at T and proceed 0.9 miles to small parking area next to tall palms.

Time / Distance
To beach road: 6.3 mi. / 10 min
Beach road to beach: 1.3 mi. / 7.5 min

From points south
Total travel time: 3.0 mi. / 10.5 min
From Governor's Harbour intersection proceed north for 1.7 miles. Make right just before Worker's Complex buildings and proceed 0.4 miles straight through intersection to end. Make left at T and proceed 0.9 miles to small parking area next to tall palms.

Time / Distance
To beach road: 1.7 mi. / 3 min
Beach road to beach: 1.3 mi. / 7.5 min

What You Should Know	
Privacy	Semi-private
Shade	Plenty
Accessibility	4WD recommended
Beach Path	Sandy
Water Entry	Sandy
Water Condition	Deep ocean
Litter/Seaweed	Light
Nearest Town	Governor's Harbour
Snorkeling	Good
Shelling	No
Beach Size	30 yards x 10 yards

Sandpiper Beach

This is one of those secluded Eleuthera beaches that you expect to have all to yourself. It is just the right size, about 80 yards long and 20 yards wide, set in a straight line between two high rocky points. It almost looks like a football field of sand because it is so rectangular. Isolated rocks poke out of the sand in various places adding to the overall beauty here. While it is not hard to find this beach, you do have to crawl your car over the rutted paved road next to the Worker's Complex before getting on a long sandy path that runs parallel to the houses and beaches. A small parking area that is big enough for maybe two vehicles points towards a short sandy beach path leading to this little gem.

There is a massive reef system here just offshore so the area is excellent for snorkeling. You can even do some body surfing here when the conditions are right. Nice sandy water access the entire length of the beach makes getting in and out of the water easy. Two elevated houses are partially visible to the south, but they are separated from this beach by a lush vegetated rocky cliff, which protects this beach from their general access. In other words, someone would have to drive to this beach to go here.

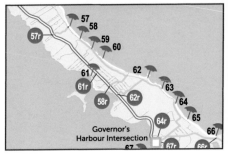

Beach ★★★ Road ★☆☆

Beach: 25° 13.414, -76° 15.761
Road (58r): 25° 12.818, -76° 15.484

How to Get There

From points north

Total travel time: 7.5 mi. / 17 min
From GHB proceed south for 6.3 miles. Make left just after Worker's Complex buildings and proceed 0.4 miles straight through intersection to end. Make left at T and proceed 0.8 miles to small parking area and access path on right.

Time / Distance
To beach road: 6.3 mi. / 10 min
Beach road to beach: 1.2 mi. / 7 min

From points south

Total travel time: 2.9 mi. / 10 min
From Governor's Harbour intersection proceed north for 1.7 miles. Make right just before Worker's Complex buildings and proceed 0.4 miles straight through intersection to end. Make left at T and proceed 0.8 miles to small parking area and access path on right.

Time / Distance
To beach road: 1.7 mi. / 3 min
Beach road to beach: 1.2 mi. / 7 min

What You Should Know

Privacy	Semi-private
Shade	None
Accessibility	4WD recommended
Beach Path	Dune
Water Entry	Sandy
Water Condition	Deep ocean
Litter/Seaweed	Light
Nearest Town	Governor's Harbour
Snorkeling	Good
Shelling	No
Beach Size	80 yards x 20 feet

The amount of seaweed and debris here is really insignificant. The only real negative is that there is absolutely no shade, so plan accordingly. Also, because the beach is small, if it is occupied, you really won't have any privacy. The rocky points are fun to explore with any number of large boulders broken up and lying about randomly at the points. Several other beaches back this way provide good options should this one be occupied, but we recommend getting here early, claiming your area and staying all day. This is one of our top rated beaches.

North Balara Bay Beach

This is a hike-to beach that isn't worth the hike. It's rated low for accessibility as well as overall beach quality, making it one that you can cross off your list — unless you are looking for a lot of privacy and a place to do some shelling. Several attempts were made to access this beach, but due to beach roads being marked private or being thwarted by chains across the road access, the trek had to be made on foot. A beach road was ultimately found that led to the north end of this triple horseshoe beach and bay. The road probably could have been driven, but it was so overgrown and narrow that hiking seemed like a better choice. Beware of spiny-backed orb-weavers, small triangular spiders, which resemble miniature crabs weaving the stickiest of webs that always seem to be at face

level. If you choose to hike back here it is advised to walk with one arm out in front of you in a permanent karate chop stance to avoid getting a face full of sticky web.

The beach is a skinny sliver of Caribbean sand that barely reaches 20' at its widest. While the beach is sandy, the water entry to the north is not. It's extremely rocky and almost ridiculously shallow. Water shoes are a must to go swimming. The good news is that because this beach is difficult to get it is also isolated. The few houses to the far north do not have beach access as they are built on the rocky shoreline and there are no roads connecting those houses to the beach. There are a couple of old docks that are eroding badly, many fallen Casuarinas and large clumps of seaweed giving the beach an overall feel of

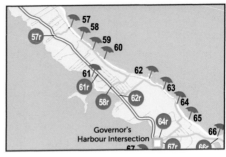

Governor's
Harbour Intersection

Beach ⭐☆☆   Road ⭐☆☆

Beach: 25° 12.975, -76° 15.808
Road: 25° 13.044, -76° 15.725

What You Should Know

Privacy	Semi-private
Shade	Some
Accessibility	Car; Hike
Beach Path	Dirt
Water Entry	Rocky
Water Condition	Shallow Caribbean
Litter/Seaweed	Moderate
Nearest Town	Governor's Harbour
Snorkeling	Poor
Shelling	Yes
Beach Size	1.0 miles x 20 feet

How to Get There

From points north
Total travel time: 6.3 mi. / 12 min
From GHB proceed south for 6.2 miles. Turn right and proceed cautiously 0.1 mile to water. Beaches area is to left of dock.

Time / Distance
To beach road: 6.2 mi. / 10 min
Beach road to beach: 0.1 mi. / 2 min

From points south
Total travel time: 1.9 mi. / 5 min
From Governor's Harbour intersection proceed north 1.8 miles. Turn left and proceed cautiously 0.1 mile to water. Beach area is to left of dock.

Time / Distance
To beach road: 1.8 mi. / 3 min
Beach road to beach: 0.1 mi. / 2 min

desolation. If you walk to the left you will find a large amount of small shells especially on the part of the beach that acts as the connecting horseshoe. Continuing in this direction leads to the inhabited portion of the bay where privacy ends, but sandy water access begins. The views also change for the better, with Cupid's Cay quite visible in the distance. It's safe to say that the southern end of the beach is much more picturesque.

To summarize, this is a good beach for privacy on the northern end, but you'll need water shoes. The middle is a good place for shelling. The southern portion is the most swimmable. In total you have approximately 1 mile of beach across three separate horseshoes. The main reason to go is for shells.

Twin Coves Beach

There are a number of access points to this beach, and while the twin half-moon beaches are small, about 0.25 miles each, selecting the right beach access point will make a huge difference. First off, the road getting back to the beach may earn the moniker of 'worst paved road' in Eleuthera. There used to be several choices of roads leading back to the beach, but it looks like the better ones were purposely cut off to keep people from accessing this great beach. For a short drive on a paved road it feels like a long drive on a bumpy road due to how damaged it is. Still, if you spend the 8 minutes getting back to the beach from Queen's Highway it's sure to delight.

There is what can best be described as a sand runway between the two little beaches that lead to a small peninsula which sports its own little beach making it very picturesque. The water is a beautiful mix of light and dark turquoise on both sides of the little bridge. The water here is shallow, the peninsula well protected. Be aware that the beach to the south has a long ring of rocks a few paces into the water that runs almost the complete length of the beach. You need water shoes to access the southern twin. Walking about 0.2 miles to the north from the main beach path takes you to the bridge and also to the northern twin where the tradeoff is privacy versus sandy water entry. The north beach has a private house and volleyball court sitting just above its beach line.

Really tall palm trees make the whole

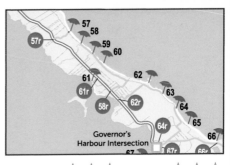

Beach 62 ★★☆ Road ★★☆
Beach: 25° 12.830, -76° 14.644
Road: 25° 12.668, -76° 15.331

Beach 62a ★★☆ Road ★★☆
Beach: 25° 12.887, -76° 14.780
Road: 25° 12.668, -76° 15.331

Beach 62b ★★☆ Road ★★☆
Beach: 25° 12.957, -76° 14.925
Road: 25° 12.668, -76° 15.331

Beach 62c ★★☆ Road ★★☆
Beach: 25° 12.813, -76° 14.622
Road: 25° 12.668, -76° 15.331

What You Should Know

Privacy	Semi-private
Shade	Some
Accessibility	Car, bumpy
Beach Path	Sandy
Water Entry	Rocks and sand
Water Condition	Shallow entry
Litter/Seaweed	Moderate
Nearest Town	Governor's Harbour
Snorkeling	Poor
Shelling	No
Beach Size	0.5 miles x 20 yards

area very scenic and there is lots of escaping sea lettuce vines running towards the water. Seaweed and debris on both beaches are not really a problem, but they do diminish the look of the beach, negatively impacting its overall grade. You can find some shady areas under the Casuarinas.

Based on its many unique features this beach would, under normal circumstances, receive our highest grade, however, there were too many issues - from the house on the beach, to the rocks in the water, to the debris and seaweed – and that moved this beach into the pack of contenders. Still, it's a great beach with many nice features, the uniqueness of the runway and peninsula making it one of the more interesting beaches on the island.

How to Get There

From points north
Total travel time: 7.5 mi. / 20 min
From GHB proceed south 6.7 miles to access road on left. Make left and proceed 0.6 miles on very bumpy paved road. Make a right at T onto dirt trail and proceed 0.2 miles to beach access on left.

Time / Distance
To beach road: 6.7 mi. / 11 min
Beach road to beach: 0.8 mi. / 9 min

From points south
Total travel time: 2.1 mi. / 11 min
From Governor's Harbour intersection proceed north 1.3 miles. Make right and proceed 0.6 miles on very bumpy paved road. Make a right at T onto dirt trail and proceed 0.2 miles to beach access on left.

Time / Distance
To beach road: 1.3 mi. / 2 min
Beach road to beach: 0.8 mi. / 9 min

Med Point Beach

Stay to the northern end of this beach to avoid several houses that are built on its southern shore. The location of this beach can best be described as north of Club Med North and south of Twin Coves. It looked accessible from both sides although an attempt to reach it was only made from the Twin Coves side. Be careful driving this road as there were some severely rutted sandy areas that looked perfect for trapping a car, and, in fact, it made more sense to park below the bad spots and walk up to the beach path.

What makes this beach so appealing is its pitch. The upper sand shelf is tilted at an almost impossible angle that appears greater than 45 degrees down to the water's edge.

Below the rocky point to the north you have a perfect little round sand bowl with exquisite water lapping at its base.

If it weren't for the lack of privacy this beach would be ideal. There is not a lot seaweed or debris primarily owing to the visible offshore breakers along with the rocky point acting as a natural filter. Also, this beach has no shade whatsoever. The tall palm trees are attractive, but they're set too far back to be useful.

This is a nice little beach if you happen to be in the vicinity. Since you can access both Club Med Beach and Twin Coves Beach on foot you get a nice sampling of a variety of good beaches within a very short walk.

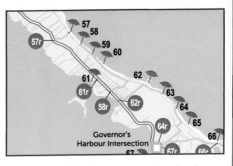

Beach ⭐⭐☆   Road ⭐⭐☆

Beach: 25° 12.787, -76° 14.572
Road (62r): 25° 12.668, -76° 15.331

How to Get There

From points north
Total travel time: 7.6 mi. / 21 min
From GHB proceed south 6.7 miles. Make left and proceed 0.6 miles on very bumpy paved road. Make a right at T onto dirt trail and proceed 0.3 miles to beach access on left.

Time / Distance
To beach road: 6.7 mi. / 11 min
Beach road to beach: 0.9 mi. / 10 min

From points south
Total travel time: 2.2 mi. / 12 min
From Governor's Harbour intersection proceed north 1.3 miles. Make right and proceed 0.6 miles on very bumpy paved road. Make a right at T onto dirt trail and proceed 0.3 miles to beach access on left.

Time / Distance
To beach road: 1.3 mi. / 2 min
Beach road to beach: 0.9 mi. / 10 min

What You Should Know	
Privacy	Semi-private
Shade	None
Accessibility	Car, bumpy
Beach Path	Sandy
Water Entry	Rocks and sand
Water Condition	Shallow entry
Litter/Seaweed	Light
Nearest Town	Governor's Harbour
Snorkeling	Poor
Shelling	No
Beach Size	0.25 miles x 20 yards

Club Med Beach North

There are quite a few reasons why this beach earned its own description and is separately cataloged in our inventory. Even though this is the northern part of what is known as the Club Med beach, it was different enough in a variety of ways to warrant a separate evaluation and grading. One of the major differences between this beach and Club Med Central is protection from wind. The beach access sits in front of a forest of Casuarinas that provide natural protection from both the wind and sun. Several trees have fallen and they provide some natural, albeit firm, places to sit if you've forgotten a beach chair. There's even a rope swing on the beach to get out your inner Tarzan or Jane.

The rock formations that frame the left side of the beach are quite beautiful and unique. The first cutout resembles an open half door that was left ajar to give you unimpeded access to the sand and water. Further to the left is an even bigger semi-cave beach. The water has eroded enough of the rock to offer a little protected sand hideaway.

Most of the water access is friendly, but there are a few rocky areas that can be easily

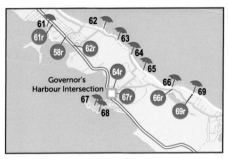

Beach ⭐⭐☆   Road ⭐⭐☆

Beach: 25° 12.531, -76° 14.298
Road: 25° 11.763, -76° 14.655

How to Get There

From points north
Total travel time: 0.8 mi. / 6 min
Proceed south to intersection in Governor's Harbour. Make a left and drive straight up hill 0.2 miles. Continue straight through intersection 0.3 miles to bottom of hill. Make a left onto gravel path and proceed 0.1 miles. Make a right and proceed 0.2 miles to beach access road on right.

Time / Distance
To beach road: 0.8 mi. / 6 min
Beach road to beach: 0.0 mi. / 0 min

From points south
Total travel time: 0.8 mi. / 6 min
Proceed north to intersection in Governor's Harbour. Make a right and drive straight up hill 0.2 miles. Continue straight through intersection 0.3 miles to bottom of hill. Make a left onto gravel path and proceed 0.1 miles. Make a right and proceed 0.2 miles to beach access road on right.

Time / Distance
To beach road: 0.8 mi. / 6 min
Beach road to beach: 0.0 mi. / 0 min

What You Should Know	
Privacy	Semi-private
Shade	Some
Accessibility	Car, bumpy
Beach Path	Sandy
Water Entry	Sandy
Water Condition	Deep ocean
Litter/Seaweed	Light
Nearest Town	Governor's Harbour
Snorkeling	Good
Shelling	No
Beach Size	1.0 miles x 60 yards

avoided. The coral heads are plentiful and are sticking out of the ocean. One small cay to the north is near shore and is good for snorkeling. The beach is moderately clean. There is some debris and seaweed, although it is generally not a problem.

This wide, pink-sand beach is an excellent choice and is slightly better than location 65 due to its unique rocks, natural protection and superior privacy. This beach almost earned our highest grade, but fell short due to not having any particular feature that was truly outstanding or unique.

Club Med Beach Central

Picture everything you could possibly want in a beach resort's beach - great sand, clear water and lots of reef. Now remove the beach resort and that's what you've got at this ultra-wide expanse of sand that used to front the Eleutheran version of Club Med. Hurricane Floyd wreaked its havoc back in 1999, and the resort never re-opened, however, the vestige of what was once there can still be seen in the old shells of buildings. The tall palm trees still stand as protective pillars around the border of what was once one of the jewels of the island.

The beach is still excellent and is perhaps the widest beach on the island stretching 60 to 70 yards at its max, very reminiscent of the great expanse of the Pink Sands beach on Harbour Island, sans the people. What you get here is a vibrant, sunny, and very private beach with just a few houses well off in the distance.

Located just a few minutes from the island's capital, Governor's Harbour, this beach is an excellent choice due to its central location and the ease with which it can be found. The beach road is reasonably good

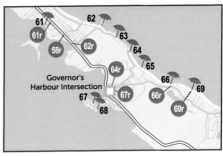

Beach ★★☆ Road ★★☆

Beach: 25° 12.248, -76° 14.168
Road: (64r): 25° 11.763, -76° 14.655

How to Get There

From points north
Total travel time: 0.7 mi. / 6 min
Proceed south to intersection in Governor's Harbour. Make a left and drive straight up hill 0.2 miles. Continue straight through intersection 0.3 miles to bottom of hill. Make a left onto gravel path and proceed 0.1 miles. Make a right and proceed 0.1 miles to beach access road on right.

Time / Distance
To beach road: 0.7 mi. / 5 min
Beach road to beach: 100 feet / 1 min

From points south
Total travel time: 0.7 mi. / 6 min
Proceed north to intersection in Governor's Harbour. Make a right and drive straight up hill 0.2 miles. Continue straight through intersection 0.3 miles to bottom of hill. Make a left onto gravel path and proceed 0.1 miles. Make a right and proceed 0.1 miles to beach access road on right.

Time / Distance
To beach road: 0.7 mi. / 5 min
Beach road to beach: 100 feet / 1 min

What You Should Know	
Privacy	Semi-private
Shade	None
Accessibility	Car, bumpy
Beach Path	Sandy
Water Entry	Sandy
Water Condition	Deep ocean
Litter/Seaweed	Light
Nearest Town	Governor's Harbour
Snorkeling	Good
Shelling	No
Beach Size	1.0 miles x 60 yards

with parking for several cars leading to a generous sandy beach path. The coral heads here are almost unreasonably high cresting the water in places making snorkeling a rather circuitous adventure. From the beach dune, sea lettuce grows towards the ocean in long stretchy vines escaping its bounds and heading towards saltwater.

Choose this beach for its location, its unique length and width, and to see a testament of times past, ever changed by a hurricane's wrath. Keep track of your sun exposure as this beach lacks shade.

French Leave Beach North

The entry to this popular and very well known beach is covered with Casuarina trees making it a little difficult to see the beach road from the Bank's Road. The beach road itself is very short and has ample shaded parking. The beach looks well used. When it was evaluated there were the makings of a small homemade beach bar/pavilion leading to the assumption that parties may be held here on occasion.

The beach path and beach road are within walking distance to the Bahamas Beach House restaurant, an excellent choice for tapas and cold drinks. They even have a little gift shop with some unique island made items.

At French Leave you can find both sun and some shade on its vast and wide 2 mile long stretch. The lack of privacy, due to nearby private residences and the restaurant, can be overcome by moving further north, to the left of the beach path. There was also a lot of seaweed up on the beach especially right at the beach entry that would cause me to pitch my beach blanket and chairs away from the beach path. If you want more privacy you are better off walking left beyond the sight of the houses and away from the seaweed. To the right you will be in front of houses and the restaurant, offering some convenience to that amenity.

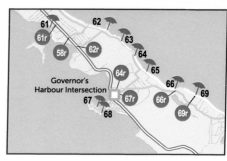

Beach ★★☆   Road ★★☆

Beach: 25° 11.898, -76° 13.727
Road: 25° 11.872, -76° 13.737

How to Get There

From points north
Total travel time: 1.1 mi. / 7 min
Proceed south to intersection in Governor's Harbour. Make a left and drive straight up hill 0.2 miles. At intersection make a right and proceed 0.9 miles. Make left and go a few hundred feet to parking on left.

Time / Distance
To beach road: 1.1 mi. / 6 min
Beach road to beach: 200 feet / 1 min

From points south
Total travel time: 1.1 mi. / 6 min
Proceed north to intersection in Governor's Harbour. Make a right and drive straight up hill 0.2 miles. At intersection make a right and proceed 0.9 miles. Make left and go a few hundred feet to parking on left.

Time / Distance
To beach road: 1.1 mi. / 6 min
Beach road to beach: 200 feet / 1 min

What You Should Know

Privacy	Semi-private
Shade	Some
Accessibility	Car
Beach Path	Sandy
Water Entry	Sandy
Water Condition	Deep ocean
Litter/Seaweed	Moderate
Nearest Town	Governor's Harbour
Snorkeling	Good
Shelling	No
Beach Size	2.0 miles x 40 yards

Coral heads and one small cay can be reached easily from shore for snorkeling.

French Leave North has a lot of pluses. It is close to the Bahamas Beach House, is easy to find, and has a nice sandy water entry with a good nearby reef system. However, if privacy is of paramount importance then you should look for more isolated beaches. Also, you can probably expect some road noise here from vehicles passing by on the Bank's Road. Be prepared for the lack of shade.

Governor's Harbour Beach

This is the larger of the two beaches that are part of Eleuthera's capital city of Governor's Harbour. The beach sits in front of the retaining wall that protects the road leading from Governor's to Cupid's Cay. It is a quaint public beach that is best suited for youngsters. It seems to always be bustling with activity and you can often engage in many activities like swimming, sailing and kayaking.

The water is a gorgeous shade of turquoise and the entire area has a very protected bay-like feel. The town of Governor's Harbour is right down the road. You are within easy walking distance of shops, restaurants and grocers. You will also be directly across the street from the beautiful Hayne's Public Library. The adults can get Internet service there while the kids play in the shallow waters. Access to the water is nice and sandy over all its 150 yards.

What we don't like is the obvious lack of privacy and audible road noise. The flipside of that is the convenience of being right in the heart of Governor's with access to all of its amenities. There are a generous number of benches and picnic tables that are set up underneath the shade of nearby palm trees once again making this a good area for parents to relax while the kids experience a great day of vacation.

Beach ⭐☆☆ Road ⭐⭐☆

Beach: 25° 11.560, -76° 14.796
Road: 25° 11.759, -76° 14.657

How to Get There

From points north
Total travel time: 0.4 mi. / 2 min
Proceed south to intersection in Governor's Harbour. Make a right and proceed 0.4 miles towards Cupid's Cay. There is parking both left and right.

Time / Distance
Beach road to beach: 0.4 mi. / 2 min

From points south
Total travel time: 0.4 mi. / 2 min
Proceed north to intersection in Governor's Harbour. Make a left and proceed 0.4 miles towards Cupid's Cay. There is parking both left and right.

Time / Distance
Beach road to beach: 0.4 mi. / 2 min

What You Should Know	
Privacy	Public
Shade	Some
Accessibility	Car
Beach Path	None
Water Entry	Sandy
Water Condition	Shallow Caribbean
Litter/Seaweed	None
Nearest Town	Governor's Harbour
Snorkeling	Poor
Shelling	No
Beach Size	150 yards x 15 feet

Governor's Harbour Beach South

The smaller beach of the two town beaches set on the south side of Cupid's Cay is only about 50 yards long and has the Friday night Fish Fry hut as its focal point. Similar to beach 67, this is a beach for small children. The water is very shallow, the bay very protected. The benefit of using this beach as compared to the larger one on the other side of the road is there is less boat traffic and activity. It's more like a child's wading pool complemented by a couple of scenic cays off in the distance.

You have all the conveniences of Governor's Harbour just a few hundred feet away including shops, restaurants, groceries, and the Haynes Public Library. Walking around Cupid's Cay is an adventure, and the whole colorful scene is something to experience.

Tables and benches that are part of the regular weekly fish fry are available for use in shaded areas for a picnic lunch. What we found problematic at this location, in addition to the lack of privacy and people noise, is the overflowing garbage cans, which were aesthetically unpleasant and smelly.

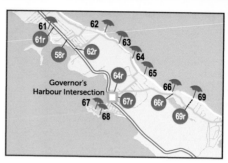

Governor's Harbour Intersection

Beach ☆☆☆   Road ☆☆☆

Beach: 25° 11.560, -76° 14.796
Road (67r): 25° 11.759, -76° 14.657

How to Get There

From points north
Total travel time: 0.4 mi. / 2 min
Proceed south to intersection in Governor's Harbour. Make a right and proceed 0.4 miles towards Cupid's Cay. There is parking both left and right.

Time / Distance
Beach road to beach: 0.4 mi. / 2 min

From points south
Total travel time: 0.4 mi. / 2 min
Proceed north to intersection in Governor's Harbour. Make a left and proceed 0.4 miles towards Cupid's Cay. There is parking both left and right.

Time / Distance
Beach road to beach: 0.4 mi. / 2 min

What You Should Know	
Privacy	Public
Shade	Some
Accessibility	Car
Beach Path	None
Water Entry	Sandy
Water Condition	Shallow Caribbean
Litter/Seaweed	None
Nearest Town	Governor's Harbour
Snorkeling	Poor
Shelling	No
Beach Size	60 yards x 10 feet

French Leave Beach Central

Sometimes the road less traveled is the best one to take especially when it leads to a beach that is so lovely and so isolated. This hike-to beach, while difficult to find and get to, is one of the island's best due to its utter privacy and overall neatness. The first step in getting here is finding the beach path. This beach was visited and reviewed several times and each time, even after knowing where to go, proved to be a bit of a challenge. What you are looking for as a landmark off of the Bank's Road is a 12' high sand dune with a rope hung conveniently from a small palm tree to aid the ascension up the dune to the beach path that leads through the jungle. The sandy path at the top of the dune was cut out and marked with waist high wooden

property markers indicating a more or less straight line back to the beach. Sure enough, after a 5 to 10 minute hike down this slightly up and down path you crest another small sand dune and then voila! Always look for tall Casuarinas or palms as they generally indicate you are nearing the beach, hope in the form of a tree.

Miles of sun and sand stretch from Palmetto Point all the way to Governor's Harbour. However, be prepared for absolutely no shade. A very clean beach with almost no seaweed and hardly any debris complements the crystal clear water. The beach has cool, firm sand that is great for walking and running. Lots of coral heads are visible along with one large cay in front of the breaker reef, which

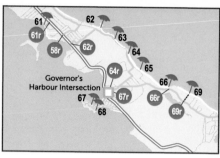

Governor's
Harbour Intersection

Beach ★★★   Road ★☆☆

Beach: 25° 11.778, -76° 13.156
Road: 25° 11.645, -76° 13.272

What You Should Know

Privacy	Secluded
Shade	None
Accessibility	Car; Hike
Beach Path	Dune; rope climb
Water Entry	Sandy
Water Condition	Deep ocean
Litter/Seaweed	Light
Nearest Town	Governor's Harbour
Snorkeling	Good
Shelling	No
Beach Size	2.0 miles x 40 yards

can be reached by swimming. It is probably the protection created by this cay and reef that explains why it's so clean.

The beach features a low-lying dune wall littered with sea oats and tall Casuarinas as its backdrop. The beach is great for walking, hiking, swimming or snorkeling. We wouldn't recommend trying to get a kayak back to this top-notch beach only because the climb up and down the dune rope along with the hike back to the beach would be a bit strenuous. The only negatives in our evaluation were the absence of shade, little parking, difficult to find and difficult to get to. However, the level of privacy and great setting of this beach easily offset those blemishes.

How to Get There

From points north
Total travel time: 1.8 mi. / 18 min
Drive south to intersection in Governor's Harbour. Make a left and drive straight up hill 0.2 miles. At intersection make a right and go 1.4 miles to small parking area on left. Look for rope to assist climbing dune. Hike sandy path 0.2 miles to beach.

Time / Distance
To beach road: 1.6 mi. / 8 min
Beach road to beach: 0.2m hike / 10 min

From points south
Total travel time: 4.5 mi. / 27 min
Drive north to intersection in Palmetto Point. Make a right and proceed 0.7 miles to T. Make a left, bear right at first fork, and proceed a total of 3.6 miles to small parking area on right. Look for rope to assist climbing dune. Hike sandy path 0.2 miles to beach.

Time / Distance
To beach road: 4.3 mi. / 17 min
Beach road to beach: 0.2m hike / 10 min

French Leave Beach South

Just south of the very popular island restaurant, Tippy's, you'll find the beach path, which is currently marked by a wooden fence just off of the Bank's Road. The beach is quite visible through the trees. This looked like the easiest place to access the beach with just a short stroll down a clear path. All other reasonable access points appeared to be on private property or associated with the restaurant.

The location and convenience to Tippy's is probably the best attribute of the beach. This beach also differentiates itself by its width.

At low tide the beach can reach almost 100 yards wide, and on average it's still a very wide 60 to 80 yards stretching almost a mile, mostly to the north, from this vantage point.

This beach is not very private, however. It is exposed to the road and car noise. With many private homes, Tippy's, and Pineapple Fields surrounding this access point you shouldn't expect to have the beach to yourself. Parking on the road was also a bit precarious since there really wasn't any defined parking area. You simply pull off on the side of the road.

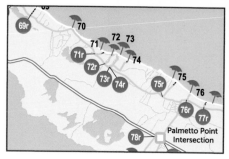

Beach ★★☆ Road ★★★

Beach: 25° 11.373, -76° 12.473
Road: 25° 11.373, -76° 12.473

How to Get There

From points north

Total travel time: 2.5 mi. / 12 min
Drive south to intersection in Governor's Harbour. Make a left and drive straight up hill 0.2 miles. At intersection make a right and proceed 2.3 miles. The access path is a few hundred feet past Tippy's on the left. Access path currently has a small wooden fence pointing the way.

Time / Distance
To beach road: 2.5 mi. / 12 min
Beach road to beach: 0.0 mi. / 0 min

From points south

Total travel time: 3.4 mi. / 14 min
Drive north to intersection in Palmetto Point. Make a right and proceed 0.7 miles to T. Make a left, bear right at first fork, and proceed a total of 2.7 miles to access path on right. Access path currently has a small wooden fence pointing the way.

Time / Distance
To beach road: 3.4 mi. / 14 min
Beach road to beach: 0.0 mi. / 0 min

What You Should Know	
Privacy	Semi-private
Shade	Some
Accessibility	Car
Beach Path	Stairs
Water Entry	Sandy
Water Condition	Deep ocean
Litter/Seaweed	Moderate
Nearest Town	Governor's Harbour
Snorkeling	Good
Shelling	No
Beach Size	2.0 miles x 40 yards

The big wide open beach is good for snorkeling, walking, and running. There was a fair amount of wash up and seaweed. You can find shade towards the back of the beach, but then you are sitting on its worst part. Most of the water entry is good although there are some rocky ledges that extend into the water in several places. They are easily avoided, though. This is a good beach around lunchtime. Grab a meal or drink at Tippy's, and then lounge the day away on one of Eleuthera's widest beaches.

North Rocks Beach

The overall opinion of this beach was jaded significantly due to the condition it was in when it was evaluated. The problem here was a huge amount of seaweed both in the water and on the beach along with a fair amount of wash-up. Due to the seaweed the beach was uninviting and the water even worse. There was nothing overly interesting about this spot. It was just a big wide sandy beach that could be used for sunning. To make matters worse, it lacks shade

The appearance of the overall location seemed to indicate that it was mostly cleared to show off residential lots so the beach path and associated beach road may not exist for much longer. The beach road itself was a bit tricky, as you have to keep to the right shortly after leaving the highway into a jungle path that looks like it's the wrong way. However, if you continue you will find a dirt path between a series of palm trees. There's no real parking area here and just before the beach is a lot of sand so be careful to avoid getting your car stuck.

All in all, this was a very average location and would really only be useful for tanning or beachcombing. Even snorkeling would require some inconvenience, as you would need to walk further north to where the coral heads come closer to shore. You can find better beaches to both the north and south of North Rocks.

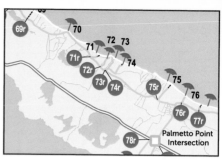

Beach ★★☆ Road ★★☆

Beach: 25° 10.984, -76° 11.955
Road: 25° 10.936, -76° 12.034

How to Get There

From points north
Total travel time: 3.6 mi. / 16 min
Drive south to intersection in Governor's Harbour. Make a left and drive straight up hill 0.2 miles. At intersection make a right and go 3.2 miles. Make a left and proceed 0.2 miles bearing right up hill through narrow dirt path. Stop short of sanded area to avoid getting car stuck.

Time / Distance
To beach road: 3.4 mi. / 14 min
Beach road to beach: 0.2 mi. / 2 min

From points south
Total travel time: 2.7 mi. / 14 min
Drive north to intersection in Palmetto Point. Make a right and proceed 0.7 miles to T. Make a left, bear right at first fork, proceed a total of 1.8 miles and make a right. Proceed 0.2 miles bearing to the right up hill through narrow dirt path. Stop short of sanded area to avoid getting car stuck.

Time / Distance
To beach road: 2.5 mi. / 12 min
Beach road to beach: 0.2 mi. / 2 min

What You Should Know	
Privacy	Semi-private
Shade	None
Accessibility	Car, bumpy
Beach Path	Dune
Water Entry	Sandy
Water Condition	Deep ocean
Litter/Seaweed	Extensive
Nearest Town	Palmetto Point
Snorkeling	Poor
Shelling	No
Beach Size	1.0 miles x 40 yards

Next 2 Rocks Beach

Sometimes, driving just a short distance from one beach location to another means a lot in terms of quality and experience. Next 2 Rocks is physically located just north of Ji-Kan and a wee bit south of North Rocks. However, because this location is extremely protected by an extended rock formation, the overall cleanliness of the beach was improved by orders of magnitude.

There was little seaweed on the beach or in the water and very little debris. The water was crystal clear and had very appealing light turquoise hues not unlike that of a shallow Caribbean-side beach. The view was also much more alluring than nearby beaches due to its proximity to the unique rock formation.

The main negative is that the beach sits very close to a single large property. If that house is occupied this beach would likely not be very private.

The hard packed sand is of excellent quality and easy to walk on. Overall, the setting is very nice and offers a lot of choices for those seeking sun, good swimming, exploring and snorkeling.

Be aware that there is not a lot of shade except in a couple of isolated spots. To compare this beach with others that are within a short walk of the rock formation, this one is superior to North Rocks, but not quite as nice as Ji-Kan simply because of privacy.

Beach ★★☆ Road ★★☆

Beach: 25° 10.952, -76° 11.769
Road: 25° 10.798, -76° 11.891

How to Get There

From points north

Total travel time: 3.9 mi. / 15 min
Drive south to intersection in Governor's Harbour. Make a left and drive straight up hill 0.2 miles. At intersection make a right and go 3.5 miles. Make a left and proceed 0.2 miles to beach.

Time / Distance
To beach road: 3.7 mi. / 14 min
Beach road to beach: 0.2 mi. / 1 min

From points south

Total travel time: 2.6 mi. / 12 min
Drive north to intersection in Palmetto Point. Make a right and proceed 0.7 miles to T. Make a left, bear right at first fork, and proceed a total of 1.7 miles. Make a right and proceed 0.2 miles to beach.

Time / Distance
To beach road: 2.4 mi. / 12 min
Beach road to beach: 0.2 mi. / 1 min

What You Should Know	
Privacy	Semi-private
Shade	None
Accessibility	Car, bumpy
Beach Path	Dune
Water Entry	Sandy
Water Condition	Deep ocean
Litter/Seaweed	Light
Nearest Town	Palmetto Point
Snorkeling	Poor
Shelling	No
Beach Size	1.0 miles x 40 yards

Ji-Kan Beach

This picturesque location received our high-est rating primarily due to its unique rock formations to the north of the beach path along with the overall cleanliness, beautiful water, and level of privacy. You know you're on the right beach road when you start seeing above ground water pipes leading through cement stanchions. Why would water pipes be going to a beach, you might ask? At one time or another there was a functioning bath-room just off to the side of the parking area. Although no longer functioning you know you've found the right beach when you find the High Can to the left of the beach path!

There are nice vista views from the shaded parking area leading you to a very wide beach path. Miles of beach to the south are perfect for walking. Crossing the jagged rocks to the north leads to a whole different expanse of gorgeous pink sand. Separating the two sides of beach is a large striated rock formation with cutouts that have been formed from the surf leaving protected little beach caves between the rock. Sandy ledges beside the rocks spill down to the ocean. Across the rocks is a private little beach cove with a few houses which may squander some of your privacy. These rock steps jut out a good 150' into the ocean

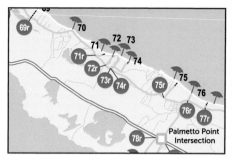

Beach ★★★ Road ★★☆

Beach: 25° 10.919, -76° 11.624
Road: 25° 10.718, -76° 11.798

How to Get There

From points north
Total travel time: 4.1 mi. / 17 min
Drive south to intersection in Governor's Harbour. Make a left and drive straight up hill 0.2 miles. At intersection make a right and go 3.7 miles. Make a left and proceed past wooden posts. Continue straight for a total of 0.2 miles to parking area.

Time / Distance
To beach road: 3.9 mi. / 15 min
Beach road to beach: 0.2 mi. / 2 min

From points south
Total travel time: 2.4 mi. / 11 min
Drive north to intersection in Palmetto Point. Make a right and proceed 0.7 miles to T. Make a left, bear right at first fork, and proceed a total of 1.5 miles. Make a right and proceed past wooden posts. Continue straight for a total of 0.2 miles to parking area.

Time / Distance
To beach road: 2.2 mi. / 11 min
Beach road to beach: 0.2 mi. / 2 min

What You Should Know	
Privacy	Semi-private
Shade	Some
Accessibility	Car, bumpy
Beach Path	Dune
Water Entry	Sandy
Water Condition	Deep ocean
Litter/Seaweed	Light
Nearest Town	Palmetto Point
Snorkeling	Good
Shelling	No
Beach Size	0.75 miles x 20 yards

forming an above water road to Atlantis.

The overall privacy at this location is good with only one other house immediately to the north and set way back on the cliff. The views are great. The water is beautiful with no rocks to contend with and there is a good reef system out front for snorkeling. The only negative with this beach is that there's not much shade except at the parking area so bring suntan lotion and an umbrella. Enjoy this super-long and super-wide beach where you have dunes, rugged cliffs, interesting rocks to climb and several hidden beaches nearby.

Ji-Kan Beach South

This beach is really the same long beach on the North Palmetto shoreline as Sol, Poponi, Ji-Kan and several others and is just up the road from the 'Rocks' beaches of Governor's Harbour. This is just a different access point and probably one that you shouldn't have to go out of your way to find since it offers nothing especially unique. There are two private houses next to the beach access, which affects privacy.

What's interesting about this location is that there's a sandy elevated beach on a plateau near the parking area up and away from the main beach. You could use that upper plot of sand to have a protected place to gather some sun and then use the beach path down to the main beach when you want to swim or snorkel.

Moving left from the beach path offers much more privacy since the beach path is just to the left of the two private houses. It's a little tricky to reach this beach as you need to drive up a hill, cross a small a path, and then drive through a narrowing beach road as it leads up to the parking area. It is easy to get discouraged, as the beach road doesn't always appear to be a road that should be driven.

Choose this beach for its elevated second beach, which affords additional protection since it is away from the ocean. Otherwise, choose one of the nearby access points for a better overall experience.

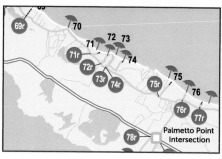

Palmetto Point
Intersection

Beach ★★☆ Road ★☆☆

Beach: 25° 10.828, -76° 11.486
Road: 25° 10.626, -76° 11.623

How to Get There

From points north
Total travel time: 4.1 mi. / 18 min
Drive south to intersection in Governor's Harbour. Make a left and drive straight up hill 0.2 miles. At intersection make a right and go 3.7 miles. Make a left and proceed up steep hill after passing cement stanchions. Pass over small dirt road and continue back to beach bearing right as road gets overgrown. Continue up hill to level parking area and walk down sanded path to beach on right.

Time / Distance
To beach road: 3.9 mi. / 16 min
Beach road to beach: 0.2 mi. / 2 min

From points south
Total travel time: 2.2 mi. / 10 min
Drive north to intersection in Palmetto Point. Make a right and proceed 0.7 miles to T. Make a left, bear right at first fork, and proceed a total of 1.3 miles. Make a right and proceed up steep hill after passing cement stanchions. Pass over small dirt road and continue back to beach bearing right as road gets overgrown. Continue up hill to level parking area and walk down sanded path to beach on right.

Time / Distance
To beach road: 2.0 mi. / 10 min
Beach road to beach: 0.2 mi. / 2 min

What You Should Know	
Privacy	Semi-private
Shade	None
Accessibility	4WD recommended
Beach Path	Dune
Water Entry	Sandy
Water Condition	Deep ocean
Litter/Seaweed	Light
Nearest Town	Palmetto Point
Snorkeling	Good
Shelling	No
Beach Size	0.75 miles x 20 yards

Sol Beach

Sol beach is hot, literally! This is a very sunny spot with no shade whatsoever. Regardless of that it's quite an interesting beach. There's lots of privacy, however, this beach had the look of a place that would soon be developed so it may not exist as an accessible beach once houses get built here.

It requires a little bit of work to get to and it is difficult to get up the beach road with a car. Look out for burs as you walk across the dune and down to the beach. You'll have to descend down a sandy beach access path to reach the beach.

The beach has very little debris. What remains has mostly been picked up and turned into beach art, hung from a dead Casuarina, like a summertime Christmas tree.

There are no houses directly above or near the beach. There are some in the distance, but they are much further away both north and south and the parking area is small so you shouldn't get a lot of people traffic. The parking area, because it's set on a small dune, gives you a nice elevated view of the Atlantic. The water gets deep quickly and there could be heavy surf so be careful with tides on windy or otherwise rough days.

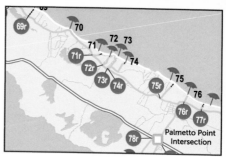

Palmetto Point
Intersection

Beach ★★☆   Road ★★☆

Beach: 25° 10.458, -76° 10.595
Road: 25° 10.216, -76° 10.816

How to Get There

From points north
Total travel time: 5.0 mi. / 22 min
Drive south to intersection in Governor's Harbour. Make a left and drive straight up hill 0.2 miles. At intersection make a right and go 4.6 miles. Make a left and proceed 0.2 miles back to beach. Walk down dune to beach.

Time / Distance
To beach road: 4.8 mi. / 20 min
Beach road to beach: 0.2 mi. / 2 min

From points south
Total travel time: 1.3 mi. / 7 min
Drive north to intersection in Palmetto Point. Make a right and proceed 0.7 miles to T. Make a left, bear right at first fork, and proceed a total of 0.4 miles. Make a right and proceed 0.2 miles back to beach. Walk down dune to beach.

Time / Distance
To beach road: 1.1 mi. / 7 min
Beach road to beach: 0.2 mi. / 2 min

What You Should Know	
Privacy	Secluded
Shade	None
Accessibility	4WD recommended
Beach Path	Dune
Water Entry	Sandy
Water Condition	Deep ocean
Litter/Seaweed	Light
Nearest Town	Palmetto Point
Snorkeling	Good
Shelling	No
Beach Size	1.2 miles x 40 yards

Poponi Beach

This astounding beach, perfectly centrally located, is simply beautiful. What makes Poponi special is its size relative to the amount of wash-up and seaweed. Most unprotected Atlantic beaches have lots of debris, but Poponi has less.

It's very close to Palmetto Point as well as Unique's restaurant where you can go to grab lunch or a nice cold drink. There is ample parking, a very short beach path and ample shade especially at the access point. Large coral heads just offshore afford the ocean sea life a perfect hideaway and give you an ideal spot to snorkel. Walk or run up and down the beach to your heart's content, as Poponi stretches for more than a mile.

There are some houses in the area especially up the cliffs to the south. It will be hit or miss whether you'll have privacy or not, however the beach feels more secluded because there are fewer homes, they're further apart and most are high up on cliffs. Choose Poponi for a blend of big ocean, small waves, good snorkeling, expansive beach and nearby amenities.

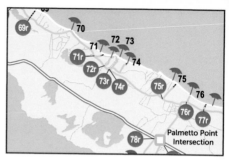

Beach ☆☆☆ Road ☆☆☆

Beach: 25° 10.207, -76° 10.276
Road: 25° 10.154, -76° 10.368

How to Get There

From points north
Total travel time: 1.1 mi. / 7 min
Drive south to intersection in Palmetto Point. Make a left and proceed 0.7 miles to T. Make a right and proceed 0.1 miles to access road road with Poponi sign. Make a left and proceed 0.3 miles to parking area.

Time / Distance
To beach road: 0.8 mi. / 5 min
Beach road to beach: 0.3 mi. / 2 min

From points south
Total travel time: 1.1 mi. / 7 min
Drive north to intersection in Palmetto Point. Make a right and proceed 0.7 miles to T. Make a right and proceed 0.1 miles to road with Poponi sign. Make a left and proceed 0.3 miles to parking area.

Time / Distance
To beach road: 0.8 mi. / 5 min
Beach road to beach: 0.3 mi. / 2 min

What You Should Know	
Privacy	Semi-private
Shade	Plenty
Accessibility	Car, bumpy
Beach Path	Sandy
Water Entry	Sandy
Water Condition	Deep ocean
Litter/Seaweed	Light
Nearest Town	Palmetto Point
Snorkeling	Good
Shelling	No
Beach Size	1.2 miles x 40 yards

Unique's Beach

This very nice beach, reached by descending a 55-step staircase, sits below the vacation resort Unique's with its large restaurant, bar, swimming pool, hotel, and vacation rentals. There are commanding views from its elevated perch with most of the Eastern shore of Eleuthera visible.

The beach itself is high quality with very little debris or wash-up. A freshwater shower is available at the base of the steps as an added amenity. Other than one rocky outcropping right where the steps lead to sand there is good sandy water access for more than a mile. This beach is excellent for walking and running. There are numerous coral heads offshore for snorkeling on calm days.

Expect no privacy due to the proximity to the resort although the beach is well beyond the restaurant and hotel so you won't have the feeling of being watched. This is a great beach if you are looking for a perfect beach road, ample shade, the benefits of a bar, restaurant, shower and bathroom within a few paces and a lovely scenic overview. Just be cautious of the steps down to the beach as you're going to have to climb back up after you've had your sun and swim.

Beach ★★☆ Road ★★★

Beach: 25° 10.085, -76° 10.023
Road: 25° 10.009, -76° 10.057

How to Get There

From points north
Total travel time: 1.2 mi. / 9 min
Drive south to intersection in Palmetto Point. Make a left and proceed 0.7 miles to T. Make a right and proceed 0.4 miles to entrance marked by Unique's and Atlantic Resort sign. Make a left and proceed 0.1 miles back to restaurant on right. Walk to back of restaurant and take 60 steps down to beach.

Time / Distance
To beach road: 1.1 mi. / 8 min
Beach road to beach: 0.1 mi. / 1 min

From points south
Total travel time: 1.2 mi. / 9 min
Drive north to intersection in Palmetto Point. Make a right and proceed 0.7 miles to T. Make a right and proceed 0.4 miles to entrance marked by Unique's and Atlantic Resort sign. Make a left and proceed 0.1 miles back to restaurant on right. Walk to back of restaurant and take 60 steps down to beach.

Time / Distance
To beach road: 1.1 mi. / 8 min
Beach road to beach: 0.1 mi. / 1 min

What You Should Know	
Privacy	Semi-private
Shade	Plenty
Accessibility	Car
Beach Path	Stairs
Water Entry	Sandy
Water Condition	Deep ocean
Litter/Seaweed	Light
Nearest Town	Palmetto Point
Snorkeling	Good
Shelling	No
Beach Size	1.2 miles x 40 yards

Papaw Bay Beach

One of the more interesting panoramas on the island greets you as you crest the access path onto this narrow double half-moon beach. The beach stretches approximately 0.3 miles with each half-moon providing 0.15 miles of luscious soft sand. There are a total of four nearby cays although one is hidden behind the others and only becomes visible from the center of the beach, arguably the best spot to pitch your beach chairs since that's the prime water entry spot.

Papaw is a very protected bay. When the wind comes from the west it is one of the few Caribbean beaches that will remain flat and calm. There are several rocky ledges leading into the water at both the northern and southern ends of the beach. This is the poorest water entry and this is also where the private properties are located meaning less privacy. For the best sandy water access and the most privacy, head to the middle of the beach or swim out to the cay that is to the left as it has its own little private beach.

This beach is clean, fun to walk and can provide some good opportunities to collect prized miniature shells. The beach access points have been reduced to one spot and parking is limited so if you find a car already there expect to have some company on the beach. One of the other nice things about this beach is that it is one of the few that actually has formal road signage. It is easy to find and sure to please.

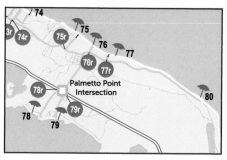

Beach ★★☆   Road ★★☆

Beach: 25° 9.055, -76° 11.326
Road: 25° 9.490, -76° 10.949

How to Get There

From points north
Total travel time: 5.5 mi. / 14 min
From Governor's Harbour intersectionintersection drive south for 4.9 miles. Make a right at Papaw Bay Road and proceed 0.6 miles following bend to right to beach access.

Time / Distance
To beach road: 4.9 mi. / 8 min
Beach road to beach: 0.6 mi. / 6 min

From points south
Total travel time: 0.7 mi. / 7 min
From Palmetto Point intersection drive north for 0.1 miles. Make a left at Papaw Bay Road and proceed 0.6 miles following bend to right to beach access.

Time / Distance
To beach road: 0.1 mi. / 1 min
Beach road to beach: 0.6 mi. / 6 min

What You Should Know	
Privacy	Semi-private
Shade	Some
Accessibility	Car, bumpy
Beach Path	Sandy
Water Entry	Rocky
Water Condition	Shallow Caribbean
Litter/Seaweed	Light
Nearest Town	Palmetto Point
Snorkeling	Good
Shelling	Yes
Beach Size	0.3 miles x 10 yards

South Palmetto Point Beach

The Bahamian community beaches are usually not the best choice for visitors due to their lack of privacy compared to some of the more difficult to reach beaches on the island. South Palmetto Point is an exception as it has a lot of characteristics and features that make it quite pleasant. First off, it is extremely easy to access on a short perfectly paved road. The view is outstanding with several small cays off to the north along with sweeping views of southern Eleuthera to the south. Even Ten Bay Beach, 3 miles away, can be easily seen.

The beach area serves the community during celebrations. Several beach huts line the shore for use during Homecomings. Don't worry about this interrupting your use of the beach during the day. The raucous celebrations begin after dark and go into the wee hours of the morning.

There are two sides to this beach that are separated by a large dilapidated dock at the center. The sand is clean and pink and there is little debris or seaweed on either side. There are some rocky water entry spots that can be easily avoided. The light turquoise water is very shallow for quite a distance from shore

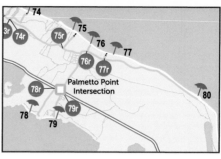

Beach ★★☆   Road ★★★

Beach: 25° 8.976, -76° 10.972
Road: 25° 9.417, -76° 10.815

How to Get There

From points north
Total travel time: 0.5 mi. / 3 min
Drive south to intersection in Palmetto Point.
Make right and proceed 0.5 miles.

Time / Distance
Beach road to beach: 0.5 mi. / 3 min

From points south
Total travel time: 0.5 mi. / 3 min
Drive north to intersection in Palmetto Point.
Make left and proceed 0.5 miles.

Time / Distance
Beach road to beach: 0.5 mi. / 3 min

What You Should Know

Privacy	Public
Shade	Some
Accessibility	Car
Beach Path	None
Water Entry	Sandy
Water Condition	Shallow Caribbean
Litter/Seaweed	Light
Nearest Town	Palmetto Point
Snorkeling	Good
Shelling	Yes
Beach Size	0.3 miles x 20 yards

making this a good swimming spot for young
children. Shade can be found away from the
beach access point, but very few trees are close
to the beach and none are by the water's edge.
Expect no privacy as houses and several small
resorts line both sides of the beach.

In general, this is a nice community beach
and probably the best one in that class. The
broken down dock and nearby cemetery do
spoil the atmosphere a bit, but if you are
looking for a very easy to get to beach that is
clean, has shallow water, and a nice view then
South Palmetto Point fits the bill.

Between the Rocks Beach

This is a unique, scenic beach, which has a large ocean tidal pool, perfect for swimming or wading. While the beach is quite nice with attractive tall palms interspersed along the back of the dune, it was really the gorgeous, shallow sandy water channel that earned this beach our highest grade. We didn't find any other formations like this on the island that compares.

The beach path is on a small sandy road. Parking and access is found in a semi-private spot between private houses. Cross a little dune to reach a flat sandy shelf, which then gives way to a sloping sand shelf leading to the water. There you'll find two sets of low lying rock ledges split by a turquoise channel that runs between the rocks on out to the ocean. The color contrast is simply amazing. If you want just regular beach with clear sandy water access you only have to move a few hundred feet to either side of the rocky point.

The tidal pool is roughly 50 yards long and 15 feet wide. You can follow it all the way out into the deep blue ocean where a significant reef system provides good

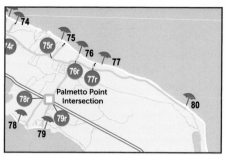

Beach ★★★ Road ★★☆

Beach: 25° 9.334, -76° 8.331
Road: 25° 9.334, -76° 8.331

How to Get There

From points north
Total travel time: 3.3 mi. / 12 min
Drive south to intersection in Palmetto.
Make a left and proceed 0.7 miles to T. Make
a right and proceed 2.6 miles to beach path
on left.

Time / Distance
To beach road: 3.3 mi. / 12 min
Beach road to beach: 0.0 mi. / 0 min

From points south
Total travel time: 3.3 mi. / 12 min
Drive north to intersection in Palmetto.
Make a right and proceed 0.7 miles to T.
Make a right and proceed 2.6 miles to beach
path on left.

Time / Distance
To beach road: 3.3 mi. / 12 min
Beach road to beach: 0.0 mi. / 0 min

What You Should Know

Privacy	Semi-private
Shade	None
Accessibility	Car, bumpy
Beach Path	Dune
Water Entry	Sandy
Water Condition	Deep ocean, shallow channel
Litter/Seaweed	Light
Nearest Town	Palmetto Point
Snorkeling	Good
Shelling	No
Beach Size	3.2 miles x 40 yards

snorkeling. The entire contiguous beach area runs almost 3.5 miles from North Palmetto all the way to the end of Double Bay so you have plenty of pink sand to sink your toes in.

This is a beautiful and very interesting geographic formation that receives an 'A' for uniqueness. The only real negatives are the proximity to several houses and lack of shade. Also, be aware that the sandy road to the south of this point is blocked off and impassable past the house. You will have to reverse your way back out to return to the Bank's Road.

Double Bay Beach

This long expansive ocean beach stretches north for 3 miles or more from the beach path, which starts at the southern tip. Double Bay is a prime real estate market and there are many large homes up and down its short dune banks making them quite visible. While there are no houses at the access point there are many houses further north so don't expect complete privacy.

The beach and beach road have changed somewhat over the years and what is first noticeable is the deterioration of the paved road leading back to the beach. What used to be one of the smoothest roads on the island is now very washed out and should be driven with care. The beach is still reachable by car, but expect a longer driving time than one would expect for a 1 mile paved road. Additionally, at the end of your drive the road turns to dirt and then to sand up a small hill. Use caution if you drive up the hill as the sand is quite soft and a car can easily get stuck.

Double Bay is very exposed and therefore gets quite a bit of debris and seaweed, making it unattractive. One can see Gut Island far to the north where the beach wraps around and ultimately connects into the beaches of North

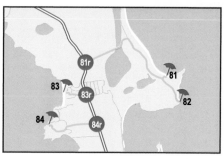

Beach ★★☆   Road ★☆☆

Beach: 25° 7.563, -76° 7.244
Road: 25° 7.799, -76° 8.694

What You Should Know

Privacy	Semi-private
Shade	None
Accessibility	Car, bumpy
Beach Path	Dune
Water Entry	Sandy
Water Condition	Deep ocean
Litter/Seaweed	Moderate
Nearest Town	Palmetto Point
Snorkeling	Good
Shelling	No
Beach Size	3.2 miles x 40 yards

Palmetto Point. A loosely connected reef system exists although better snorkeling is to the south along the rocky shoreline. There is at least one and possibly two shipwrecks in this southern quadrant, one that is visible above the waterline. The ocean water gets deep quickly creating waves, usually small ones that provide a lovely swashing sound as they break against the shore.

The tall scenic palms provide an elegant backdrop for a beach ideal for sunning and swimming. This is a good choice if you are looking for a beach that is easy to find and has miles of wide shoreline.

How to Get There

From points north
Total travel time: 4.1 mi. / 13 min
From Palmetto Point intersection drive south 2.0 miles. Make a left between stone pillars. There is a High Voltage sign as a landmark on the right. Proceed 1.0 miles to T. Make a right and proceed 1.0 miles. Make a left at fork at end onto overgrown beach path for 0.1 miles.

Time / Distance
To beach road: 2.0 mi. / 3 min
Beach road to beach: 2.1 mi. / 10 min

From points south
Total travel time: 5.6 mi. / 15 min
From Savannah Sound intersection drive north 3.5 miles. Make a right between stone pillars. There is a High Voltage sign as a landmark on the left. Proceed 1.0 miles to T. Make a right and proceed 1.0 miles. Make a left at fork at end onto overgrown beach path for 0.1 miles.

Time / Distance
To beach road: 3.5 mi. / 5 min
Beach road to beach: 2.1 mi. / 10 min

Girt Bay Beach

There's something about this beach that gives it a different sound quality. Maybe it's the roughness of the water crashing along the shore or it could be the ocean bubbling up through the rocky formations. Whatever it is, if you want the complete sensation of sight, sound and sea smell then this beach fits the bill. If the volume of the surf was a characteristic that was considered in our ratings then this beach would win hands down.

Stuck way out on the point at Girt Bay, it feels like it's almost set into the middle of the ocean. It has a rugged 10' high dune wall as its backdrop leading to a steeply pitched beach that angles sharply into the water. The beach is a small half-moon that barely stretches 100 yards. It is completely secluded and you are likely to have it all to yourself unless someone beats you to it. The water gets deep quickly and can be dangerous with waves and current. There is a good amount of debris and seaweed. There is also no shade so if you plan on staying for any length of time bring an umbrella and plenty of sunscreen.

This beach is interesting, unique and well worth the little extra effort to get there. A 4WD vehicle is recommended due to high vegetation on a beach road that is not well maintained. Once you are parked you will need to walk a few hundred feet over a dune and rocky shelf to get to the sandy part of the beach. Choose this beach for seclusion, big waves and natural ocean soundtrack.

Beach ★★☆ Road ★☆☆

Beach: 25° 7.122, -76° 6.974
Road (81r): 25° 7.799, -76° 8.694

How to Get There

From points north
Total travel time: 4.6 mi. / 24 min
From Palmetto Point intersection drive south 2.0 miles. Make a left between stone pillars. There is a High Voltage sign as a landmark on the right. Proceed 1.0 miles to T. Make a right and proceed 1.0 miles. Go straight at fork at end onto overgrown beach path for 0.6 miles.

Time / Distance
To beach road: 2.0 mi. / 10 min
Beach road to beach: 2.6 mi. / 14 min

From points south
Total travel time: 6.1 mi. / 19 min
From Savannah Sound intersection drive north 3.5 miles. Make a right between stone pillars. There is a High Voltage sign as a landmark on the left. Proceed 1.0 miles to T. Make a right and proceed 1.0 miles. Go straight at fork at end onto overgrown beach path for 0.6 miles.

Time / Distance
To beach road: 3.5 mi. / 5 min
Beach road to beach: 2.6 mi. / 14 min

What You Should Know	
Privacy	Secluded
Shade	None
Accessibility	4WD recommended
Beach Path	Dune
Water Entry	Sandy
Water Condition	Deep ocean
Litter/Seaweed	Extensive
Nearest Town	Palmetto Point
Snorkeling	Poor
Shelling	No
Beach Size	0.2 miles x 15 yards

Ten Bay Beach

One of the finest beaches on the island, and certainly one of the best of the shallower Caribbean beaches, Ten Bay sets the bar for what can be considered the cream of the crop.

One of the chief qualities that stand out is cleanliness. There was no debris or wash-up owing to its unique protected position on the island. It stretches a full half-mile giving it a much greater length relative to other Caribbean beaches, which are usually quite compact and sometimes rocky. On a non-windy day the flat calm water seems to spread in an endless rainbow of blue and turquoise, painting a lovely palette of color against the sun drenched sky. The quality of the shallow sandy water access up and down the beach and the exquisite color of the soft pink sand

make this an ideal beach for both wading and swimming. Be aware that the bay is very shallow and you won't be in water up to your waist for at least 30 yards from shore.

You can easily find equal doses of sun and shade as the towering Casuarinas provide a natural canopy over soft-needled sitting areas. Additionally, the beach is easy to find and the beach road is of good quality.

The main issues are the lack of privacy along with some leftover seaweed towards the back of the beach from a recent hurricane. There are several homes on the beach and along the southern rocky shoreline. You should not expect to have this beach without company. For more privacy head either north or south and set up camp away from

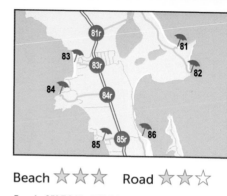

Beach ★★★ Road ★★☆

Beach: 25° 7.245, -76° 9.041
Road: 25° 7.243, -76° 8.677

What You Should Know	
Privacy	Semi-private
Shade	Plenty
Accessibility	Car, bumpy
Beach Path	Sandy
Water Entry	Sandy
Water Condition	Shallow Caribbean
Litter/Seaweed	None
Nearest Town	Savannah Sound
Snorkeling	Average
Shelling	Yes
Beach Size	0.5 miles x 25 feet

How to Get There

From points north
Total travel time: 3.4 mi. / 11 min
From Pametto Point intersection drive south 3.0 miles. Make right and proceed 0.3 miles. Make a right away from private driveway and proceed 0.1 miles. Make left away from a second private driveway and proceed 0.2 miles to beach.

Time / Distance
To beach road: 3.0 mi. / 5 min
Beach road to beach: 0.4 mi. / 6 min

From points south
Total travel time: 2.9 mi. / 9 min
From Savannah Sound intersection drive north 2.5 miles. Make left and proceed 0.3 miles. Make a right away from private drive-way and proceed 0.1 miles. Make left away from a second private driveway and proceed 0.2 miles to beach.

Time / Distance
To beach road: 2.5 mi. / 3 min
Beach road to beach: 0.4 mi. / 6 min

the main beach access. There is a second beach access, offering greater privacy towards the southern end of the beach, which can be reached by making a left a few 10ths of a mile before the main beach access. It requires a 4WD vehicle due to dense jungle vegetation.

Ten Bay Beach is a half-mile of sun and sand and sea. It is excellent for kayaking and good for snorkeling around the rocky shore-lines. The beach is kid and pet friendly due to the shallowness of the water, the easy water entry and the abundance of shade. Overall, the combination of positive key features against very few negatives earned Ten Bay Beach our highest rating.

Kemp's Creek Beach

This beach is less of a beach and more of a swimming or snorkeling spot as the tide will dictate whether or not there is any sand above the water. A creek runs from the mangroves into what amounts to a saltwater swimming hole set between a circular rock fortress with a 30 yard wide opening that leads to the ocean. At the time of our visit a new house was being built on the southern rock ledge making this a much less private spot than it was previously. However, the benefit of the community being developed is that the beach road is wider and flatter making the beach much easier to find and get to.

Choose this location for its unique view and as a protected swimming spot. Good snorkeling can be found just to the left of the ocean mouth where submerged rocks attract the gamut of sea life. Bring water shoes or dive booties as the water entry has jagged rocks all the way around. This is also a good spot to launch a kayak or other small boat.

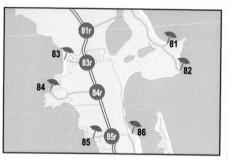

Beach ★☆☆   Road ★★☆

Beach: 25° 6.660, -76° 9.346
Road: 25° 6.693, -76° 8.485

How to Get There

From points north
Total travel time: 4.5 mi. / 14 min
From Palmetto Point intersection drive south for 3.6 miles. Make right just after small lake bed. Road is further identified by a series of telephone poles leading away from highway. Proceed 0.9 miles without making any turns.

Time / Distance
To beach road: 3.6 mi. / 6 min
Beach road to beach: 0.9 mi. / 8 min

From points south
Total travel time: 2.8 mi. / 10 min
From Savannah Sound intersection drive north 1.9 miles. Make left just before small lake bed. Road is further identified by a series of telephone poles leading away from highway. Proceed 0.9 miles without making any turns.

Time / Distance
To beach road: 1.9 mi. / 2 min
Beach road to beach: 0.9 mi. / 8 min

What You Should Know	
Privacy	Semi-private
Shade	None
Accessibility	Car, bumpy
Beach Path	Rocky
Water Entry	Rocky
Water Condition	Deep cove
Litter/Seaweed	None
Nearest Town	Savannah Sound
Snorkeling	Good
Shelling	Yes
Beach Size	50 feet x 10 feet

Little Bay Beach

The condition of this beach is poor due to the volume of seaweed that has been deposited on its shores by Hurricane Sandy (2012). While nature will eventually return Little Bay to its ideal state, it currently leaves a lot to be desired.

The raw beauty of the land is unseemly due to the seaweed. It made the interesting beach amenities—a hammock, a beach shack and some chairs—completely unusable due to the amount of build-up.

The beach itself is very small lending to its name. It stretches a mere 20 yards in length and is only 10 feet wide. While there are some rocks around the sandy portion of the beach there is a good shallow, sandy entry area making it fine for swimming. A large cay in the distance provides some nice perspective to an otherwise flat view.

Overall, this is a pretty little area, but due to the recent development of a residential community it lacks privacy. One house sits very close to the beach on the northern shore with another off in the distance to the south. Other houses sit along the rocky northern shoreline, but are not visible from the beach.

The short beach road drive makes Little Bay easy to get to and find – which are the best things about it. Until nature returns it to its previous pristine state this beach is one worth avoiding.

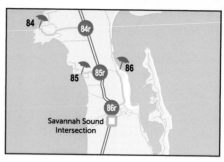

Beach ⭐☆☆ Road ⭐⭐☆

Beach: 25° 5.876, -76° 8.515
Road: 25° 5.898, -76° 8.208

How to Get There

From points north
Total travel time: 4.9 mi. / 9 min
From Palmetto Point intersection drive south 4.6 miles. Make right into dirt access road marked by cement stanchions with metal balls on top. Proceed 0.3 miles to beach path on left.

Time / Distance
To beach road: 4.6 mi. / 7 min
Beach road to beach: 0.3 mi. / 2 min

From points south
Total travel time: 1.2 mi. / 3 min
From Savannah Sound intersection drive north 0.9 miles. Make left into dirt access road marked by cement stanchions with metal balls on top. Proceed 0.3 miles to beach path on left.

Time / Distance
To beach road: 0.9 mi. / 1 min
Beach road to beach: 0.3 mi. / 2 min

What You Should Know	
Privacy	Semi-private
Shade	Some
Accessibility	Car, bumpy
Beach Path	Sandy
Water Entry	Sandy
Water Condition	Shallow Caribbean
Litter/Seaweed	Extensive
Nearest Town	Savannah Sound
Snorkeling	Average
Shelling	No
Beach Size	50 feet x 10 feet

Savannah Sound Beach

The color contrast of the water as it changes from shallow to deep is the most interesting and unique feature of this beach with soft pastels, bright blue-greens, and then ultimately dense blue out into the ocean beyond the bay. The Sound itself is well protected by the northern tip of Windermere Island to the right and the point of Girt Bay to the left, which helps to keep the beach almost free of debris. It is much cleaner than many other Atlantic beaches with only small amounts of seaweed towards the rear of the beach.

The beach road becomes a little dense as you proceed further north. It eventually winds through two cement pillars where you will park by an abandoned hut. There are several other access points along this beach road with the main difference between them being the size of the parking areas and the amount of shade under the trees. At the recommended access point, there are two half-moon beaches split by a large cement dock - the smaller to the south and a long wrap-around to the north. Overall, the beach is long and fairly narrow. Due to the shallowness of the flats this beach offers a good opportunity to land a bonefish. Water entry is sandy and shallow with the deep ocean several hundred feet from shore.

The view at Savannah Sound is quite

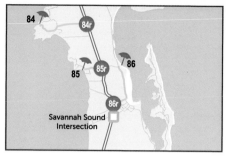

Beach 86 ⭐⭐☆　Road ⭐⭐☆

Beach: 25° 5.962, -76° 7.846
Road: 25° 5.245, -76° 7.985

Beach 86a ⭐⭐☆ Road ⭐⭐☆

Beach: 25° 5.679, -76° 7.767
Road: 25° 5.245, -76° 7.985

What You Should Know	
Privacy	Semi-private
Shade	Some
Accessibility	Car, bumpy
Beach Path	Sandy
Water Entry	Sandy
Water Condition	Shallow entry
Litter/Seaweed	Light
Nearest Town	Savannah Sound
Snorkeling	Poor
Shelling	No
Beach Size	2.0 miles x 10 yards

How to Get There

From points north

Total travel time: 6.0 mi. / 14 min
From Palmetto Point intersection drive south 5.3 miles. Make left at Beach Access sign and proceed 0.2 miles on paved road. Proceed onto dirt road and follow bend to the left 0.5 miles. Go through cement stanchions and abandoned hut to beach and dock on right.

Time / Distance
To beach road: 5.3 mi. / 8 min
Beach road to beach: 0.7 mi. / 6 min

From points south

Total travel time: 0.9 mi. / 7 min
From Savanah Sound intersection drive north 0.2 miles. Make right at Beach Access sign and proceed 0.2 miles on paved road. Proceed onto dirt road and follow bend to the left 0.5 miles. Go past cement stanchions and abandoned hut to beach and dock on right.

Time / Distance
To beach road: 0.2 mi. / 1 min
Beach road to beach: 0.7 mi. / 6 min

scenic and the area fairly private considering its proximity to a large Bahamian community. You will be far enough away that no houses or buildings are within sight. The further north you go on this beach the more protected it gets as there are no other access points past this one. Beware of biting ants below the shaded Casuarinas if seeking refuge from the sun.

Savannah Sound is a good beach for swimming, fishing, kayaking and walking. It has great views out to the ocean, outstanding water coloration and is ideal for families with young children due to the shallow, sandy water entry.

Little Mangrove Cay Beach

Take a short walk down the beach path to the right from the parking area to find this cute little beach, approximately 75 yards long x 15 feet wide. Its dominating feature is a shoreline dotted with sea lettuce and other vines growing at the water's edge. The beach offers some of the best views of the bayside homes on the southern end of Windermere Island. There are no homes directly on the beach, however, there are houses visible on Windermere and another private residence to the left of the beach so temper any expectations of complete privacy.

The water at Little Mangrove is very shallow and more suitable for wading than snorkeling. This body of water can best be described as the bayside of Windermere Island with a large channel leading out to the deep ocean in the distance. A few small cays can be seen, but were not accessible. Several other similar small beaches are visible to the right, but are not reachable by land but can be accessed by wading across the water.

There is some shade to the back of the beach, but beware of biting ants and other insects that have taken up residence here. The water's edge and beach are rocky in places, but you can find ample sand to sit on and a shallow, sandy water entry. Some debris is visible to the left and at the beach entry, but the

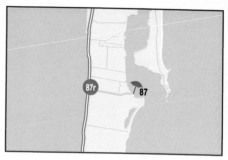

Beach ☆☆☆ Road ★★☆

Beach: 25° 2.162, -76° 7.626
Road: 25° 2.229, -76° 8.432

How to Get There

From points north

Total travel time: 4.1 mi. / 9 min
From Savannah Sound intersection drive south 3.3 miles. Make a left just after Christian Sports Camp and proceed 0.8 miles to end. Park in small area before private driveway. Walk jungle path on right a few hundred feet to beach.

Time / Distance
To beach road: 3.3 mi. / 7 min
Beach road to beach: 0.8 mi. / 2 min

From points south

Total travel time: 4.7 mi. / 11 min
From Tarpum Bay intersection drive north 3.9 miles. Make a right just before Christian Sports Camp and proceed 0.8 miles to end. Park in small area before private driveway. Walk jungle path on right a few hundred feet to beach.

Time / Distance
To beach road: 3.9 mi. / 9 min
Beach road to beach: 0.8 mi. / 2 min

What You Should Know

Privacy	Semi-private
Shade	Some
Accessibility	Car, bumpy; Hike
Beach Path	Sandy
Water Entry	Rocks and sand
Water Condition	Shallow bay
Litter/Seaweed	Light
Nearest Town	Savannah Sound
Snorkeling	Poor
Shelling	No
Beach Size	75 yards x 15 feet

beach itself is clean. A small deposit of seaweed didn't detract from the entire experience.

Come to this beach for the interesting views, to experience a watery mangrove and if you prefer shallow water. This beach showed promise as a place to kayak as well.

The abundance of miniature palm trees on the dunes provides a very interesting backdrop to a beach that is made for tanning. Further enhancing the landscape, water has created multiple shelves, or sand plateaus, that dip and ebb to the water's edge. Overall, this is a very nice spot. We just hope it lasts for a while since new construction might restrict access.

Islandia Beach

One of the best characteristics of this beach is that it is probably the most private beach that requires the least amount of work to get to meaning that the beach road is relatively easy to find and quite passable with good pavement almost the entire way in. However, don't be tempted to continue to follow the pavement to the end. Follow our directions and leave the road to go onto a short path through the jungle because the paved road becomes impassable after awhile.

The better water access on this beach can be found by walking either north or south from the beach path just past where you'll park. You can certainly get in the water where you first come onto the beach, but there is a long, flat rocky ledge that you would need to cross first.

Islandia is exquisitely long reaching almost 2 miles with an extremely well developed reef system that offers both beginners and experienced snorkelers an excellent opportunity to explore. Coral heads start just offshore and lead to long ledges of reef that run the entire length of the beach at varying distances from shore.

If you want to find shade there is a little natural cutout in the rocks approximately a quarter mile south from the access path. There, you'll find a little rectangular patch of sand set back between two rocky shelves with a bed of Casuarina needles under tall trees. This area is loaded with burs as is the upper shelf of the beach. Use caution and bring tweezers just in case. Proceeding a bit further south from this point reveals several

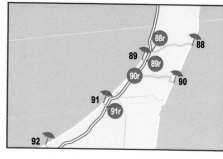

Beach ★★☆ Road ★★☆

Beach: 25° 0.445, -76° 7.920
Road: 25° 0.307, -76° 8.670

What You Should Know

Privacy	Secluded
Shade	Some
Accessibility	Car, bumpy
Beach Path	Dune
Water Entry	Sandy
Water Condition	Deep ocean
Litter/Seaweed	Extensive
Nearest Town	Tarpum Bay
Snorkeling	Good
Shelling	No
Beach Size	2.0 miles x 40 yards

little cave-like overhangs with natural seats carved out of the rocks. These are good resting places that complement a nice long beach walk.

The main negatives here are the debris, wash up, seaweed and trash that littered the flat back shelf of the beach - along with the lack of shade. You can avoid most of this eyesore by moving away from the beach path. The further south you go the better the beach becomes especially when factoring in the improved sandy water access. Choose this beach for its isolation, its length and for its massive reef system.

How to Get There

From points north
Total travel time: 6.4 mi. / 19 min
From Savannah Sound intersection drive south 5.5 miles. Make left and proceed 0.8 miles on paved access road. Make left and proceed 0.1 miles on dirt road to beach path.

Time / Distance
To beach road: 5.5 mi. / 12 min
Beach road to beach: 0.9 mi. / 7 min

From points south
Total travel time: 2.6 mi. / 11 min
From Tarpum Bay intersection drive north 1.7 miles. Make right and proceed 0.8 miles on paved access road. Make left and proceed 0.1 miles on dirt road to beach path.

Time / Distance
To beach road: 1.7 mi. / 4 min
Beach road to beach: 0.9 mi. / 7 min

Comber's Beach

This was the best beach on the island for shelling, hands down. With a 3.5-mile stretch of sand that extends all the way into Tarpum Bay, there is a huge amount of unique shells. They cluster in a wide, uniform grouping that covers almost everything that isn't rock. You'll also find an abundance of natural sponges washed up on shore. If you are looking for a beach littered with those natural treasures, look no further.

Except for the shells, there are not too many other reasons to come here. Our opinion was certainly jaded by the conditions we found on a day when wind from the west brought in some ugly water and the usually calm Caribbean rippled with almost

an almost constant series of small, petulant waves. On the Caribbean beaches we expect to find calm and clear turquoise waters lapping the shores of very pristine pink sand. Instead, we found brackish green water splashing up against a fairly extensive jagged and uneven rock ledge that would definitely necessitate the use of water shoes when entering the ocean. It was most uninviting.

A narrow line of sand runs between a Casuarina needle / seaweed covered beach back and the rock ledge that leads out into the water. There is a nice mix of sun and sand here. Plus, as compared to many of the beaches in the area, the access road is a pleasant and stress free 1-minute ride from

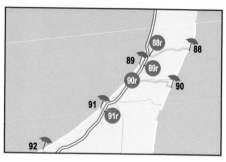

Beach ★★☆   Road ★★★

Beach: 25° 0.148, -76° 8.811
Road: 25° 0.142, -76° 8.753

How to Get There

From points north
Total travel time: 5.8 mi. / 14 min
From Savannah Sound intersection drive south for 5.7 miles. Make right and proceed 0.1 miles to beach.

Time / Distance
To beach road: 5.7 mi. / 13 min
Beach road to beach: 0.1 mile / 1 min

From points south
Total travel time: 1.6 mi. / 4 min
From Tarpum Bay intersection drive north for 1.5 miles. Make left and proceed 0.1 miles to beach.

Time / Distance
To beach road: 1.5 mi. / 3 min
Beach road to beach: 0.1 mile / 1 min

What You Should Know

Privacy	Semi-private
Shade	Plenty
Accessibility	Car, bumpy
Beach Path	Sandy
Water Entry	Rocky
Water Condition	Shallow Caribbean
Litter/Seaweed	Extensive
Nearest Town	Tarpum Bay
Snorkeling	Poor
Shelling	Yes
Beach Size	3.5 miles x 10 feet

the highway to the beach. Some houses have been built here and there are other signs of development in the area. It is quite possible that this access road will be closed off for exclusive use by private residents in the near future. The good news is that there are other ways to access parts of this beach although they would require much more work.

Choose this beach for beach combing. Wear a good set of water shoes and allow ample time to work up and down its length of periwinkles, junonias, conchs, mussels, angel wings, arks and scotch bonnets along with a variety of large sponges and tiny bits of coral.

Tarpum Northside Beach

This beach access point is at the southern end of Islandia Beach (88). Because there is one large house right on the beach, and what looks like renewed development in the area, you will not have the same level of privacy as you would on Islandia. What you get, though, is perfect sandy water access. At Islandia you either have to cross a rocky ledge or proceed well away from the beach path to have this kind of ocean access. Better water access versus absolute privacy. Those are the choices.

All of the same beach characteristics that Islandia offers are found here. The same well developed reef system is easily reachable

just offshore. There is an abundance of sun without much shade except under one small cluster of trees just south of the beach path. There is seaweed on the back of the beach and a fair amount of wash up especially in the shady area.

The beach is just shy of 2 miles long by almost 40 yards wide so an excellent choice for walking and running. Due to excellent water access it is also good for swimming. The massive reef system makes snorkeling here a prime objective. This is not a great beach for very small children due to limited shade, and also because the path to get to the beach is very overgrown with brush, sea

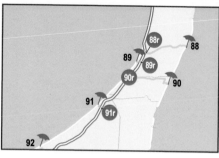

Beach ⭐⭐☆ Road ⭐⭐☆

Beach: 24° 59.670, -76° 8.261
Road: 24° 59.866, -76° 8.956

What You Should Know

Privacy	Semi-private
Shade	None
Accessibility	Car, bumpy
Beach Path	Dune
Water Entry	Sandy
Water Condition	Deep ocean
Litter/Seaweed	Extensive
Nearest Town	Tarpum Bay
Snorkeling	Good
Shelling	No
Beach Size	2.0 miles x 40 yards

How to Get There

From points north
Total travel time: 6.8 mi. / 19 min
From Savannah Sound intersection drive south for 5.9 miles. Make left and proceed 0.9 miles on gravel access road bearing right past private house. Make first left past house and proceed up hill to parking area and beach path.

Time / Distance
To beach road: 5.9 mi. / 14 min
Beach road to beach: 0.9 mi. / 5 min

From points south
Total travel time: 2.2 mi. / 7 min
From Tarpum Bay intersection drive north 1.3 miles. Make right and proceed 0.9 miles on gravel access road bearing right past private house. Make first left past house and proceed up hill to parking area and beach path.

Time / Distance
To beach road: 1.3 mi. / 2 min
Beach road to beach: 0.9 mi. / 5 min

lettuce and other small vegetation. Wearing a pair of shoes or sturdy sandals is necessary to access the beach.

One other interesting aspect of the beach is its dunes. They have extremely lush vegetation and a wide variety of plants, trees, shrubs and brush. It forms a very beautiful backdrop to the sand and heightens the overall experience. This area does have the look of a community under development and access to this beach may change rapidly. Take advantage of a reasonably well-maintained road to find a beach that is easy to get to and easy to find. Bring your sandals, snorkel, umbrella and enjoy a day at the beach!

Bullard Bay Beach

Further to the south of 89, Comber's Beach, is a beach road identified with signage as Bullard's Bay. This is the same long strip of Caribbean beach that leads all the way to Tarpum Bay. It is easy to find and easy to access, but once down the beach road it becomes less inviting. There is one house at the end of this road and signage points you away from this property and onto the beach through either a cement wall that you need to jump down from or through a bunch of fallen Casuarinas. This is not a big problem, but perhaps not the preferred way to start your beach day.

Owing to the northwest wind we had, this day the beach was somewhat unsightly. The water was brown and full of seaweed.

The beach was also littered with seaweed. When combined with the lack of privacy and the uninviting signs, there aren't too many reasons to seek out this spot. To contrast this area with Comber's, the water is much more accessible here with good sandy water entry, but the abundance of shells was missing, which was the main attraction of the access point to the north. There were, however, a lot of sponges and conch shells here.

On a calm day this could be a nice spot, but this would depend on whether houses are occupied and where the wind is coming from. There are better beaches for your money. Come here if you want a beach that is well marked and easy to find.

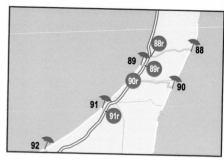

Beach ⭐⭐☆   Road ⭐⭐☆

Beach: 24° 59.341, -76° 9.506
Road: 24° 59.316, -76° 9.468

How to Get There

From points north
Total travel time: 5.0 mi. / 11.5 min
From Savannah Sound intersection drive south for 5.0 miles. Make right and proceed 300 feet to beach. Access is to right of private house.

Time / Distance
To beach road: 5.0 mi. / 11 min
Beach road to beach: 300 feet / 0.5 min

From points south
Total travel time: 2.2 mi. / 6.5 min
From Tarpum Bay intersection drive north for 2.2 miles. Make left and proceed 300 feet to beach. Access is to right of private house.

Time / Distance
To beach road: 2.2 mi. / 6 min
Beach road to beach: 300 feet / 0.5 min

What You Should Know	
Privacy	Semi-private
Shade	Plenty
Accessibility	Car, bumpy
Beach Path	Sandy
Water Entry	Sandy
Water Condition	Shallow Caribbean
Litter/Seaweed	Extensive
Nearest Town	Tarpum Bay
Snorkeling	Poor
Shelling	No
Beach Size	3.0 miles x 10 feet

Tarpum Bay Beach

Traveling a bit north from the interesting and colorful village of Tarpum Bay brings you to an easy to find paved access road leading to Ingraham's Beach Inn. After swift passage down this street you'll find plenty of parking next to the quaint Bahamian resort. The reason to come here is to have a short, easy access ride.

The beach access is right next to the resort so expect no privacy. Most of the time the water is a gorgeous turquoise blue, but wind from the west means this unprotected bay will churn with seaweed causing the water to go somewhat green so pay attention to the tide and weather reports. The sand ledge is very narrow, less than 10 feet in most places. There is little shelling, and the only shade you'll find is next to a strand of fallen Casuarinas.

The beach is good for a long sunny walk. It also offers some shelling opportunities, but not right in front of this access point. You are better off heading north to have more privacy and better shelling opportunities.

Overall, this is a fairly plain, narrow beach that didn't offer a compelling reason to visit it. Come here if you don't want to risk driving down a difficult road or because you want to be close to the wonderful conch shacks in Tarpum Bay.

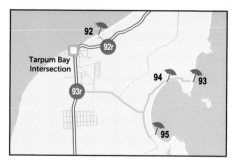

Beach ★☆☆   Road ★★★

Beach: 24° 58.582, -76° 10.567
Road: 24° 58.459, -76° 10.457

How to Get There

From points north
Total travel time: 6.7 mi. / 16 min
From Savannah Sound intersection drive south for 6.5 miles. Make right and proceed 0.2 miles. Access is to right of small beach hotel.

Time / Distance
To beach road: 6.5 mi. / 15 min
Beach road to beach: 0.2 mi. / 1 min

From points south
Total travel time: 0.9 mi. / 3 min
From Tarpum Bay intersection drive north for 0.7 miles. Make left and proceed 0.2 miles. Access is to right of small beach hotel.

Time / Distance
To beach road: 0.7 mi. / 2 min
Beach road to beach: 0.2 mi. / 1 min

What You Should Know	
Privacy	Public
Shade	None
Accessibility	Car
Beach Path	Sandy
Water Entry	Sandy
Water Condition	Shallow Caribbean
Litter/Seaweed	Light
Nearest Town	Tarpum Bay
Snorkeling	Poor
Shelling	Yes
Beach Size	3.0 miles x 10 feet

Crossing Bluff Beach

The two beaches at Crossing Bluff came close to earning our highest grade. If not for a serious amount of seaweed and debris they probably would have. It is almost wrong to call them two separate beaches. If not for the rocky point that causes a natural geographical separation, they would probably be considered a single beach. The beach to the south is about a quarter mile while the bigger beach to the north reaches more than twice that length.

What makes these beaches unique is their position in the water relative to Winding Bay and the ensuing contrast that provides. As you drive back here, the only body of water you see is calm, protected and pristine. But, as you head out to the point past a small sand pit you find these two big Atlantic-type beaches. I say, Atlantic-type, because they share the same characteristics of deep blue ocean, wide sand, and big surf that most of the beaches on the eastern side of the island seem to have.

The rocky point has a set of natural steps that lead to shady, albeit hard, sitting areas, and that is the only relief from the sun. The reef system, just away from the beach, is mature and extensive. This beach, depending on the wind, offers big waves, deep surf, awesome snorkeling, and lots of beach to roam and explore. The debris and seaweed are the biggest detractors and it really takes away from the overall experience. That's the price you sometimes pay for this amount of privacy and seclusion.

Beach ★★☆   Road ★★☆

Beach: 24° 57.780, -76° 8.887
Road: 24° 57.583, -76° 10.970

How to Get There

From points north
Total travel time: 4.3 mi. / 12 min
From Tarpum Bay intersection drive south for 0.9 miles. Make left after Esso station and proceed 1.9 miles. Bear left at fork and proceed 1.2 miles. Bear left at fork and proceed 0.3 miles to sand pit.

Time / Distance
To beach road: 0.9 mi. / 2 min
Beach road to beach: 3.4 mi. / 10 min

From points south
Total travel time: 10.2 mi. / 20 min
From Rock Sound marketplace drive north for 6.8 miles. Make right before Esso station and proceed 1.9 miles. Bear left at fork and proceed 1.2 miles. Bear left at fork and proceed 0.3 miles to sand pit.

Time / Distance
To beach road: 6.8 mi. / 10 min
Beach road to beach: 3.4 mi. / 10 min

What You Should Know	
Privacy	Secluded
Shade	Some
Accessibility	Car, bumpy
Beach Path	Sandy
Water Entry	Sandy
Water Condition	Deep ocean
Litter/Seaweed	Extensive
Nearest Town	Tarpum Bay
Snorkeling	Good
Shelling	No
Beach Size	1.0 miles x 30 yards

Winding Bay Beach North

The northern access points at Winding Bay offer a different experience compared to the central one. You almost feel like you are at a completely separate bay. From this location there is one access point even further north that faces due west that was not evaluated, but also has the same promise as here. The water here is calm and the view much prettier than the central access point on the beach primarily due to how well protected this beach spot is below the northern rocky point. We find it much better to sit away from the homes and see them across the bay than to sit under their doorstep.

The sand quality here is better as is the vegetation. The burs, unfortunately, are another issue. You really have to watch where you walk both entering the beach and when sitting to make sure you don't drag your feet through one of their nasty little seeding areas.

This Caribbean-like pool of water has great sandy water access and is very secluded. It provides a haven for hawksbill turtles that hang out in the area and hopefully they are yearlong residents. Besides the burs, the only real negatives were the amount of seaweed on the back of the beach and the fact that the beach was so narrow you'd almost have to sit in the water to find a suitable resting spot. We think that sitting with your toes in a warm protected pool of water watching friendly turtles forage nearby might just be the most splendid way to spend an island day.

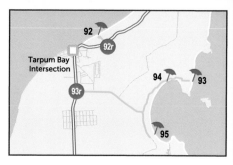

Beach ★★☆   Road ★★☆

Beach: 24° 57.812, -76° 9.244
Road (93r): 24° 57.583, -76° 10.970

How to Get There

From points north
Total travel time: 3.8 mi. / 9 min
From Tarpum Bay intersection drive south for 0.9 miles. Make left after Esso station and proceed 1.9 miles. Bear left at fork and proceed 1.0 miles to beach path on right.

Time / Distance
To beach road: 0.9m / 2 min
Beach road to beach: 2.9 mi. / 7 min

From points south
Total travel time: 9.7 mi. / 19 min
From Rock Sound marketplace drive north for 6.8 miles. Make right before Esso station and proceed 1.9 miles. Bear left at fork and proceed 1.0 miles to beach path on right.

Time / Distance
To beach road: 6.8 mi. / 10 min
Beach road to beach: 2.9 mi. / 7 min

What You Should Know	
Privacy	Semi-private
Shade	None
Accessibility	Car, bumpy
Beach Path	Sandy
Water Entry	Sandy
Water Condition	Shallow entry
Litter/Seaweed	Extensive
Nearest Town	Tarpum Bay
Snorkeling	Poor
Shelling	No
Beach Size	2.0 miles x 1 to 20 yards

Winding Bay Beach Central

This very good swimming and kayaking bay, in a well-protected cove on the Atlantic, has a number of blemishes that make this central access location particularly uninviting. This beach is generally good, but not from this access point. The beach path sits just north of the private houses on Winding Bay, one of those rare 270-degree half-moons on the Atlantic side of the island. To the left you have a decent amount of privacy although some may object to sitting in front of, or near to, the dilapidated Venta Club, an Italian version of Club Med, that closed down shortly after Hurricane Floyd in 1999. To the right you have houses, many which are exclusive villa rentals. Move in that direction and you

lose privacy. Move to the left and you have remnants of hurricane damage. Stay put and you have other problems.

What is probably the worst aspect of the beach is the amount of grass, vegetation, burs, and saplings that are growing out of the beach itself almost down to the high water mark on the sand. It looks extremely unkempt and makes you wish you had a weed whacker to make everything look more pristine. The water entry is good all around although wind conditions will alter the color of the water from a gorgeous turquoise blue when the wind is calm to an unimpressive brownish green when the wind is up.

Do be careful of the burs as they extend

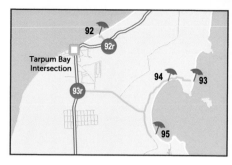

Beach ★★☆   Road ★★☆

Beach: 24° 56.874, -76° 9.595
Road (93r): 24° 57.583, -76° 10.970

How to Get There

From points north
Total travel time: 3.3 mi. / 6 min
From Tarpum Bay intersection drive south
for 0.9 miles. Make left after Esso station
and proceed 1.9 miles. Bear right at fork and
proceed 0.5 miles. Make left onto beach path
and proceed 500 feet to beach.

Time / Distance
To beach road: 0.9 mi. / 2 min
Beach road to beach: 2.4 mi. / 4 min

From points south
Total travel time: 9.2 mi. / 14 min
From Rock Sound marketplace drive north
for 6.8 miles. Make right before Esso station
and proceed 1.9 miles. Bear right at fork and
proceed 0.5 miles. Make left onto beach path
and proceed 500 feet to beach.

Time / Distance
To beach road: 6.8 mi. / 10 min
Beach road to beach: 2.4 mi. / 4 min

What You Should Know

Privacy	Semi-private
Shade	None
Accessibility	Car, bumpy
Beach Path	Sandy
Water Entry	Sandy
Water Condition	Deep ocean
Litter/Seaweed	Light
Nearest Town	Tarpum Bay
Snorkeling	Poor
Shelling	No
Beach Size	2.0 miles x 20 yards

from the beach path well onto the beach
making walking a bit treacherous. Once you
are past the grassy beach areas you still have
to make your way through piles of seaweed
that extend from the water's edge to the
woods at the time this beach was evaluated.

When this beach is clean it can be an
excellent choice with its protected Caribbean
feel, shallow entry and rapid deep-water access. However, with the amount of seaweed
and beach outgrowth we would recommend
moving further north around the bay to more
protected waters. There are several nearby
access points and several other beaches that
might be better options depending on conditions here.

The Point at Half Sound Ocean Beach

It was extremely hard not to give this beach our highest rating. It did have enough blemishes that it fell just shy, but is definitely one of those beaches that are worth going out of the way for. It is the best spot on the oceanside of Half Sound for its uniqueness and overall quality. You need to go a little more than a half-mile on a sandy road past the location for beach 98 where you'll find an easily recognizable large parking area with a cement slab to mark its location. A fairly steep, sandy descent takes you down onto this gorgeous beach. If climbing up and down the hill is going to be an issue, avoid this spot.

What you notice right away is a great little swimming area, a natural ocean cutout, carved amongst the reef and rocks. It's not a large area, but resembles a small, ocean swimming pool with crystal clear turquoise water offset by the dark hues of the reef and deep blue ocean. A rocky point to the left provides an interesting exploration climb where you can find another hidden beach set below the rock wall, a little two person, romantic tropical hideaway that also has ocean access.

The well-developed reef system has good snorkeling. The water is accessed via an angled stretch of sand pitched at an inviting slope away from its level upper half. Trees had been arranged on the beach in a temporary artistic configuration to form a primitive open-aired sand teepee.

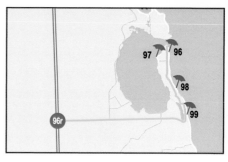

Beach ★★☆   Road ★☆☆

Beach: 24° 56.011, -76° 8.953
Road: 24° 54.738, -76° 10.934

What You Should Know	
Privacy	Secluded
Shade	None
Accessibility	4WD recommended
Beach Path	Dune
Water Entry	Sandy
Water Condition	Deep ocean
Litter/Seaweed	Light
Nearest Town	Tarpum Bay
Snorkeling	Good
Shelling	No
Beach Size	1.0 miles x 50 yards

The main con, beside the sandy climb down to the beach, is its debris and seaweed fields. This beach was cleaner than the other beaches on this stretch, but it was still enough of a detraction to affect the beach's overall score.

Casuarinas at the back of the beach provided ample shade. Be careful when climbing to the little hidden beach as what looks like a solid pile of sand can turn out to be soft and deep, like thigh high deep, which is a little tricky to extricate oneself from.

This is a very scenic and picturesque beach. Its look is unique with high dunes, lush trees, large rock walls and rocky outcroppings. The water quality, access and reef system are all excellent.

How to Get There

From points north
Total travel time: 8.4 mi. / 41 min
From Tarpum Bay intersection drive south for 4.2 miles. Make left where telephone wires cross the road and proceed on bumpy road for 4.2 miles. Road will bend to the left past part of Half Sound on the left and eventually turn sandy with overhanging palm trees. Park at cement slab. Beach path is to right of cement.

Time / Distance
To beach road: 4.2 mi. / 9 min
Beach road to beach: 4.2 mi. / 32 min

From points south
Total travel time: 7.7 mi. / 37 min
From Rock Sound marketplace drive north for 3.5 miles. Make right where telephone wires cross the road on long straightaway and proceed on bumpy road for 4.2 miles. Road will bend to the left past part of Half Sound on the left and eventually turn sandy with overhanging palm trees. Park at cement slab. Beach path is to right of cement.

Time / Distance
To beach road: 3.5 mi. / 5 min
Beach road to beach: 4.2 mi. / 32 min

Half Sound Bayside Beach

On some days a little exploration and hard work led to some truly unique beaches, and the little bayside beaches at Half Sound fall into that category. This little journey into the jungle had equal amounts of promise and pain, as the road to get back here seemed to not be the correct one and was almost impassable in spots. It was quite overgrown, and while you can make it in a car, you probably want some extra clearance below your vehicle to avoid leaving a muffler behind.

At the end of the journey there is a little grassy parking area that is the heavenly gateway to one of the cleanest, most pristine beaches on the island. It earned our highest grade because of how perfect it looked, with sand that seemed to glow hot white and pink in the sunlight. It was so immaculate we didn't dare walk on the sand lest we upset a single grain.

It's just lovely here with an outstanding view that soaks in the entire bay. The water is shallow, flat, and calm. The two small beaches total 175 yards and sit on either side of a rocky point. There's not a single rock in or near the water to stub your toe on with flawless sandy water access. The only thing we couldn't tell is whether the floor of the bay

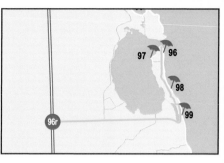

Beach ★★★ Road ★☆☆

Beach: 24° 55.819, -76° 9.092
Road (96r): 24° 54.738, -76° 10.934

What You Should Know	
Privacy	Secluded
Shade	Some
Accessibility	4WD recommended
Beach Path	Sandy
Water Entry	Sandy
Water Condition	Shallow bay
Litter/Seaweed	None
Nearest Town	Tarpum Bay
Snorkeling	Poor
Shelling	No
Beach Size	175 yards x 20 feet

How to Get There

From points north
Total travel time: 8.4 mi. / 41 min
From Tarpum Bay intersection drive south for 4.2 miles. Make left where telephone wires cross the road and proceed on bumpy road for 4.0 miles. Road will bend to the left past part of Half Sound on the left and eventually turn sandy with overhanging palm trees. Make a left and proceed 0.2 miles through overgrown sand road to beach.

Time / Distance
To beach road: 4.2 mi. / 9 min
Beach road to beach: 4.2 mi. / 32 min

From points south
Total travel time: 7.7 mi. / 37 min
From Rock Sound marketplace drive north for 3.5 miles. Make right where telephone wires cross the road on long straightaway and proceed on bumpy road for 4.0 miles. Road will bend to the left past part of Half Sound on the left and eventually turn sandy with overhanging palm trees. Make a left and proceed 0.2 miles through overgrown sand road to beach.

Time / Distance
To beach road: 3.5 mi. / 5 min
Beach road to beach: 4.2 mi. / 32 min

is extremely soft as many bay waters are. We leave that for you to explore.

Rocks on both sides of the point offer shade and added privacy. To the right is a dense Casuarina forest that provides shade and a lush, green backdrop. It's proximity to the Point at Half Sound is an added plus, and it only takes a few minutes to drive from here to the ocean to experience other unique beaches.

Due to its privacy, cleanliness, gorgeous view and outstanding sand this beach earned our highest rating.

Half Sound Ocean Beach 1

Roughly a half mile further north past the Half Sound Ocean Beach 2 beach path, and to the north of its rocky point, you will find Ocean Beach 1. It feels like a different experience due to how different its terrain is. This is the more rugged and picturesque of the two beaches, but is also the dirtier of the two in terms of seaweed and wash up. Fortunately, the debris seems concentrated to the upper ledge.

After crossing the path and some rocks on the back of the beach that definitely require protective footwear you come out onto a short 5' long sand ledge, which then has a short, steep vertical drop-off leading onto the lower beach which is carved out between rocks. The vertical ledge seems to twist, turn, jut out and recede in places, a formless slave to its ocean master. These ledges offer interesting photo opportunities.

If it's possible, this beach is even more secluded than its southern sister due to it being a little further away from the highway. There is good sandy water access, but only in the places where you don't have rock ledges. Even where there is good beach you'll find some

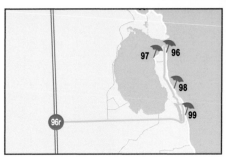

Beach ★★☆ Road ★☆☆

Beach: 24° 55.399, -76° 8.861
Road (96r): 24° 54.738, -76° 10.934

What You Should Know

Privacy	Secluded
Shade	Some
Accessibility	4WD recommended
Beach Path	Dune
Water Entry	Rocks and sand
Water Condition	Deep ocean
Litter/Seaweed	Moderate
Nearest Town	Tarpum Bay
Snorkeling	Good
Shelling	No
Beach Size	1.0 miles x 30 yards

rocks scattered about, but it's not anything that would prohibit you from entering the water or necessitate the need for water shoes.

The reef system here is good. The abundance of rocks limits your exploring to a walking / climbing pace and this is not a place to go for a jog. Pockets of shade under various Casuarinas are a welcome relief.

This beach rates high for seclusion and uniqueness. Its debris, seaweed, and difficult access make it less desirable. All in all this is a good beach for seclusion, photography and snorkeling.

How to Get There

From points north
Total travel time: 7.6 mi. / 34 min
From Tarpum Bay intersection drive south for 4.2 miles. Make left where telephone wires cross the road and proceed on bumpy road for 3.4 miles. Road will bend to the left past part of Half Sound on the left and eventually turn sandy with overhanging palm trees. Park on left. Overgrown beach path is on right.

Time / Distance
To beach road: 4.2 mi. / 9 min
Beach road to beach: 3.4 mi. / 25 min

From points south
Total travel time: 6.9 mi. / 30 min
From Rock Sound marketplace drive north for 3.5 miles. Make right where telephone wires cross the road on long straightaway and proceed on bumpy road for 3.4 miles. Road will bend to the left past part of Half Sound on the left and eventually turn sandy with overhanging palm trees. Park on left. Overgrown beach path is on right.

Time / Distance
To beach road: 3.5 mi. / 5 min
Beach road to beach: 3.4 mi. / 25 min

Half Sound Ocean Beach 2

Excellent privacy and good snorkeling are what you get at the various access points on the ocean side of Half Sound, a body of water that resembles a large lake with a narrow mouth spilling into the ocean at its northern tip. Ocean Beach 2 is the most southerly access point on the ocean side of Half Sound. While it is the first you will come to it may not be the best choice.

The road leading here is easy to miss from the highway, the most visible landmark being the electric wires that cross Queen's Highway when heading south on the long straightaway after you exit the town of Tarpum Bay. Expect a fairly long, bumpy ride back to the beach path, which also is not in such great shape. It's noticeable as a path, but is narrow and overgrown. The best way

to spot the beach access is to look for the first place on the side of the beach road that is large enough to park a car. The path is just across from there on your right.

What you normally find when you have to work a bit to get to the beach is lots of seclusion and this beach is no exception. There are no houses or other signs of civilization anywhere nearby save for an occasional fisherman who might explore the established reef systems. As is usually the case with a beach that is not visited frequently, vast quantities of seaweed and wash up greet you immediately thereby negatively influencing our opinion of this location. There is also a rock shelf that makes water entry difficult. It extends to the north for quite a ways. You will want to head south, if on foot, to find

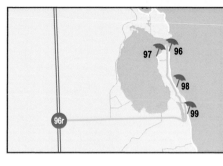

Beach ★★☆ Road ★☆☆

Beach: 24° 54.936, -76° 8.607
Road (96r): 24° 54.738, -76° 10.934

What You Should Know

Privacy	Secluded
Shade	None
Accessibility	4WD recommended
Beach Path	Dune
Water Entry	Rocks and sand
Water Condition	Deep ocean
Litter/Seaweed	Moderate
Nearest Town	Tarpum Bay
Snorkeling	Good
Shelling	No
Beach Size	2.75 miles x 30 yards

How to Get There

From points north
Total travel time: 6.9 mi. / 27 min
From Tarpum Bay intersection drive south for 4.2 miles. Make left where telephone wires cross the road and proceed on bumpy road for 2.7 miles. Road will bend to the left past part of Half Sound on the left. Park on left. Beach path is on right.

Time / Distance
To beach road: 4.2 mi. / 9 min
Beach road to beach: 2.7 mi. / 18 min

From points south
Total travel time: 6.2 mi. / 23 min
From Rock Sound marketplace drive north for 3.5 miles. Make right where telephone wires cross the road on long straightaway and proceed on bumpy road for 2.7 miles. Road will bend to the left past part of Half Sound on the left. Park on left. Beach path is on right.

Time / Distance
To beach road: 3.5 mi. / 5 min
Beach road to beach: 2.7 mi. / 18 min

better sandy swimming access.

The debris field is largely towards the back of the beach next to the dune. The dune rises 10' high and has a nice variety of vegetation. Tall towering palms complement the lush green tropics that grow on the dune.

You will likely have this beach all to yourself given the difficulty in finding and reaching it. It's a great place to snorkel with reasonably good water access. Its overall length is almost 3 miles so a good choice for walking and running. The debris and seaweed on the upper plateau are mildly un-pleasant and there is nothing truly outstand-ing here. We found the other access points on Half Sound to all be more interesting and cleaner. Choose this spot if you don't feel like looking for them.

The Southern Beaches

The rugged south covers both the eastern and western shores of Eleuthera, from Cape Eleuthera to Lighthouse Beach. It extends north through the towns of Wemyss Bight, Waterford, Green Castle, and ultimately Rock Sound. We refer to it as the rugged south when it should really be described as the natural south. Tourism fades as the island shows more of its roots. The towns are poorer, the buildings more destitute and the land less populated. As the population dwindles so do the amenities that most visitors expect. That's the price you pay for a more genuine island experience.

The southern part of Eleuthera is fascinating. Every time we go there we find something new, some raw natural beauty overlooked on a previous visit. Everything is more natural and raw — even the beaches.

Many of the best and most interesting beaches on the island can be found in Rock Sound or south of it. You will immediately feel a sense of adventure, like you are leaving civilization in search of unexplored territories. The beaches are fascinating because they are as nature left them; pure, untouched and unspoiled. The natural features, rock formations, limestone caves, and sand cliffs have been created through time.

You will most certainly enjoy the southern beaches, but like many things in life, the best sometimes comes with a cost. Many of the beaches, especially those on the 'northern' shores of the southern wings often have a lot of debris. They are not visited very often and thus are not maintained. They are also more difficult to find and generally the hardest to access. Roads that should normally take a few minutes based on their length take close to fifteen and feel like they take even longer due to the constant bumps, and ruts. We are not the first, nor will we be the last, to have turned back on some of these trips, feeling for sure that we must be on the wrong road. But here's the good news, we've traveled all of these roads. We have verified what's at their end. Don't get discouraged. Press on. Enjoy the island in its purest form. The South.

White Road Beach

This beach is easy to find with a nice straight path in a well-marked area. The road deteriorates rapidly, but it's not one of those jungle paths that are difficult to traverse. Follow the road to the end and you have your choice of beach paths, with the more defined of the two leading off to the left under a grouping of sea grape trees. Just before the beach is a shaded area that shows evidence of being a hang out spot for locals replete with the remains of a grill and other cooking implements. Pass the last few sea grapes to get onto the beach, which is the southern extension of the Atlantic beaches up at Half Sound. As such it has many of the same characteristics as beaches 98 and 99 along with similar blemishes.

The beach is well suited for walking, jogging, and swimming due to almost perfect sandy water access. This is the kind of beach you can come to for a day and really bask in the sun while repeatedly cooling off in the ocean. What you won't like is the amount of debris and seaweed, and that is typical of Atlantic beaches that are private and secluded. This beach is set back away from the community and has no houses or other development around it, but that also means that anything that washes up on shore is not going to be removed unless the sea reclaims it.

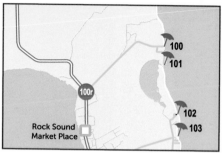

100
101
100r
102
103
Rock Sound
Market Place

Beach ★★☆ Road ★☆☆

Beach: 24° 53.862, -76° 8.391
Road: 24° 53.059, -76° 9.716

How to Get There

From points north
Total travel time: 8.9 mi. / 22.5 min
From Tarpum Bay intersection drive south for 7.0 miles. Make left and proceed 1.9 miles on paved road that turns to bumpy gravel. There are two access point to left of T shaped parking area and one to the right through the brush.

Time / Distance
To beach road: 7.0 mi. / 14 min
Beach road to beach: 1.9 mi. / 8.5 min

From points south
Total travel time: 2.6 mi. / 9.5 min
From Rock Sound marketplace drive north for 0.7 miles. Make right and proceed 1.9 miles on paved road that turns to bumpy gravel. There are two access point to left of T shaped parking area and one to the right through the brush.

Time / Distance
To beach road: 0.7 mi. / 1 min
Beach road to beach: 1.9 mi. / 8.5 min

What You Should Know

Privacy	Secluded
Shade	Some
Accessibility	4WD recommended
Beach Path	Sandy
Water Entry	Sandy
Water Condition	Deep ocean
Litter/Seaweed	Moderate
Nearest Town	Rock Sound
Snorkeling	Good
Shelling	No
Beach Size	2.0 miles x 50 yards

Snorkeling here is not as good as up north. The reef is more spread out and pod-like with the more well developed reef systems residing further offshore. An advanced snorkeler or good swimmer would find this location suitable, but it's probably not the best spot for a novice.

This is a beach that is not spectacular. It's a good solid Atlantic-side beach, but not one that you would go out of your way for. Beaches further south or north are much more unique. The best part of this beach is its convenience. It's a good beach if you are staying in or around Rock Sound.

Red Pond Beach

This is one of the most beautiful places on the island and its geography may be the most unique of them all. It is dramatic, beautiful, pristine and breathtaking all in one. What sets it apart is the vertical sand wall on the opposite shore away from where you park. It resembles a giant clam with a huge lip up top that supports the island vegetation. Then, you have an undulating vertical drop off that could be twenty feet in places creating what resembles a snowy mountain. It's truly amazing and can't be found anywhere else on Eleuthera.

A very protected reef just outside a little bay funnels to a channel that reaches back into the pond helping to keep the beach in such an unspoiled state. The beach area seems inconsequential compared to the beauty of the view and surrounding area. The protected bay is very good for swimming and is relatively shallow. Just beyond the breakers you have deep blue sea and a very mature reef system.

This location has everything; fantastic and unique geography, awesome swimming, great snorkeling, extreme seclusion, perfect water access, and an amazing amount of diversity. The only thing you'll give up is shade as there is not much to find here and one lonely tall palm tree almost seems out of place given the

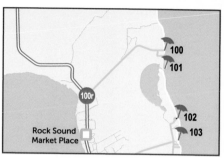

100
101
100r
102
103

Rock Sound
Market Place

Beach ★★★ Road ★☆☆

Beach: 24° 53.539, -76° 8.369
Road (100r): 24° 53.059, -76° 9.716

How to Get There

From points north
Total travel time: 9.2 mi. / 28 min
From Tarpum Bay intersection drive south for 7.0 miles. Make left and proceed 1.7 miles on paved road that turns to bumpy gravel. Make right and proceed 0.5 miles to beach.

Time / Distance
To beach road: 7.0 mi. / 14 min
Beach road to beach: 2.2 mi. / 14 min

From points south
Total travel time: 2.9 mi. / 15 min
From Rock Sound marketplace drive north for 0.7 miles. Make right and proceed 1.7 miles on paved road that turns to bumpy gravel. Make right and proceed 0.5 miles to beach.

Time / Distance
To beach road: 0.7 mi. / 1 min
Beach road to beach: 2.2 mi. / 14 min

What You Should Know

Privacy	Secluded
Shade	Some
Accessibility	4WD recommended
Beach Path	Sandy
Water Entry	Sandy
Water Condition	Shallow bay and deep ocean
Litter/Seaweed	None
Nearest Town	Rock Sound
Snorkeling	Good
Shelling	No
Beach Size	100 yards x 25 yards

exquisiteness of everything else around.

The beach extends quite far although we didn't have a chance to fully explore past the mouth of the pond. Several smaller beaches wrap around the pond, which resembles the bay at Half Sound with even a few sand bars poking their heads above the waterline.

Make Red Pond one of your must-see beaches on your tour of the island. This beach is worth going out of your way for if you want to see a natural wonder that is as raw a beauty as you will find.

Nort'side Beach Resort

There are a number of reasons to come to the beach that sits below this quaint, elevated seaside resort the least of which might be the beach, which is no slouch itself. Just behind the restaurant and sandy floored bar, take the 33 steps down to this idyllic Atlantic beach that stands out from others on this part of the island due to its relative cleanliness. This is a big dramatic beach that extends all the way to the vertical-lipped wall that hovers over Red Pond (101). Its total length is slightly more than a mile; its width 20 to 30 yards most of the way. Water access is very good in front of the resort. There are a couple of small rock formations to the right that break up the view and a rock ledge a bit further down to the left.

Past the rock ledge is where you'll have improved water access and the most privacy.

There is a moderate reef system here, mostly small roundish pods, until you get much farther from shore where the more contiguous reef resides. The water gets deep almost immediately and there is usually some light wave action.

We think the best reason to come here, though, is to meet Rose Gibson and to delight in her restaurant and bar. Rose is the owner of Nort'side Beach Resort and a more wonderful person is hard to find. She is always eager to engage in conversation that sometimes borders on a spiritual sermon. We find her to be both entertaining and enlightening. Make

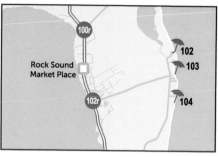

100r

Rock Sound Market Place

102r

102
103
104

Beach ★★☆   Road ★★☆

Beach: 24° 52.688, -76° 8.160
Road: 24° 51.827, -76° 9.555

How to Get There

From points north
Total travel time: 2.7 mi. / 8 min
From Rock Sound Market Place drive south 0.7 miles. Make a left and proceed 1.6 miles on paved road to T. Make a left and bear to right as paved road turns to gravel up hill to resort. Steps behind restaurant lead to beach.

Time / Distance
To beach road: 0.7 mi. / 2 min
Beach road to beach: 2.0 mi. / 6 min

From points south
Total travel time: 8.8 mi. / 16 min
From Chris Brown Boulevard / Cotton Bay drive north 6.8 miles. Make a right and proceed 1.6 miles to T. Make a left and bear to right as paved road turns to gravel up hill to resort. Steps behind restaurant lead to beach.

Time / Distance
To beach road: 6.8 mi. / 10 min
Beach road to beach: 2.0 mi. / 6 min

What You Should Know	
Privacy	Semi-private
Shade	None
Accessibility	Car, bumpy
Beach Path	Stairs
Water Entry	Rocks and sand
Water Condition	Deep ocean
Litter/Seaweed	Light
Nearest Town	Rock Sound
Snorkeling	Good
Shelling	No
Beach Size	1.15 miles x 20 yards

sure to try her fresh, fried snapper or cracked conch. The view from the elevated outside patio is outstanding, the sandy floored bar unique and her huge, furry dog Teddy, a riot.

Since this is a small resort it isn't a secluded spot, but the beach is large enough that you can walk a bit to have some solitude. The access road is reasonably good. The end of the road gets a bit bumpy, but this is not a wild jungle ride by any stretch of the imagination. The beach is good for walking and running. If you don't mind the steps then it's a good beach to choose because of the resort amenities. Rose is a lovely lady and a wonderful cook. It's worth going here just to meet her.

Nort'side Beach Central

A smaller half-monish beach can be found just south of the Nort'side Beach Resort. It is a little harder to get to with two separate access points that are both short jungle trails that might make you want for a 4WD vehicle. The first access point puts you onto the sand after a short walk over a small dune, the second, onto the rocks at the southern point of this beach, which is about 1/3rd of a mile long in total.

You have two main differences here compared to beach 102. There is a lot more debris and it's a lot more secluded with no houses on or around the beach. You are still within eyesight of the resort and it's easy to just drive up there for lunch or a drink without feeling like you are right underneath it

There is good sandy water access here and a more well developed reef system that is just offshore so an excellent place for children to snorkel within your watchful eye. You can find cleaner sections of this beach as well as shade by moving more to the north with several isolated Casuarinas providing some limited natural coverage.

Beach 103 ★★☆ Road ★☆☆

Beach: 24° 52.250, -76° 8.117
Road (102r): 24° 51.827, -76° 9.555

Beach 103a ★★☆ Road ★☆☆

Beach: 24° 52.212, -76° 8.091
Road (102r): 24° 51.827, -76° 9.555

How to Get There

From points north
Total travel time: 2.4 mi. / 7 min
From Rock Sound Market Place drive south 0.7 miles. Make a left and proceed 1.6 miles on paved road to T. Make a right and proceed 300 feet. Make a left and poceed 300 feet to parking area.

Time / Distance
To beach road: 0.7 mi. / 2 min
Beach road to beach: 1.7 mi. / 5 min

From points south
Total travel time: 8.5 mi. / 15 min
From Chris Brown Boulevard / Cotton Bay drive north 6.8 miles. Make a right and proceed 1.6 miles to T. Make a right and proceed 300 feet. Make a left and poceed 300 feet to parking area.

Time / Distance
To beach road: 6.8 mi. / 10 min
Beach road to beach: 1.7 mi. / 5 min

What You Should Know	
Privacy	Semi-private
Shade	Some
Accessibility	4WD recommended
Beach Path	Dune
Water Entry	Rocks and sand
Water Condition	Deep ocean
Litter/Seaweed	Moderate
Nearest Town	Rock Sound
Snorkeling	Good
Shelling	No
Beach Size	0.33 miles x 20 yards

Nort'side Beach South

This small sliver of beach is actually the head of a much larger beach that stretches about 1.75 miles to the south although we found no other access points other than this one. The beach immediately in front of the beach road is about 100 yards wide and 20 yards deep between two sharp, scraggly rocky points. As we proceeded south away from the Nort'side Beach Resort the beaches, such as this one, become more isolated and much more debris laden. There were serious amounts of collected seaweed and debris here especially to the left of the access point.

The good news is this beach is easy to find and easy to get to. There is good water access directly in front of where you enter the beach and then again past the rocky point to the

right. We didn't fully explore this beach to the end, but there's plenty of beach to the south to walk or run on.

In front of the seaweed is a modestly angled slope that takes you into the water. The water looks good here and this front part of the beach was clean. The reef system is better to the right with a larger mature reef system further offshore. One lone cay is within view a little over a quarter mile away. Finally, a few isolated Casuarinas can be found for some shade.

There was nothing overly special about this beach, and the main reason we could think of to drive down this far would be if the other beaches were occupied or if you wanted more seclusion on a larger exploration-oriented beach.

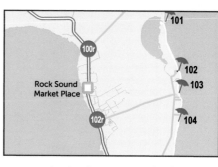

Rock Sound
Market Place

101
102
103
104
100r
102r

Beach ★★☆   Road ★☆☆

Beach: 24° 51.949, -76° 8.108
Road (102r): 24° 51.827, -76° 9.555

How to Get There

From points north
Total travel time: 2.5 mi. / 9 min
From Rock Sound Market Place drive south 0.7 miles. Make a left and proceed 1.6 miles on paved road to T. Make a right and proceed 0.1 miles. Make a left and proceed 300 feet to parking area.

Time / Distance
To beach road: 0.7 mi. / 2 min
Beach road to beach: 1.8 mi. / 7 min

From points south
Total travel time: 8.6 mi. / 17 min
From Chris Brown Boulevard / Cotton Bay drive north 6.8 miles. Make a right and proceed 1.6 miles to T. Make a right and proceed 0.1 miles. Make a left and proceed 300 feet to parking area.

Time / Distance
To beach road: 6.8 mi. / 10 min
Beach road to beach: 1.8 mi. / 7 min

What You Should Know	
Privacy	Secluded
Shade	None
Accessibility	4WD recommended
Beach Path	Dune
Water Entry	Rocks and sand
Water Condition	Deep ocean
Litter/Seaweed	Moderate
Nearest Town	Rock Sound
Snorkeling	Good
Shelling	No
Beach Size	100 yards x 40 yards

Whiteland Beach 1

One of the unique features of this beach is a geographic formation at the northernmost tip of the beach. The Blue Window is a cave with no entry or exit. It has a floor and a ceiling, and is then open to let the light through. It's large enough for several people to sit in and when the light shines through it is nirvana, one of the most beautiful natural features of the island with pastel blue light filtering through greyish white rock. The dramatic colors and shape look like the glow of a dragon's fiery blue eye. The Blue Window is reached by heading north about 6/10ths of a mile from this access point and is a must see.

Now, the rest of the beach is not too shabby. It resembles three Nike swooshes back to back. The swooshes are actually curving

rocky points that hug the turquoise water underneath them like a loving child under her mother's protective arms. These little 'bays' are natural wading pools sitting inside of the ocean's deep blue waters. What you get is a swimming hole surrounded by both deep blue ocean and a very well developed reef system.

The beach is very secluded. This is the northernmost tip of a super long stretch of sand that reaches almost four miles south to Cotton Bay. While it is one contiguous beach we recommend using a car to find the other accessible southern areas due to a number of ponds that cut off access most of the way.

Due to its length, this beach is naturally good for walking or running. It is charming, peaceful, beautiful, quaint and spectacular all at the same

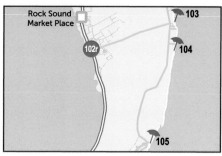

Beach ★★★   Road ★★☆

Beach: 24° 50.270, -76° 8.549
Road (102r): 24° 51.827, -76° 9.555

What You Should Know

Privacy	Secluded
Shade	Some
Accessibility	4WD recommended
Beach Path	Dune
Water Entry	Sandy
Water Condition	Deep ocean
Litter/Seaweed	Moderate
Nearest Town	Rock Sound
Snorkeling	Good
Shelling	Yes
Beach Size	0.8 miles x 40 yards

How to Get There

From points north
Total travel time: 4.8 mi. / 25 min
From Rock Sound Market Place drive south 0.7 miles. Make a left and proceed 1.6 miles on paved road to T. Make a right and proceed 2.3 miles. Make a left and proceed 0.2 miles. Make a left and proceed 300 feet to parking area.

Time / Distance
To beach road: 0.7 mi. / 2 min
Beach road to beach: 4.1 mi. / 23 min

From points south
Total travel time: 10.9 mi. / 33 min
From Chris Brown Boulevard / Cotton Bay drive north 6.8 miles. Make a right and proceed 1.6 miles to T. Make a right and proceed 2.3 miles. Make a left and proceed 0.2 miles. Make a left and proceed 300 feet to parking area.

Time / Distance
To beach road: 6.8 mi. / 10 min
Beach road to beach: 4.1 mi. / 23 min

time. The only negative is, due to its location, there is a fair amount of seaweed and debris on the upper level of the beach. We also found the remains of several boats, which were both interesting and reminders that this area does not get cleaned up except by natural means. Water access is good, but there are a few rocky places that are easily avoided. This is not a great shelling beach, but you can find very fine miniature shells with some patience. This seemed to also be the pinkest of the pink sand beaches. Foraminifera, the organism that causes the beaches to have this color and also its cool temperature, seem to be in abundance here.

Don't miss Whiteland Beach 1. This is the cream of the crop. It is worth the extra time to find and explore it.

Whiteland Beach 2

This secluded beach is a beauty and one of the most picturesque on the island. This is just like one of those tropical oasis beaches that you sometimes see on a postcard. Only this time it's real, and you're there. It's that pristine. It's that quaint. It's that delectable.

The beach is shaped like an almost perfect semi-circle, which aids its appeal, but what makes it stand out is the color of the water. The bay is somewhat shallow with a white sandy bottom that creates a translucent shade of aquamarine. This brightly colored swimming hole sits in front of a massive reef system with deep blue ocean all around. The bay is excellent for swimming and snorkeling.

Because the bay is just one part of this super long Atlantic beach that stretches all the way south to Cotton Bay you have plenty of room to walk, run, and explore both north and south. A high sand dune marks the end of this quarter mile bay which is Casuarina lined all around with a pod of tall palms towards the south.

Whiteland has just the right amount of sun and shade with a natural picnic area set amongst the Casuarina needles at the entrance by the parking area. The fact that it is set back a bit from the surrounding long

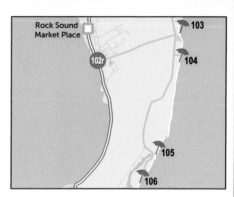

Rock Sound Market Place

102r

103

104

105

106

Beach ★★★ Road ★★☆

Beach: 24° 49.993, -76° 8.705
Road (102r): 24° 51.827, -76° 9.555

What You Should Know

Privacy	Secluded
Shade	Plenty
Accessibility	4WD recommended
Beach Path	Sandy
Water Entry	Sandy
Water Condition	Shallow bay
Litter/Seaweed	Light
Nearest Town	Rock Sound
Snorkeling	Good
Shelling	No
Beach Size	0.2 miles x 30 yards

How to Get There

From points north
Total travel time: 5.2 mi. / 29 min
From Rock Sound Market Place drive south 0.7 miles. Make a left and proceed 1.6 miles on paved road to T. Make a right and proceed 2.3 miles. Make a left and proceed straight for 0.6 miles to parking area.

Time / Distance
To beach road: 0.7 mi. / 2 min
Beach road to beach: 4.5 mi. / 27 min

From points south
Total travel time: 11.3 mi. / 37 min
From Chris Brown Boulevard / Cotton Bay drive north 6.8 miles. Make a right and proceed 1.6 miles to T. Make a right and proceed 2.3 miles. Make a left and proceed straight for 0.6 miles to parking area.

Time / Distance
To beach road: 6.8 mi. / 10 min
Beach road to beach: 4.5 mi. / 27 min

beach, coupled with a rocky northern point, makes all the difference in terms of debris and wash up. While the neighboring beaches were loaded with wash up, Whiteland Beach 2 was almost comically clean in comparison. The only problem with this beach is that it's a bit of a hike to get here through a slightly overgrown jungle road that is a bit tricky to find, but well worth the trip.

With water this inviting, a beach this clean, and the view this lovely, this beach must really be seen in person. Pack a picnic and plan to spend a day on this outstanding and highly rated beach.

Rocky Point Beach

Tough to find, tough to get to, loaded with debris and wash up. These are generally good indicators that if you work a little bit to make the trek back to this beach you are likely to have your own beach for the day. It is quite lovely in its own way, but also seems lonely, too.

This is the same stretch of sand that runs from Whiteland in the north down to Cotton Bay to its south. A lone rocky point separates two beach halves that form a short half-moon with another half-moon directly around the point to the north. The beach has nice sand and good water access that gets deep immediately.

The fallen Casuarinas are its most distinguishing feature. Like giant pieces of driftwood they offer a somewhat unique contrast with their grey trunks standing out against the pink sand and blue ocean. They create some unique photo opportunities. You'll find a good combination of sun and shade here with a dense set of Casuarinas to the north.

This is a good beach for the more adventurous who are willing to go out of their way to find a secluded beach. The main issues with the beach are the multitude of seaweed and debris. You'll definitely want a 4WD vehicle especially to cover the last 4/10ths of a mile that go through dense jungle, this after leaving a very bumpy back road. Snorkeling can be done here although the major reef system is a bit farther offshore as compared to other beaches in the area.

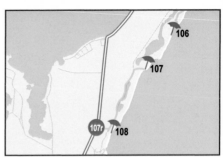

Beach ★★☆   Road ★☆☆

Beach: 24° 49.201, -76° 9.283
Road: 24° 48.180, -76° 10.120

How to Get There

From points north
Total travel time: 7 mi. / 20 min
From Rock Sound Market Place drive south 5.1 miles to Northshore Drive. Make a left and proceed 1.3 miles bearing left at 0.2 miles. Make right and proceed 0.4 miles on very overgrown road to beach on right.

Time / Distance
To beach road: 5.1 mi. / 8 min
Beach road to beach: 1.9 mi. / 12 min

From points south
Total travel time: 4.3 mi. / 15 min
From Chris Brown Boulevard / Cotton Bay drive north 2.4 miles to Northshore Drive. Make a right and proceed 1.3 miles bearing left at 0.2 miles. Make right and proceed 0.4 miles on very overgrown road to beach on right.

Time / Distance
To beach road: 2.4 mi. / 4 min
Beach road to beach: 1.9 mi. / 12 min

What You Should Know	
Privacy	Secluded
Shade	Plenty
Accessibility	4WD recommended
Beach Path	Sandy
Water Entry	Sandy
Water Condition	Deep ocean
Litter/Seaweed	Moderate
Nearest Town	Green Castle
Snorkeling	Good
Shelling	No
Beach Size	2.0 miles x 40 yards

Cotton Bay Estates Beach

This is the beach where we had the most discomfort on the walk. It's a semi hike-to beach and one that we discovered almost by accident as a result of making a wrong turn. Seeing a path leading off into the jungle, curiosity took over. We proceeded through a very narrow, thorny, spidery, and otherwise treacherous trail back to a six foot tall dune that dropped us down onto, what was expected to be, an extremely beautiful secluded beach. With the unstoppable itch from the seed-pods of the Warri trees just beginning, what we found was an extremely debris covered beach that lacked

privacy due to its proximity to the large new development at Cotton Bay Estates, which was about a quarter mile to the south.

The worst part of the beach was to the north. It was rocky on the beach as well as into the water. Because there is no protective rocky point extending into the water to the north it seems that the debris has nowhere to go but up on shore where a fairly steep dune helps to capture it on the rocks. Overall, this was extremely unattractive and spoiled any thoughts of staying here for any length of time.

To quickly summarize, there is nothing

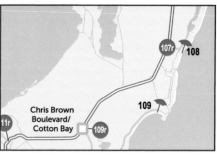

Chris Brown
Boulevard/
Cotton Bay

Beach ★☆☆ Road ★☆☆

Beach: 24° 48.132, -76° 9.919
Road (107r): 24° 48.180, -76° 10.120

How to Get There

From points north

Total travel time: 5.3 mi. / 10 min
From Rock Sound Market Place drive south
5.1 miles to Northshore Drive. Make a left
and proceed 0.2 miles. Make right and proceed to end. On left, just before road ends, is
a foot path. Proceed on foot a few hundred
feet to beach. Foot path has sharp vegetation.
Use caution.

Time / Distance

To beach road: 5.1 mi. / 8 min
Beach road to beach: 0.2 mi. / 2 min

From points south

Total travel time: 2.6 mi. / 6 min
From Chris Brown Boulevard / Cotton Bay
drive north 2.4 miles to Northshore Drive.
Make a right and proceed 0.2 miles. Make
right and proceed to end. On left, just before
road ends, is a foot path. Proceed on foot
a few hundred feet to beach. Foot path has
sharp vegetation. Use caution.

Time / Distance

To beach road: 2.4 mi. / 4 min
Beach road to beach: 0.2 mi. / 2 min

What You Should Know

Privacy	Semi-private
Shade	None
Accessibility	4WD recommended
Beach Path	Dirt
Water Entry	Sandy
Water Condition	Deep ocean
Litter/Seaweed	Extensive
Nearest Town	Green Castle
Snorkeling	Good
Shelling	No
Beach Size	1.5 miles x 20 yards

overly special here. When you take into con-
sideration the difficult short hike through the
jungle, a vast amount of debris, and the close
proximity to Cotton Bay Estates development, there were very few reasons to embark
on this particular adventure unless you really
want to see or experience the prickly sea-pods
of the Warri trees. What should be noted is
there was a reasonably good reef system offshore and there was good sandy water access
where you come out onto the beach and to
the south. However, we don't feel this is worth
the time or trouble.

Jack's Bay Beach

We like Jack's Bay and you will too. It almost feels like two different beaches with a very well protected and private north shore complemented by a very exposed and rugged southern shore. There is evidence of a new golf course being built along the southern shore as well as back behind the beach, but out of sight. Knowing that, we're not sure how much longer Jack's will stay as nice and private as it is.

One of the better beach roads, one in which we actually got the vehicle over 20mph in places, leads to the central access point to one of the longest contiguous Atlantic-side bays on the island. It stretches almost one mile in a gently contouring slope away from its tall pinnacle point on the northern tip.

This tip protects the bay in such a way that it resembles a cove, one that attracts numerous Hawksbill turtles to feed in its shallow waters. The northern part of the beach is more private, better protected and cleaner.

As you move further south you give up the protection from the northern pinnacle. A few homes are built along the beach, and based on how land is being cleared; we expect others to join those in the future. There is more seaweed, debris, and much more wave action to the south.

Be careful to avoid the abundance of burs in the grass especially in front of the shady Casuarinas. You can find good bur-free areas to sit, but you really need to look for them. Wear shoes or look closely before sitting down.

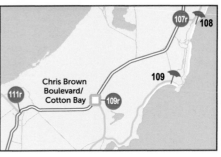

Chris Brown
Boulevard/
Cotton Bay

Beach ★★☆   Road ★★☆

Beach: 24° 47.091, -76° 10.387
Road: 24° 46.812, -76° 11.612

What You Should Know

Privacy	Semi-private
Shade	Some
Accessibility	Car, bumpy
Beach Path	Sandy
Water Entry	Sandy
Water Condition	Deep ocean
Litter/Seaweed	Moderate
Nearest Town	Green Castle
Snorkeling	Good
Shelling	No
Beach Size	1.0 miles x 20 yards

How to Get There

From points north
Total travel time: 1.9 mi. / 11 min
Proceed south to Chris Brown Boulevard / Cotton Bay. Make a left followed by making your 3rd left at 0.7 miles. Proceed 1.2 miles. Make right to beach.

Time / Distance
Beach road to beach: 1.9 mi. / 11 min

From points south
Total travel time: 1.9 mi. / 11 min
Proceed north to Chris Brown Boulevard / Cotton Bay. Make a right followed by making your 3rd left at 0.7 miles. Proceed 1.2 miles. Make right to beach.

Time / Distance
Beach road to beach: 1.9 mi. / 11 min

There is not a lot of reef structure compared to other areas, but this is still a good snorkeling bay. The water access is excellent, which makes it easy to get in and out of the water with no rocks to inhibit safe passage. Tall majestic palms to the south of the beach complete the scene at this fine beach.

This is a lovely, beautiful well-protected bay. It is longer, wider, and rounder as compared to most other Atlantic side bays. We recommend moving to the more protected northern part of the beach where the turtles feed so you can enjoy sun, shade, snorkeling and a commanding ocean view that extends far south on the island.

Cotton Bay Beach

The Cotton Bay Golf Course is still the best landmark for finding the accessible oceanside beach at Cotton Bay. There are actually two beaches with several access points, but due to the private residences, retired bungalows, and an ample supply of No Trespassing signs, there is really only one good access point at the middle of the more southerly half-moon bay.

To the left of this access point you can still see the vestiges of the old resort and its cottages, some of which appear to be occupied. There are also remnants of the elevated green of the par 5 sixth hole, which from my experience, was the most severely sloped triple tier green that one might ever see. Perched precariously over the northern tip of the beach, it was

a very difficult little target with winds sometimes blowing shots 30 or 40 yards off line into the sea.

The beach has a similar look as Jack's Bay, but what sets it apart is its width, which easily reaches 80 yards in places especially to its south. There was a wide line of seaweed that seemed to surround the beach all the way around along with some moderate debris towards the back, but nothing that was too troubling. This is a pretty beach with crystal clear water, good swimming and decent snorkeling. The terrain is more interesting than at many other beaches because of the abundance of tall palms to its south, which really make for a charming backdrop. Sea lettuce and shrubbery

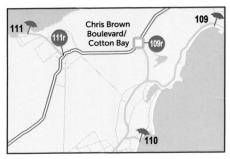

Beach ★★☆ Road ★★☆

Beach: 24° 45.155, -76° 11.608
Road (109r): 24° 46.812, -76° 11.612

What You Should Know

Privacy	Semi-private
Shade	Some
Accessibility	Car, bumpy
Beach Path	Sandy
Water Entry	Sandy
Water Condition	Deep ocean
Litter/Seaweed	Light
Nearest Town	Green Castle
Snorkeling	Good
Shelling	No
Beach Size	1.0 miles x 80 yards

How to Get There

From points north
Total travel time: 2.3 mi. / 6 min
Proceed south to Chris Brown Boulevard / Cotton Bay. Make a left and proceed 2.1 miles. Make left before picket fence and proceed 0.2 miles. Make right and proceed 500 feet to beach.

Time / Distance
Beach road to beach: 2.3 mi. / 6 min

From points south
Total travel time: 2.3 mi. / 6 min
Proceed north to Chris Brown Boulevard / Cotton Bay. Make a right and proceed 2.1 miles. Make left before picket fence and proceed 0.2 miles. Make right and proceed 500 feet to beach.

Time / Distance
Beach road to beach: 2.3 mi. / 6 min

surround the shaded parking area, which is easy to find and access. Most of the road was very good, but the last chunk into the community is very rutted and bumpy lowering its overall grade.

You can find ample sun and a fair amount of shade especially at the entrance. At the time we visited there was also a constant set of waves suitable for body surfing. With less burs and debris than at Jack's Bay, this is probably the better choice of the two with the only real negative being the lack of privacy. With cottages to the north, large beach houses and a community to the south, plus an ample of amount of workers around, you won't have the seclusion that is so notable on most of the southern beaches.

Green Castle Beach / Little Bay

The hardest part in describing this beach is accurately recounting the width of the beach relative to its water access. The accessible water area is tiny and rocky making it almost mandatory to use water shoes. But, the beach itself is wide and shady with the most well-manicured beach area of any of the public beaches. The base around the Casuarinas were cleared and covered with sand making the back of the beach under the trees quite inviting. If you are looking for a shaded picnic area with shallow waters ideal for children this is a good choice.

There are picnic tables, tiki huts, lots of shade and benches. A large beach hut to the back of the beach serves as a place of revelry for Bahamian evening affairs. While the sandy water access area is 10' at its widest, the beach sand extends a good 80 to 100 yards back under the trees and has good soft sand all the way to its rear.

If you want shade, tables, shallow water and a public beach that is not far from Rock Sound, this is it. Expect no privacy and bring water shoes. The nearby town of Green Castle has several places to eat and drink.

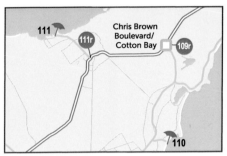

Beach ★☆☆ Road ★★★

Beach: 24° 46.988, -76° 13.401
Road: 24° 46.589, -76° 12.935

How to Get There

From points north
Total travel time: 2.2 mi. / 4 min
From Chris Brown Boulevard / Cotton Bay drive south 1.6 miles. Make a right and proceed 0.6 miles to beach access on right.

Time / Distance
To beach road: 1.6 mi. / 3 min
Beach road to beach: 0.6 mi. / 1 min

From points south
Total travel time: 3.0 mi. / 7 min
From Wemyss Bight T drive north 2.4 miles. Make a left and proceed 0.6 miles to beach access on right.

Time / Distance
To beach road: 2.4 mi. / 6 min
Beach road to beach: 0.6 mi. / 1 min

What You Should Know	
Privacy	Public
Shade	Plenty
Accessibility	Car
Beach Path	None
Water Entry	Rocky
Water Condition	Shallow bay
Litter/Seaweed	Light
Nearest Town	Green Castle
Snorkeling	Poor
Shelling	Yes
Beach Size	200 yards x 80 yards

Deep Creek Beach

Idyllic is the word that first comes to mind when trying to describe the magnificence that is the Deep Creek oceanside beach. This is an amazing beach that faces southwest, its sweeping view capturing endless miles of the Great Exuma Sound. It received our highest rating owing to a number of factors. It is unique, super clean and is the kind of place that proves the theory of relativity. Every hour spent here seems like milliseconds.

Getting here is the hardest part. Once you leave the highway in Deep Creek the beach road winds around marsh and mangrove. It is bumpy, rutted and can flood. More than

once we had to swim the vehicle across the channel through water that seemed too swift to safely pass. If the tides are up or you are a timid driver, then you should think twice before venturing here.

The beach forms an almost complete circle, surrounded by two rocky shorelines which protect its sandy shores. There is a swift moving channel to the left of the parking area where water surges into the bay purging it by pushing everything out to sea. To the right of the channel is about 0.5 miles of sand that looks hot white, but is cool to the touch. To the left of the channel

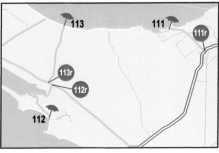

Beach ★★★   Road ★☆☆

Beach: 24° 45.496, -76° 15.646
Road: 24° 46.024, -76° 15.582

How to Get There

From points north
Total travel time: 2.9 mi. / 11 min
Drive south on Queen's Highway past Waterford to T in Wemyss Bight. Make a right and proceed 1.9 miles. Make a left just past St. Joseph's Anglican Church and proceed 1.0 miles around curvy, bumpy road that can flood to two sand parking areas at end.

Time / Distance
To beach road: 1.9 mi. / 4 min
Beach road to beach: 1.0 mi. / 7 min

What You Should Know

Privacy	Secluded
Shade	Plenty
Accessibility	4WD recommended
Beach Path	Sandy
Water Entry	Sandy
Water Condition	Shallow bay
Litter/Seaweed	None
Nearest Town	Deep Creek
Snorkeling	Poor
Shelling	No
Beach Size	0.7 miles x 20 feet

is a quarter mile strip of sand backed by a short rocky ledge. There are large rocks and small pebbles scattered about that seem to have been placed there purposely to offset the glowing white canvas. The paint, if we can call it that, comes from the hues of the water. Every shade of blue and green can be found resembling a work of fine art, the artist choosing from an infinite palette of blue and green pastels.

There is no seaweed or debris. The water entry is sandy and very shallow with sand bars occasionally popping up creating little islands that can be used as sitting spots in the middle of the ocean. Back on shore the sand is firm with pockets of shade under groupings of Casuarinas. You wouldn't choose this beach to snorkel and it's not the best swimming beach since the water doesn't get deep until much further out. What you choose this beach for is its pristineness.

We couldn't find anything wrong here. There were no imperfections other than one nearby bulldozer that made us think that sand may be harvested on occasion. It was completely secluded with nothing else in sight. All in all, this is a great beach, a special spot and well worth finding.

Deep Creek Caribbean Beach

This is not the most beautiful place on the island, but if you are looking for a good long walking beach with lots of privacy, then look no further. It was hard to truly appreciate or assess this 2.5-mile stretch of sand. Much of the shoreline is narrow and rocky while it seemed like just as much was sandy. The beach road running parallel to the sand goes for miles. We only stopped at several noticeable parking areas to check out conditions. Because the trees are spread out there were limitless access points. Just pick a place to stop and walk about 20 feet through the trees to the beach. Alternately, consider the spots

we catalogued that had better parking and were close to the beach roads leading back from the highway.

The most interesting feature of the beach was the color of the sand. Where most beaches, especially those on the Caribbean or around the sounds, have very discernible pink hues, this beach looked like Gulden's mustard with a deep golden brown tone. There was lots of shade under a dense Casuarina forest with sand extending away from the water a ways under the Casuarinas. Because of a thorough covering of needles you almost wouldn't recognize it as such.

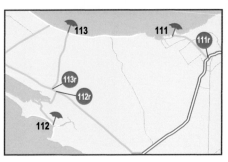

Beach 113 ★★☆ Road ★★☆

Beach: 24° 47.041, -76° 15.431
Road: 24° 46.074, -76° 15.663

Beach 113a ★★☆ Road ★★☆

Beach: 24° 47.156, -76° 15.710
Road: 24° 46.557, -76° 16.631

How to Get There

From points north
Total travel time: 3.2 mi. / 10 min
Drive south on Queen's Highway past Waterford to T in Wemyss Bight. Make a right and proceed 2.0 miles. Make a right and proceed 1.2 miles on paved road which turns to gravel and then to sand. Park on right.

Time / Distance
To beach road: 2.0m / 4 min
Beach road to beach: 1.2 mi. / 6 min

There was very little debris or seaweed here, and we found no shells to speak of, which was somewhat surprising. This beach is interesting, but probably not the beach you would go out of your way to find. However, if you are craving privacy and want a sound side beach with shallow water and a view of Rock Sound, then this is it. The water is good for wading. It's also a very short walk from the parking spot to where the beach is located. Just seek out a spot away from some of the rocky shoreline for the best experience.

What You Should Know	
Privacy	Secluded
Shade	Plenty
Accessibility	Car, bumpy
Beach Path	Sandy
Water Entry	Rocky
Water Condition	Shallow bay
Litter/Seaweed	Light
Nearest Town	Deep Creek
Snorkeling	Poor
Shelling	No
Beach Size	2.5 miles x 10 feet

The Beaches at Guinea Corn Cay

Heading out towards Cape Eleuthera the beaches become few and far between, but this cute little location showed up on our radar and didn't disappoint. The two beaches are separated by a small rocky mangrove outcropping with the first beach barely reaching 100 yards while the beach to the east is almost a quarter mile long. The bays are both mostly straight with good sandy water access, shallow waters and can best be described as Caribbean-like.

Visually, they are interesting with several nearby cays visible in the distance. Small mangroves break up the landscape in an appealing way. The sand here was not the deep golden brown that we experienced further east in Deep Creek, but it's not exactly that pristine pink sand that you find everywhere else, landing somewhere in between.

Lots of shade can be found under Casuarina trees especially at the point that separates the bays. It's also very secluded

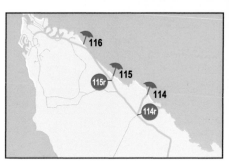

Beach ★★☆ Road ★★☆

Beach: 24° 48.900, -76° 18.536
Road: 24° 48.575, -76° 18.693

How to Get There

From points north
Total travel time: 7.2 mi. / 18 min
Drive south on Queen's Highway past Waterford to T in Wemyss Bight. Make a right and proceed 6.8 miles. Make a right and proceed 0.4 miles on gravel road.

Time / Distance
To beach road: 6.8 mi. / 15 min
Beach road to beach: 0.4 mi. / 3 min

What You Should Know	
Privacy	Secluded
Shade	Plenty
Accessibility	Car, bumpy
Beach Path	Sandy
Water Entry	Sandy
Water Condition	Shallow bay
Litter/Seaweed	Light
Nearest Town	Deep Creek
Snorkeling	Poor
Shelling	No
Beach Size	0.2 miles x 10 feet

here although there was one fishing boat on shore that was obviously getting some use. Some minor debris and seaweed was strewn about the narrow beaches.

There's nothing wrong here, but nothing really special either. The cays and mangroves are cute. The seclusion is nice. The water entry is excellent. These are two nice beaches, but don't necessarily warrant a long drive to get here.

Cape Eleuthera Public Beach

There is one beach that sticks out as an example of everything a beach should not be and unfortunately, this is it. The only positive thing we can say about this location is that it's easy to get here, but even that is offset by the fact that you'll definitely hear cars driving by if one should happen to pass. Of all the beaches that made it into this book, combined with a number that we found but purposely left out because they seemed borderline illegal to access, the Cape Eleuthera Public Beach wins the award for worst beach on Eleuthera.

Upon entering the beach area you are greeted by dead trees, piles of black conch shells, wash-up, litter, seaweed, rocks and fallen Casuarina spikes that jut out of the sand making it difficult to find a place to sit. There is no shade and the Casuarinas that are still standing are spindly saplings that probably won't survive the next hurricane. There didn't seem to be any reasonable place to access the water nor would you really want to. This would be an ok boat launch, but you'd still probably scrape your hull on the debris and rocks just getting the vessel launched.

In short, this beach stinks. There are some more sandy areas past the mangroves to the right, but we didn't feel it was worth exploring. If not for some interesting mangroves both onshore and sticking out of the water there would be nothing here to even look at. If you want to see the bottom of the barrel then spend 60 seconds here, otherwise just keep going.

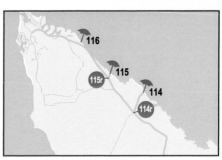

Beach ★☆☆ Road ★★☆

Beach: 24° 49.262, -76° 19.156
Road: 24° 49.231, -76° 19.201

How to Get There

From points north
Total travel time: 7.2 mi. / 16.5 min
Drive south on Queen's Highway past Waterford to T in Wemyss Bight. Make a right and proceed 7.2 miles. Make a right and proceed 300 feet on gravel road.

Time / Distance
To beach road: 7.2 mi. / 16 min
Beach road to beach: 300 feet / 0.5 min

What You Should Know	
Privacy	Secluded
Shade	None
Accessibility	Car, bumpy
Beach Path	Sandy
Water Entry	Rocky
Water Condition	Shallow bay
Litter/Seaweed	Extensive
Nearest Town	Deep Creek
Snorkeling	Poor
Shelling	No
Beach Size	50 yards x 10 feet

Cape Eleuthera Institute Beach

It would probably be more interesting to tell the stories of the beaches we found down this way, but aren't going to publish because of restricted access. We found several at the Cape, however, we were left with the Cape Eleuthera Institute Beach as the only one in the area that you can access without risking a trip to the hoosegow and that's a shame.

The big southern ocean beach at Cape Eleuthera is now closed off and private. It is reserved for those staying at the Powell Pointe Resort or other local lodging within the gates of the marina. We were able to get access to view the beach by stopping in for a drink at the resort, but when we tried to simply access the beach we were turned away.

There are several smallish beaches that run around the old golf course that is set behind the old American Airlines terminal and roadways. Huge boulders blocked off all the roads that we tried to access. We did find one place to sneak by, and, after a difficult traipse through the jungle, eventually found what looked like long sand traps next to fairways. At one point they probably protected errant golf shots from finding the ocean. They didn't resemble beaches you would willingly choose to spend time on. Finding our way out proved even more difficult. The community being developed there appears to be private and exclusive.

The Cape Eleuthera Institute facilitates research for the nearby Island School, which hosts international high school students. It

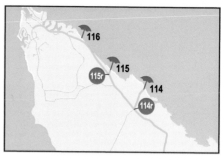

Beach ☆☆☆   Road ★★☆

Beach: 24° 49.726, -76° 19.613
Road: 24° 49.726, -76° 19.613

How to Get There

From points north
Total travel time: 7.9 mi. / 18 min
Drive south on Queen's Highway past Waterford to T in Wemyss Bight. Make a right and proceed 7.9 miles. Beach path is on right.

Time / Distance
To beach road: 7.9 mi. / 18 min
Beach road to beach: 0.0 mi. / 0 min

provides a very unique learning experience that specializes in teaching sustainable aquaculture. I was introduced to the school back in 1999, a year after they opened and it is always a pleasure to see how the community continues to evolve as a result of their influence. The Institute was very glad to welcome us in, give us a tour and answer questions.

But, what about the beach? It is accessed just before reaching the Institute. It's very rocky for the most part so if you want to swim you'll need water shoes. There is much shade with several small cays and one sandy island providing interesting geographic relief. There is no privacy due to the proximity of the nearby buildings of the Institute, but that's the reason to come here in the first place.

What You Should Know	
Privacy	Semi-private
Shade	Plenty
Accessibility	Car
Beach Path	Sandy
Water Entry	Rocky
Water Condition	Shallow bay
Litter/Seaweed	Moderate
Nearest Town	Cape Eleuthera
Snorkeling	Poor
Shelling	No
Beach Size	0.25 miles x 10 feet

Wemyss Bight Beach

The public beach within the town of Wemyss Bight is one of the nicest community beaches on the island. You never need to leave a paved road. Getting back to the beach is very straight forward so if you don't want to risk losing a tire or scratching the side of the car while still enjoying a bottomless view to the south, this beach is for you.

Wemyss Bight is typical of most of the beaches on the southern shore in that it is very shallow with unobstructed views that seem to go on forever, a boat being the only object

that occasionally dots your seascape. Also, typical of the community beaches, the town cemetery is set against the back of the beach with a large cropping of tall Casuarinas providing a liberal amount of shade.

The beach is about 0.25 miles long and narrow resembling Caribbean side beaches to the north. The better sand is towards the back of the beach. The front, leading into the water, has numerous tiny pebbles and shells. This is not a beach where you really need water shoes unless your feet are extremely sensitive.

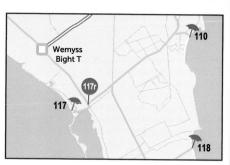

Beach ★★☆   Road ★★★

Beach: 24° 43.825, -76° 13.606
Road: 24° 43.906, -76° 13.335

How to Get There

From points north
Total travel time: 4.5 mi. / 11.5 min
Drive south on Queen's Highway to Chris Brown Boulevard / Cotton Bay. Make a left and proceed a total of 4.2 miles passing through first Stop sign. Make a left at T and proceed 300 feet. Make right and proceed 0.3 miles.

Time / Distance
To beach road: 4.2 mi. / 10.5 min
Beach road to beach: 0.3 mi. / 1 min

The ocean has the look of a place where you're likely to find conch or see stingrays. A big party hut with lights plus a couple of conch huts to the left indicate that this is probably a fun place to be during the Homecoming.

Overall, this is not a beach that you would go out of your way for. It is not a real good swimming or snorkeling beach due to how shallow the water is. It's more of a wading beach with a sweeping southerly view that is to die for.

What You Should Know	
Privacy	Public
Shade	Plenty
Accessibility	Car
Beach Path	None
Water Entry	Sandy
Water Condition	Shallow bay
Litter/Seaweed	Light
Nearest Town	Wemyss Bight
Snorkeling	Poor
Shelling	Yes
Beach Size	0.25 miles x 10 yards

Arvida Bay Beach North

If you are looking for a deserted beach, interesting landscape, and lots of room to explore then look no further. Be prepared to deal with the inherent problems associated with a deserted beach, however. There is extensive wash up plus the beach to the west was loaded with seaweed both in and out of the water making it difficult to assess typical water conditions.

For starters, this is not an easy beach to find or get to. This is the start of the upside down 'T' that most people use to mentally picture the south of the island. Thus, you are on the Atlantic side, but in a more exposed, secluded area on its northeastern shore. The beach road is one that will make you feel like you've been through the agitation cycle in a washing machine. If you are prone to motion sickness, then skip this one. Also, the road is relatively long and you have to pretend your car is a snail where winning the race isn't nearly as important as finishing. Bring a 4WD or avoid this beach.

When you leave the small parking area you have a dreadful bur field to cross before coming to a tall solitary rock that separates the left beaches from the beach on the right. The left side looks like a lowercase letter 'e' with the quarter mile upper beach separated by a small rocky point from the hundred-yard half-moon beach at the entry point.

There are no houses or signs of any other type of civilization. You have a view of one cay to your immediate right. Crossing over the rocks at the mid-point you'll be on another long 1.5 mile beach, which has several other less littered beach access points further east.

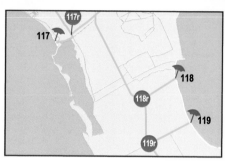

Beach ★★☆ Road ★☆☆

Beach: 24° 43.218, -76° 11.539
Road: 24° 42.836, -76° 12.140

How to Get There

From points north
Total travel time: 6.3 mi. / 21 min
Drive south on Queen's Highway to Chris Brown Boulevard / Cotton Bay. Make a left and proceed 3.6 miles to Stop sign. Make a left and proceed 1.9 miles. Make left and proceed 0.8 miles on very bumpy road to beach.

Time / Distance
To beach road: 5.5 mi. / 12 min
Beach road to beach: 0.8 mi. / 9 min

We might have caught this beach on the wrong day, but the water color was completely different. It was a deep green rather than the aquas we'd grown to expect elsewhere on the island. The eastern beach is interesting in that it has very little flat plateau and is pitched at a steep angle into the water. With good water conditions this is a good swimming beach with excellent water access. An abundant reef system offshore offers good snorkeling. Large reef breakers help to protect the entire area from high seas.

The biggest problems here are debris, seaweed, burs, and limited shade. These are not good running beaches due to the rocks and the slope of the beach. Come here for seclusion, fishing, swimming and snorkeling.

What You Should Know	
Privacy	Secluded
Shade	Some
Accessibility	4WD recommended
Beach Path	Sandy
Water Entry	Sandy
Water Condition	Deep ocean
Litter/Seaweed	Extensive
Nearest Town	Wemyss Bight
Snorkeling	Good
Shelling	Yes
Beach Size	1.75 miles x 30 yards

Arvida Bay Beach South

Moving further east about a mile from beach 118 brings you to this access point on the same large 1.5-mile beach that extends in the general direction towards the lighthouse. Here you'll find another tricky, bumpy, overgrown road that requires stamina, intestinal fortitude and probably Dramamine to reach. If you can tolerate the ride back here then you are likely to have this beach all to yourselves as this location is isolated.

The water was murky when we were here, probably because of the wind. As such, it made the sea look greener than blue and made assessing the reef system more difficult. Reef to the left of the access point was more developed, but it looked like reef further offshore towards the breakers might offer the best snorkeling for someone who is more seasoned.

Looking left you see Arvida Bay North. There was lots of seaweed on its upper shelf grouped in a dense column that extended

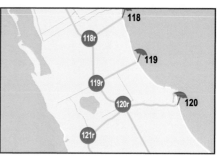

Beach ★★☆   Road ★☆☆

Beach: 24° 42.458, -76° 11.291
Road: 24° 42.107, -76° 11.976

How to Get There

From points north
Total travel time: 7.2 mi. / 23 min
Drive south on Queen's Highway to Chris Brown Boulevard / Cotton Bay. Make a left and proceed 3.6 miles to Stop sign. Make left and proceed 2.8 miles. Make left and proceed 0.8 miles on very bumpy road to beach.

Time / Distance
To beach road: 6.4 mi. / 14 min
Beach road to beach: 0.8 mi. / 9 min

for most of the beach. Water access is sandy all around.

There was only one shady spot just to the right of the access path. Pods of tall non-shade bearing Casuarinas are set back from the beach and are wind blown away from the ocean in such a way that they lean south.

This beach was nothing special and had no overwhelmingly positive traits. It was a long secluded beach that is hard to get to. Choose it for its solitude and length.

What You Should Know	
Privacy	Secluded
Shade	Some
Accessibility	4WD recommended
Beach Path	Dune
Water Entry	Sandy
Water Condition	Deep ocean
Litter/Seaweed	Extensive
Nearest Town	Millar's
Snorkeling	Good
Shelling	Yes
Beach Size	1.5 miles x 40 yards

John Miller's Atlantic Beach North

When comparing the beaches on the northern shore of the southern upside down 'T' of Eleuthera, this beach was the best of the bunch for a number of reasons. First, it was much cleaner in terms of wash-up and seaweed. While there was still a fair amount of seaweed towards the back of the beach, the seaweed field was more out of the way allowing the beautiful sand to glow in the sun like a huge reflective pink orb. Second, the color of the water was exceptionally inviting.

The water entry beckoned with a light turquoise hue before deepening into an ocean blue. Third, the sand was better quality owing to less pollution with a much flatter area to walk, jog and explore.

This beach had the same level seclusion as other north shore beaches. Its reef system is massive and easily reached. There is shade towards the back of the beach, but beware of dense areas of burs.

Ultimately, what made this beach different

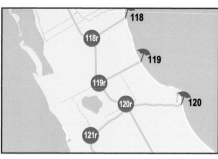

Beach ★★☆ Road ★☆☆

Beach: 24° 41.741, -76° 10.557
Road: 24° 41.743, -76° 11.513

How to Get There

From points north
Total travel time: 8.2 mi. / 25 min
Drive south on Queen's Highway to Chris
Brown Boulevard / Cotton Bay. Make a left
and proceed 3.6 miles to Stop sign. Make left
and proceed 3.5 miles. Make left and proceed
1.1 miles on very bumpy road to beach.

Time / Distance
To beach road: 7.1 mi. / 15 min
Beach road to beach: 1.1 mi. / 10 min

was its shape coupled with the amount of
driftwood we found on it. If you want some
small aquarium treasures to take home this
might be the best beach on the island. The
beach also looked like the letter 'L' with
a sharp right angle to its eastern end. You
definitely need a 4WD vehicle to come back
here, but choose this beach over 118 or 119.
It's a better beach for the long, bumpy ride.

What You Should Know	
Privacy	Secluded
Shade	Some
Accessibility	4WD recommended
Beach Path	Sandy
Water Entry	Sandy
Water Condition	Deep ocean
Litter/Seaweed	Moderate
Nearest Town	John Miller's
Snorkeling	Good
Shelling	No
Beach Size	1.5 miles x 25 yards

John Miller's Sound Beach

The first time I found this beach I rued the day. This second time, I learned from my mistakes and enjoyed a very unique southern coastal beach. The first thing you have to know is that you cannot and should not try to take your vehicle all the way to the beach. You will have to park in the vicinity of an abandoned burned out car, and cross two loosely connected rock beds that cross a set of marshes to find the beach path. It's a 5-minute walk from where you park. The walk requires some coordination and balance as the loose rocks can easily tumble. Be careful, I almost lost the

rental vehicle by trying to drive across these rocks many years ago.

After crossing the marshy areas you'll find a series of beach paths. Stay towards the right to find the center of a nice, serene beach. This is a long, narrow beach with shallow wading type water, its long, straight shore drifting to the west complemented by a wraparound half-moon to the east. Casuarinas provide enough shade, with the main negative being a fair amount of seaweed on its back shelf. There were several squatter shacks to the east and a simple, quaint cemetery set back behind a rock

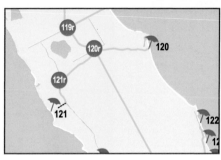

Beach ★★☆ Road ★☆☆

Beach: 24° 40.732, -76° 12.157
Road: 24° 41.213, -76° 12.123

How to Get There

From points north
Total travel time: 9.0 mi. / 26 min
Drive south on Queen's Highway to Chris Brown Boulevard / Cotton Bay. Make a left and proceed 3.6 miles to Stop sign. Make left and proceed 3.6 miles to John Miller's. Make right and proceed 0.9 miles to T. Make left and proceed 0.5 miles on dirt road. Bear right and proceed another 0.2 mile to area just before loose stones. Do NOT attempt to drive across loose stones. Walk 0.2 miles to beach bearing left at first fork on sandy path.

Time / Distance
To beach road: 8.1 mi. / 16 min
Beach road to beach: 0.9 mi. with hike / 10 min

wall to the west. Both of these 'features' are out of the way and shouldn't affect your visit.

Is it worth it to come back here? Yes, if you want seclusion. It's a tough drive and a bit of a walk, but a unique experience with an endless view, nonetheless. Off in the distance you can see the ocean drop off in the Exuma Sound, with depths of up to several thousand feet. The water here is crystal clear. This is a nice, sandy, long beach — good for walking and running. Come here, too, if you want some small shells, sand dollars and to do some general beach combing.

What You Should Know	
Privacy	Secluded
Shade	Some
Accessibility	Car, bumpy
Beach Path	Rocky
Water Entry	Sandy
Water Condition	Shallow bay
Litter/Seaweed	Light
Nearest Town	John Miller's
Snorkeling	Good
Shelling	Yes
Beach Size	0.5 miles x 20 feet

Catch Rock Beach

The view of Catch Rock, a hunk of Eleuthera that seems to just sit offshore, is the most distinctive feature of this reasonably long north shore beach. Because there is no shade it may make sense to begin your adventure at this far beach, and then work your way back to the smaller beaches (123 & 124) where you can have ample overhead coverage.

The road back here, while really not far from Rock Island Beach, was completely overgrown with extremely tall vegetation making it almost impossible to find the road. It felt more like driving by braille and we just had to hope that what our tires were touching was solid enough to create the necessary friction

to move forward. Fortunately, we found the beach access and decided not to push our luck any further as the road did continue on. It was also necessary to keep the windows cranked up on this drive as the pollen and seedlings from the tall brush were covering us even inside the vehicle. Don't take a car back here. You probably won't make it.

The beach path is overgrown and difficult to find as is the parking area. Keep your eyes peeled for the very narrowest of cutouts amongst the tall vegetation. Cross a short sloping sandy dune to a beach that stretches for nearly half a mile and is quite wide. The debris and seaweed has collected at the back

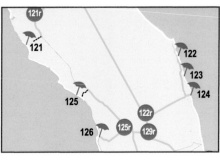

Beach ★★☆　　Road ★☆☆

Beach: 24° 40.406, -76° 9.631
Road: 24° 39.417, -76° 10.185

How to Get There

From points north
Total travel time: 11.7 mi. / 33 min
Drive south on Queen's Highway to Chris Brown Boulevard / Cotton Bay. Make a left and proceed 3.6 miles to Stop sign. Make left and proceed 6.5 miles. Make left just across street from old abandoned Bannerman Town gas station and sign for Bannerman Town and proceed 0.8 miles. Make left and proceed 0.8 miles to single parking spot on left with tiny beach path on right. Walk 50 feet on overgrown sandy path to beach.

Time / Distance
To beach road: 10.1 mi. / 17 min
Beach road to beach: 1.6 mi. / 16 min

of the beach making that part the least inviting. Once on the beach you have good sun, sandy water entry, and a really interesting snorkel spot with massive reef system. Catch Rock and the barrier reef are almost 700 yards offshore so really not swimmable.

Start your Bannerman Town back road exploration here. We recommend starting here, getting some sun in the morning, and then moving to the smaller beaches down the road later in the day. This is a very secluded beach with cleanliness and accessibility being its only negative factors.

What You Should Know	
Privacy	Secluded
Shade	None
Accessibility	4WD recommended
Beach Path	Sandy
Water Entry	Sandy
Water Condition	Deep ocean
Litter/Seaweed	Moderate
Nearest Town	Bannerman Town
Snorkeling	Good
Shelling	No
Beach Size	0.5 miles x 20 yards

Rock Island Beach

Another interesting beach with one tall massive boulder completely surrounded by sand can be found on the same back road away from Bannerman Town on the north shore of the eastern 'T' of southern Eleuthera. You almost feel like you have two beautiful beaches due to how they're naturally separated with rock formations, the right side being only about 10 feet wide, while the left is closer to 30 yards. A unique view of the south side of Catch Rock completes the scene.

There is beautiful water access here with a large snorkeling reef system easily accessible via a sandy water entry. There are any number of smaller rocks set against tall rocks that form little coves that can be explored. If not for fallen Casuarinas here and there plus some debris, this beach would have received our highest grade. Again, the debris issue generally results from how secluded this beach is with nobody around to pick up what washes up from the ocean.

In addition to the main island rock, some of the rocks are set at almost impossible angles.

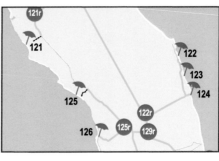

Beach ★★☆ Road ★☆☆

Beach: 24° 40.251, -76° 9.569
Road (122r): 24° 39.417, -76° 10.185

How to Get There

From points north
Total travel time: 11.4 mi. / 30 min
Drive south on Queen's Highway to Chris Brown Boulevard / Cotton Bay. Make a left and proceed 3.6 miles to Stop sign. Make left and proceed 6.5 miles. Make left just across street from old abandoned Bannerman Town gas station and sign for Bannerman Town and proceed 0.8 miles. Make left and proceed 0.5 miles on sand road to two small beaches on right across from pond.

Time / Distance
To beach road: 10.1 mi. / 17 min
Beach road to beach: 1.3 mi. / 13 min

The striations bury in the sand at 30-degree angles pointing skyward giving them a very distinctive look. You almost expect them to crawl out of the sand and start moving.

This is another beach that takes a little work to reach. The road is bumpy, long, and seems to never end. If not for a clearing between the trees we might never have found the shaded access spot, as there is little parking here. If you like interesting rock formations, and absolute peace and quiet then plan a trip to beautiful Rock Island Beach.

What You Should Know	
Privacy	Secluded
Shade	Some
Accessibility	4WD recommended
Beach Path	Dune
Water Entry	Sandy
Water Condition	Deep ocean
Litter/Seaweed	Light
Nearest Town	Bannerman Town
Snorkeling	Good
Shelling	No
Beach Size	30 yards x 20 yards

Bannerman Town Beach North

It's hard to penalize a beach for being too secluded, but these two dramatic beaches are a victim of their own inability to stay clean. As unique as they look and as interesting as the geography is, there was still too much debris and wash-up to receive the highest grade.

The smaller of the two beaches on the left is probably the more swimmable with a little protected turquoise swimming hole set below a steep rocky point. Large rocks and boulders scattered about the sand provide a very interesting look. They are easily avoided to enter the water. The beach to the right is about 30 yards long with almost no rocks on the beach face. It is set in front of a sandy limestone cliff that stands about 12 feet high. Having a pink sand back wall is always alluring, but this one is different in that it is curved, sloping gently around the back of the beach plate. Water access here is very good and completely sandy.

The area is overwhelmingly secluded. To have this kind of seclusion you can expect the usual long, bumpy ride that necessitates a 4WD vehicle. An ample reef system provides decent snorkeling with large pods widely separated. Watch for dangerous

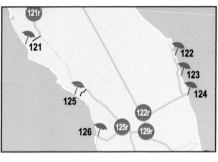

Beach ★★☆   Road ★☆☆

Beach: 24° 39.823, -76° 9.424
Road (122r): 24° 39.417, -76° 10.185

How to Get There

From points north

Total travel time: 11.0 mi. / 26 min
Drive south on Queen's Highway to Chris Brown Boulevard / Cotton Bay. Make a left and proceed 3.6 miles to Stop sign. Make left and proceed 6.5 miles. Make left just across street from old abandoned Bannerman Town gas station and sign for Bannerman Town and proceed 0.9 miles straight to beach.

Time / Distance
To beach road: 10.1 mi. / 17 min
Beach road to beach: 0.9 mi. / 9 min

currents as the water can be rough and there are large boulders out in the ocean, too, that should be avoided.

This very scenic spot is one of those picturesque places that have a wide variety of features. There is one shady spot on the point between the two beaches and then another deep Casuarina forest to the left. There is also one sandy plateau where a high concentration of shells has amassed. You can have almost any experience you want. If not for the debris and seaweed this would have been a 3-star rated beach.

What You Should Know	
Privacy	Secluded
Shade	Plenty
Accessibility	4WD recommended
Beach Path	Sandy
Water Entry	Rocks and sand
Water Condition	Deep ocean
Litter/Seaweed	Light
Nearest Town	Bannerman Town
Snorkeling	Good
Shelling	Yes
Beach Size	40 yards x 20 feet

Raineys Point Beach

There are several reasons that you might consider going out of your way to try to find this beach that is visible from Bannerman Town West. Because it's difficult to find and equally difficult to get to you can expect to have this beach all to yourself. While it has many of the same qualities as Bannerman Town West, the beach is much nicer. The water entry is far superior although water shoes are still recommended. This is a perfect location to take in a romantic evening sunset if only it were a little closer to civilization.

What you get here are sweeping views of the Caribbean that strain your eyes from seeing so far. A little lagoon with cloudy water to the back of the beach spills gently into the ocean. Overall, this is a very pretty, clean beach with a very thin line of seaweed.

The trick with this beach is to find it. The jungle road leading back here is extremely overgrown leading us to believe that it doesn't get used very often. The parking spot we found was by chance, then it was another 0.2-mile hike on a path that continuously narrows

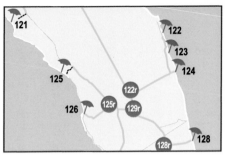

Beach ★★☆   Road ★☆☆

Beach: 24° 39.900, -76° 11.191
Road: 24° 39.181, -76° 10.408

How to Get There

From points north

Total travel time: 12.1 mi. / 27 min

Drive south on Queen's Highway to Chris Brown Boulevard / Cotton Bay. Make a left and proceed 3.6 miles to Stop sign. Make left and proceed 6.8 miles. Make a right and proceed 0.3 miles to end. Make a right and proceed 0.2 miles on dirt road. Make a right and proceed 1.0 miles on rough jungle road. There is room to park one car off of the road. Hike to the left 0.2 miles on narrowing path to beach.

Time / Distance

To beach road: 10.7 mi. / 18 min
Beach road to beach: 1.4 mi. / 9 min

as you reach the beach. We managed to get lost once, but eventually found what we were looking for. The path turns sandy. You know you're at the beach when the vegetation turns to Sea Grape trees.

The beach looked good for wading and decent for swimming if you go far enough out. There are some rocky plates leading out into the water, but they can be easily avoided. We recommend this beach to those who want to prove they can find it.

What You Should Know	
Privacy	Secluded
Shade	Some
Accessibility	4WD recommended; Hike
Beach Path	Dirt
Water Entry	Sandy
Water Condition	Shallow bay
Litter/Seaweed	None
Nearest Town	Bannerman Town
Snorkeling	Poor
Shelling	Yes
Beach Size	0.5 miles x 20 yards

Bannerman Town Beach West

This is an interesting secluded beach that has a very rugged terrain and raw feel to it. I guess that's because most of the sandy areas are set behind the ocean's rock border. There is sandy water access right at the beach center, but the more intriguing exploration areas are to the left. You'll find intriguing little tide pools and collection areas for shells that are really the highlights of this beach.

We were expecting a much rougher ride getting back to this beach, but it was really not that bad. Once you leave the main highway you follow a winding dirt road around a pond back to the beach. The shape of the beach is half-moon. Pockets of Casuarinas provide limited shade. There were signs of litter from barbecues, but for the most part, the beach was clean. We did find seaweed pushed up towards the back of the beach and in the water that we originally thought was rocks.

The water is shallow here. A mooring line in the middle of the bay looked like it was too far out to be used by boats making us

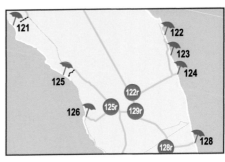

Beach ★★☆   Road ★★☆

Beach: 24° 39.112, -76° 10.989
Road (125r): 24° 39.181, -76° 10.408

How to Get There

From points north
Total travel time: 11.5 mi. / 23 min
Drive south on Queen's Highway to Chris Brown Boulevard / Cotton Bay. Make a left and proceed 3.6 miles to Stop sign. Make left and proceed 6.8 miles. Make a right and proceed 0.3 miles to end. Make a right and proceed 0.8 miles straight to beach.

Time / Distance
To beach road: 10.7 mi. / 18 min
Beach road to beach: 0.8 mi. / 5 min

think that it might be a shallow reef used by one of the nearby scuba diving boats to bring beginners. This could possibly be a good snorkeling spot.

You'll find lots of pebbles and shells strewn around in the sand. Natural rocky formations make some decent seats if you forgot to bring a beach chair. Unfortunately, there's not much else to do on this part of the island. This beach was interesting to find, but did not have any outstanding features that would make us want to go back.

What You Should Know	
Privacy	Secluded
Shade	Some
Accessibility	Car, bumpy
Beach Path	Sandy
Water Entry	Sandy
Water Condition	Shallow bay
Litter/Seaweed	None
Nearest Town	Bannerman Town
Snorkeling	Good
Shelling	Yes
Beach Size	70 yards x 20 yards

Driftrock Beach

Located just southeast of Princess Cay, where the weekly cruise ships drop off their passengers, sits this very easy to reach beach. After coming back from the Lighthouse Beaches it felt like we were on a major highway, as we never had to leave solid well-maintained pavement, which makes us think that guests of the cruise ships seeking more privacy may use this beach. We found it to be completely secluded, but your experience may vary depending on if your visit happens to coincide with a day that the cruise ships are in town.

There are two access points, the best one being at the end of the main paved road. That road gives way to a decent jungle path that runs parallel to the beach leading to a Casuarina grove. We did not venture past these points, but believe the road does extend. There may be at least one more accessible sandy beach patch just to the west.

The beach is set into a low-lying rocky platform. Most of the sand area can be found between a pair of flat rocky bookends with access into the water being extremely rocky. It's also extremely shallow. You'll want water shoes for sure, and may not even find this to

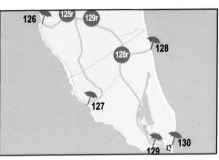

Beach ★★☆   Road ★★★

Beach: 24° 37.727, -76° 10.196
Road: 24° 37.727, -76° 10.196

How to Get There

From points north
Total travel time: 12.7 mi. / 22 min
Drive south on Queen's Highway to Chris Brown Boulevard / Cotton Bay. Make a left and proceed 3.6 miles to Stop sign. Make left and proceed 6.8 miles. Make a right and proceed 0.3 miles to end. Make a left and proceed 2.0 miles to beach.

Time / Distance
To beach road: 10.7 mi. / 18 min
Beach road to beach: 2.0 mi. / 4 min

What You Should Know	
Privacy	Secluded
Shade	Some
Accessibility	Car
Beach Path	Sandy
Water Entry	Rocky
Water Condition	Shallow bay
Litter/Seaweed	None
Nearest Town	Bannerman Town
Snorkeling	Poor
Shelling	No
Beach Size	0.1 miles x 20 yards

be a beach where swimming is even possible. We couldn't reliably tell how far out the rocks extend, but the shallow water extended significantly past a set of breakers that was about 20 yards off shore.

It's calm and quite clean here. Don't expect a good swimming or snorkeling experience due to the water qualities and lack of reef. Expect to find a good sunning spot with a decent amount of shade. If you have this beach to yourself it's a nice scenic spot that can be reached lickety-split.

Lighthouse Beach North

Normally, debris and wash-up dampens our experience and has significant impact on the grade of the beach. In this case, we felt that the positives so outweighed the negatives that we had to make an exception. This beach is purely amazing. It is 3.5 miles of the widest, most pure pink sand you'll find on Eleuthera. The topography changes continuously and dramatically showing off everything Eleuthera has to offer in one fell swoop. It's that unique variety of features that makes this beach one of our top-rated.

First, let us say that this beach is not easy to find nor easy to get to. It's access road is off of the road through the jungle that takes one to Lighthouse Beach. You will definitely want a 4WD vehicle, but the road was not nearly as

bad as expected. While there are several roads that seem to lead back to this beach, we only found one that worked, this one.

You start out with an elevated view that faces almost due east, although it feels like you are facing north. The beach extends far to the left, and also extends southeast ending at the Lighthouse, approximately 3 miles further away.

What's really interesting is that where you enter the beach, down a cliff with a short jump at the bottom, is really the worst debris spot on the beach. We chose to walk southeast towards the Lighthouse where the beach becomes more pristine with much more interesting topography. While there is little shade at the beach entrance there are numerous little caves and rock cutouts that provide

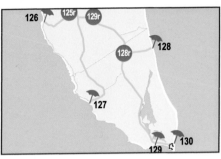

Beach ★★★ Road ★☆☆

Beach: 24° 38.638, -76° 9.136
Road: 24° 38.556, -76° 9.598

How to Get There

From points north

Total travel time: 11.9 mi. / 30 min
Drive south on Queen's Highway to Chris
Brown Boulevard / Cotton Bay. Make a left
and proceed 3.6 miles to Stop sign. Make left
and proceed 7.8 miles leaving paved road for
dirt road that leads to Lighthouse Beach just
past Bannerman Town sign. Make a left and
proceed 0.5 miles.

Time / Distance
To beach road: 11.4 mi. / 26 min
Beach road to beach: 0.5 mi. / 4 min

shade, interesting photo opportunities and an
atmosphere that can't be found elsewhere on
Eleuthera. You will feel like you are at the end
of the earth with an unobstructed view of the
infinite sea.

The water is exquisitely inviting, the reef
system intense. Tall pockmarked limestone
walls give way to a long dense Casuarina
forest. This beach is great for swimming,
running, snorkeling and exploring. It has
sun, shade and is truly scenic. It has everything that Lighthouse Beach has except the
lighthouse itself, but with way more privacy
simply because everybody goes to Lighthouse
Beach when they venture down this road.
This location is special and the beach is one of
the most beautiful on the island.

What You Should Know	
Privacy	Secluded
Shade	Some
Accessibility	4WD recommended
Beach Path	Dune
Water Entry	Sandy
Water Condition	Deep ocean
Litter/Seaweed	Moderate
Nearest Town	Bannerman Town
Snorkeling	Good
Shelling	No
Beach Size	3.5 miles x 30 yards

Lighthouse Beach Caribbean

The sand quality and color is almost indescribable. The view is ultra-delicious. The setting is as picturesque, quaint and scenic as it gets. One of the best, if not THE best, beach is found at the extreme southernmost tip of Eleuthera.

Two unique features come to mind immediately. For a beach on this side of the island, it's different because it's a big wide beach that stretches a quarter mile from its western rocky point to the base of lighthouse hill. There is more beach to the west, but we didn't have a chance to fully explore it on this excursion. There are no other sound-side beaches with shallow calm water that have this much sand depth and width. The other feature that sets it apart is its resonance. The waves are small and gently lap the beach, but the sound is like the grumble of a hungry cub. It is extremely soothing. It is easy to imagine yourself taking an afternoon siesta, tall frozen drink in hand, while gently swaying on a hammock, engrossed in the natural din of the ocean.

Past the little waves it is dead flat calm with a good snorkeling reef system not too far offshore. There are no houses or signs of civilization anywhere nearby except for the lonely remnants of the old lighthouse, which looks more like an abandoned shack on a hill. The ride here is not pleasant, but it's not one of those continuous bumpy roads that seem to shake the intestines out of you. This beach road has big, deep pockets that you must "walk" your 4WD vehicle through in places, but it's passable. It's also a long ride, which makes the journey seem longer than it actually is.

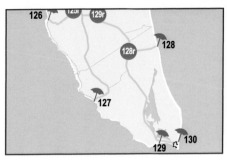

Beach 129 ★★☆ Road ★☆☆
Beach: 24° 37.023, -76° 9.062
Road: 24° 39.185, -76° 10.164

Beach 129a ★☆☆ Road ★☆☆
Beach: 24° 37.022, -76° 8.966
Road: 24° 39.185, -76° 10.164

Beach 129b ★★☆ Road ★☆☆
Beach: 24° 37.001, -76° 8.865
Road: 24° 39.185, -76° 10.164

What You Should Know

Privacy	Secluded
Shade	Some
Accessibility	4WD recommended
Beach Path	Dune
Water Entry	Sandy
Water Condition	Shallow bay
Litter/Seaweed	Light
Nearest Town	Bannerman Town
Snorkeling	Good
Shelling	No
Beach Size	0.25 miles x 30 yards

The vegetation is very complementary to the overall look of the beach. There are lots of tall sea oats, lush vegetation, and an elevated 10-foot dune that makes picture taking optimal. Big swaying palm trees and a smattering of Casuarinas seem to be sketched in just to frame the picture. The sand seems to scream, it is so bright and clean, but the lovely blue turquoise water dampens the scream into a soft hum.

It's just outstanding here. There are several other beach access paths as you move east towards the lighthouse. At the last, under the shade of several palm trees, is a grill with several homemade benches. It's a great area to BBQ, hang out, reflect and explore the tall cliffs from. What more can we say? Best beach on the island? It may be the best beach anywhere.

How to Get There

From points north
Total travel time: 13.4 mi. / 42 min
Drive south on Queen's Highway to Chris Brown Boulevard / Cotton Bay. Make a left and proceed 3.6 miles to Stop sign. Make left and proceed 6.8 miles. Leave paved road for bumpy dirt road and proceed 3.0 miles passing Big Pond to access area on right with narrow beach path.

Time / Distance
To beach road: 10.4 mi. / 18 min
Beach road to beach: 3.0 mi. / 24 min

Lighthouse Beach Atlantic

What is usually the most remote and isolated of beaches turned out to, ironically, be one of the few where there were not only people, but also lots of them. On the day of our visit the Island School had a group of students kayak over for part of a two-week spiritual campout tour around the island. I sure don't remember high school being like that!

What make this beach so great are the cliffs and caves. Not that the water and sand are anything short of spectacular, but striated limestone formations of this size can't be found anywhere else on the island. They are displayed in a picture-perfect way all the way out at the point where two oceans collide just off the tip of Eleuthera. Here you can swim between the Atlantic Ocean and Caribbean Sea, a truly exhilarating feeling.

Caves set back behind a grove of Casuarinas provide welcome shade as well as interesting exploration spots. The beach in front of this grotto is long and wide with the entire beach stretching against a Casuarina lined shore some 3.5 miles to the northwest. The nearby dense reef system looks like black volcanic rock set amongst an ever changing emerald and turquoise sea.

This is a very secluded beach. It has grown in popularity due to this and its Caribbean sister being perhaps the best set of tandem beaches on Eleuthera. Even though there is a fair amount of seaweed and some debris here, usually factors that cause a beach rating downgrade, the beach is too big for that to be an issue. Plus, the uniqueness of the land sets it apart from typical beaches.

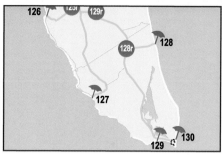

Beach ★★★   Road ★☆☆

Beach: 24° 36.982, -76° 8.811
Road (129r): 24° 39.185, -76° 10.164

How to Get There

From points north
Total travel time: 13.8 mi. / 48 min
Drive south on Queen's Highway to Chris Brown Boulevard / Cotton Bay. Make a left and proceed 3.6 miles to Stop sign. Make left and proceed 6.8 miles. Leave paved road for bumpy dirt road and proceed 3.4 miles passing Big Pond and past Caribbean side beach to sandy hill. There is a parking area to the right of the hill. You can walk up this hill to the Atlantic beach or continue driving to parking area on Atlantic side. Use caution if driving.

Time / Distance
To beach road: 10.4 mi. / 18 min
Beach road to beach: 3.4 mi. / 30 min

The main problem here is access. We chickened out from trying to drive our vehicle from the Caribbean side to the Atlantic side, as the road is fairly steep, extremely sandy and very rutted in areas. After inspecting what looked like places where vehicles often got stuck we opted to walk the path, which took about 7 minutes before reaching the beach. It seemed to be the smarter way to go considering that calling and receiving help this far away could take a half a day or more.

The island of Little San Salvador is usually visible, and on a clear day you can spot Cat Island, also due east. The old lighthouse is more easily accessed via a path from the southern side. It is perched high atop the last rocky point on the mainland and serves as the apex for great island photos.

What You Should Know	
Privacy	Secluded
Shade	Some
Accessibility	4WD recommended
Beach Path	Dune
Water Entry	Sandy
Water Condition	Deep ocean
Litter/Seaweed	Light
Nearest Town	Bannerman Town
Snorkeling	Good
Shelling	No
Beach Size	0.75 miles x 40 yards

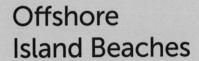

Offshore Island Beaches

Several islands north of Eleuthera are great little day trips for those seeking a little change of pace. It is interesting to see such significant differences between them when they are so close geographically. The islands of Harbour Island and Spanish Wells are reached by water taxi for a small fare from two of Eleuthera's ferry docks. Spanish Wells sits adjacent to Russell Island and is linked to it by a short bridge at the far end of the island. The best way to travel on these islands is by golf cart, which can easily be rented at the arrival dock.

Harbour Island is an eclectic, upscale and touristy locale, its two large marinas serving as temporary homes to a number of private yachts. There are several shops, fancy restaurants, luxurious boutique hotels and resplendent private villas. While the general vibe of Harbour Island is that it caters to the rich and famous, it is actually unpretentious.. It's not uncommon to see celebrities mingling with other tourists at some of the finest eateries in the Bahamas. You'll also find plenty of water activities up and down its famous east shore beach.

Spanish Wells is a sleepy and highly populated fishing village while Russell Island is more of a laid back residential community. Its large fleet of fishing boats is responsible for a significant portion of the Bahamian lobster trade and it considers itself the fishing capital of the Bahamas. If Harbour Island can be considered the happening place of these islands then Spanish Wells and Russell Island are on the opposite end of the spectrum. Their culture is quite puritanical which is very evident here.

Each little island is unique and very different from the next. They provide interesting contrasts to the sprawling and seemingly unexplored shores of Eleuthera.

Harbour Island Pink Sands Beach

Harbour Island, often characterized as the polar opposite of Eleuthera due to its populous atmosphere, is what many vacationers picture when they visualize a tropical vacation. It's the place where you might catch a glimpse of the rich and famous, but here, everyone is equal. There are opulent boutique resorts, trendy little nightclubs, expensive restaurants and just about every imaginable water activity available at your fingertips.

But, what about the beach, you ask? It's one of the best and there are some very specific reasons for that, first and foremost, being its size. Sometimes bigger is better and the massive Pink Sands beach of Harbour Island is certainly no exception. What makes it different, though, is that it's almost perfectly rectangular. Most beaches taper in places especially at the

tips, wind around, or have rock obstructions, especially on Eleuthera. This 2.5 mile long beach maintains its 100 yards of width its full length from north to south. Combined with how flat it is, you feel like you are on an endless bed of the most gorgeous pink sand that you'll ever see, complemented by fantastic water and a bustling village.

The look of the beach is also unique. You have a very tall dune at its back that looks like it was hand-painted. It is rife with exquisite tall palms, luxury homes and brightly colored resorts. It just screams 'tropics'. When you arrive here you can go from 0 to VACATION in seconds.

The color of the water is also alluring. There is an abrupt change from turquoise to deep blue that is unlike anything elsewhere.

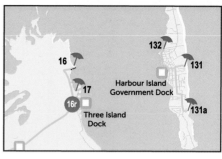

Beach 131 ☆☆☆ Road ☆☆☆
Beach: 25° 30.050, -76° 37.941
Road: 25° 30.050, -76° 37.941

Beach 131a ☆☆☆ Road ☆☆☆
Beach: 25° 29.244, -76° 37.902
Road: 25° 29.244, -76° 37.902

How to Get There

From Three Island dock to 131
Total travel time: 0.4 mi. / 3 min
Take water taxi to Harbour Island government dock. Proceed straight up hill. Make first right. Make next left on Gaol Street. Proceed straight to end. Park at access steps and walk to beach.

Time / Distance
To beach road: 0.4 mi. / 2 min
Beach road to beach: 500 feet / 1 min

From Three Island dock to 131a
Total travel time: 1.2 mi. / 6 min
Take water taxi to Harbour Island government dock. Proceed straight up hill. Make first right. Make next left on Gaol Street. Proceed 1 block on Gaol. Make right and proceed 1.0 miles. Make a left and proceed 300 feet to beach path.

Time / Distance
To beach road: 1.2 miles / 6 min
Beach road to beach: 0.0 mi. / 0 min

What You Should Know

Privacy	Public
Shade	Some
Accessibility	Golf cart recommended
Beach Path	Stairs
Water Entry	Sandy
Water Condition	Deep ocean
Litter/Seaweed	Moderate
Nearest Town	Harbour Island
Snorkeling	Good
Shelling	No
Beach Size	2.0 miles x 100 yards

The water starts shallow, but gets deep almost immediately, creating that color change. It is both dramatic and divine.

To reach Harbour Island you'll pay a small toll and take a water taxi from the Three Island dock just north of the North Eleuthera Airport (ELH). Walk over the hill or rent a golf cart to go to the beach. There are lots of other things to do here so we recommend renting a golf cart, spending the day and exploring the island. Bring money — you'll need it.

If you have become accustomed to Eleuthera where privacy and solitude is the way, then you'll be shocked by the volume of activity on Harbour Island. The beach is about as public as a beach gets and there is a fair amount of seaweed although no debris. This beach is a must-see.

Harbour Island Bayside Beach / Girl's Bank

If you look up the definition of a beach you'll generally find that it is classified as a pebbly or sandy shore by the ocean between high and low watermarks. Based on that definition this 'beach' made it into this book. However, the characteristics that you generally want in a beach – sun, shade, sand, water – are so suboptimal here that we had to bend our rules to even include this in the catalog.

This location is a photo opportunity to see the famous Lone Tree, an iconic piece of tall dead driftwood that has been painted bright white to make it further stand out. It has been placed next to another tall dead Casuarina that doesn't seem to have died from natural causes. We're not sure how the most current version of Lone Tree ended up here, but we assume previous versions might have succumbed to hurricanes. This seems like Lone Tree 2.0 to our eyes.

The sand area has a vicious odor at low tide and there are a lot of dead, abandoned boats to go with the dead trees. How this became a place to take wedding photos I'll never know.

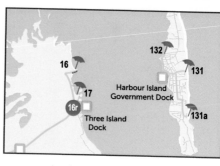

Beach ★☆☆   Road ★★★

Beach: 25° 30.366, -76° 38.314
Road (131r): 25° 30.366, -76° 38.314

How to Get There

From Three Island dock
Total travel time: 0.5 mi. / 3 min
Take water taxi to Harbour Island government dock. Make 1st left on Front Street and proceed 0.5 miles to beach on left. There is a meditation bench a few hundred feet down on the right on a small sandy beach overlooking the bay.

Time / Distance
To beach road: 0.5 mi. / 3 min
Beach road to beach: 0.0 mi. / 0 min

What You Should Know	
Privacy	Public
Shade	None
Accessibility	Golf cart recommended
Beach Path	None
Water Entry	Sandy
Water Condition	Shallow bay
Litter/Seaweed	None
Nearest Town	Harbour Island
Snorkeling	Poor
Shelling	No
Beach Size	400 yards x 50 yard

At the time we visited there were lots of industrial sounds as well as road noise making us wonder what the benefit is of having a manmade meditation area under a few palm trees on the shore nearby. It was all very chaotic and confusing.

Come for the view, but don't stay long. Choose your footwear appropriately, too, as the area stays under water most of the time. It can best be described as swampy and capable of swallowing your sandal.

Spanish Wells Beach

The island of Spanish Wells, just off the coast of northwest Eleuthera, is generally thought of as a sleepy little residential fishing village. However, it has one mile of some of the best beach sand you are likely to find in this general geography covering its entire northeastern shore. The beach is accessible from any number of its grid-like blocks.

Its sand is super clean, the water super shallow and the beach long and narrow. The surroundings are highly residential with rows of colorful houses up and down its shores. Strangely enough, at the time we reviewed this beach, there wasn't a single soul on it, however, the close proximity of all the houses made us feel like we were in a densely populated Jersey shore town as compared to Eleuthera. Of course, what you give up in privacy you get back in convenience in the form of shops, stores, and several restaurants all within an easy golf cart's drive. Be aware that Spanish Wells is a dry island. You won't find a liquor store or bar anywhere and there isn't much to do.

To get here you'll drive to the western government dock on North Eleuthera and pay $8 for a round trip water taxi to Spanish Wells. Ask the water taxi driver to phone ahead to arrange a golf cart rental for you, usually around $40 for a few hours, or pick one up

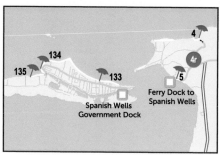

135 134 133

Spanish Wells
Government Dock

Ferry Dock to
Spanish Wells

4
4r
5

Beach ★★☆ Road ★★★

Beach: 25° 32.724, -76° 45.279
Road: 25° 32.724, -76° 45.279

How to Get There

From Eleuthera ferry dock
Total travel time: 0.5 mi. / 3 min
Take water taxi to Spanish Wells dock. From dock proceed up 5th Street. Make a left at first Stop sign and proceed to 13th Street. Make a right and proceed to end. Many other blocks other than 13th street lead to the beach. Go beyond 13th Street for northern portions of beach.

Time / Distance
To beach road: 0.5 mi. / 3 min
Beach road to beach: 0.0 mi. / 0 min

at the rental store next to the dock on Spanish Wells. A short golf cart ride will take you to the north shore beaches. You can also pre-arrange your return water taxi for a specific time if you are only planning on spending a few hours exploring the island.

The beach has nary a single rock. You'll find shade up and down the beach, which has intermittent clusters of Casuarinas, palms and sea grapes. The village is picturesque with rows and rows of brightly colored houses and a marina that is always loaded with boats. You are definitely within a community center, but one that has a terrific beach. You will have many exceptional photo opportunities.

What You Should Know	
Privacy	Public
Shade	Some
Accessibility	Golf cart recommended
Beach Path	None
Water Entry	Sandy
Water Condition	Shallow bay
Litter/Seaweed	Moderate
Nearest Town	Spanish Wells
Snorkeling	Poor
Shelling	No
Beach Size	1 miles x 20 feet

Spanish Wells Bayside Beach

Even though the bayside beach on Spanish Wells is directly connected to its sister to the east it feels like a very different beach. The setting is quaint, picturesque, and a bit more private since the community is back away from the beach. Houses in the area are across the street rather than up and down the beach itself. Super shallow water fronts a beach that reaches almost three-quarters of a mile from its northern tip all the way west to the Russell Island Bridge.

This is an excellent beach for children and kayakers. The beach is just off of the road so a very short walk and then picture perfect water access out into the bay. You have a view of Russell Island to the left and unobstructed views out towards the Devil's Backbone reef and several cays more to the north.

One large Casuarina tree provides most of the shade; it towers above a picnic table and sitting bench. Further around the bay there is a public bathroom and grilling area.

What we didn't like was how close the beach was to the main road that goes around

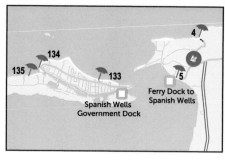

Beach ★★☆   Road ★★★

Beach: 25° 33.002, -76° 46.319
Road (133r): 25° 33.002, -76° 46.319

How to Get There

From Eleuthera ferry dock
Total travel time: 1.0 mi. / 5 min
Take water taxi to Spanish Wells dock. From dock proceed up 5th Street. Make a left at first Stop sign and proceed 1.0 miles to beach on right.

Time / Distance
To beach road: 1.0 mi. / 5 min
Beach road to beach: 0.0 mi. / 0 min

the island. Cars and golf carts seem to pass by constantly so if you want some peace and quiet head on back to Eleuthera. There is some seaweed plus a bunch of baby Casuarinas growing out of the sand making us think the beach needed a good weeding. There isn't much to do in Spanish Wells so we really only recommend making this a short day trip to experience the beach. Bring your own adult beverages, which you can pick up at the liquor store at the ferry terminal, because you won't find alcohol in Spanish Wells.

What You Should Know	
Privacy	Public
Shade	Plenty
Accessibility	Golf cart recommended
Beach Path	Sandy
Water Entry	Sandy
Water Condition	Shallow bay
Litter/Seaweed	Light
Nearest Town	Spanish Wells
Snorkeling	Poor
Shelling	No
Beach Size	300 yards x 20 yards

Russell Island Public Beach

If you have rented a golf cart on Spanish Wells then you can hop on over the little bridge that connects it to Russell Island. When you arrive you can instantly enjoy a quarter mile beach that sits on the southern side of the bridge. This is the only beach on Russell Island that is publicly accessible so there is no point going further to try to find more.

There is a channel that runs between the two islands and under the bridge. The water starts out as an almost murky green under the bridge before being magically transformed into crystal clear turquoise as you move further west. The water is extremely shallow and you'll often see sand bars stretching along the beach in all sorts of unimaginable directions glistening like private islands in the middle of the bay. The best thing about the position of this beach is its volume of shade caused by trees that seem to be pitched perfectly and

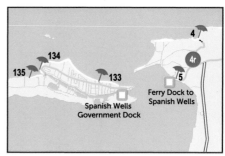

Beach ★★☆   Road ★★★

Beach: 25° 32.841, -76° 46.319
Road (133r): 25° 32.841, -76° 46.319

How to Get There

From Eleuthera ferry dock
Total travel time: 1.2 mi. / 6 min
Take water taxi to Spanish Wells dock. From dock proceed up 5th Street. Make a left at first Stop sign and proceed 1.2 mile crossing Roderick Newton Higgs bridge into Russell Island. Proceed 500 feet and make 1st right down hill onto beach.

Time / Distance
To beach road: 1.2 mi. / 6 min
Beach road to beach: 0.0 mi. / 0 min

grown to the optimal height.

This is another great beach for children and kayakers due to the depth of water and its proximity to where you'll park the golf cart. There's also a little public playground over on the Spanish Wells side that is a useful diversion. Be aware that as little as there is to do on Spanish Wells there's even less to do on Russell Island. You won't find any stores or restaurants and certainly no bars.

What You Should Know	
Privacy	Public
Shade	Plenty
Accessibility	Golf cart recommended
Beach Path	Sandy
Water Entry	Sandy
Water Condition	Shallow bay
Litter/Seaweed	Light
Nearest Town	Spanish Wells
Snorkeling	Poor
Shelling	No
Beach Size	0.5 miles x 20 yards